A Guide to Ministry Self-Care

A Guide to Ministry Self-Care

Negotiating Today's Challenges with Resilience and Grace

Richard P. Olson, Ruth Lofgren Rosell,
Nathan S. Marsh, and Angela Barker Jackson

An Alban Institute Book

ROWMAN & LITTLEFIELD
Lanham • Boulder • New York • London

Published by Rowman & Littlefield
An imprint of The Rowman & Littlefield Publishing Group, Inc.
4501 Forbes Boulevard, Suite 200, Lanham, Maryland 20706
https://rowman.com

Unit A, Whitacre Mews, 26-34 Stannary Street, London SE11 4AB,
United Kingdom

British Library Cataloguing in Publication Information Available

Library of Congress Cataloging-in-Publication Data
Names: Olson, Richard P., author.
Title: A guide to ministry self-care : negotiating today's challenges with resilience and grace / Richard P. Olson, Ruth Lofgren Rosell, Nathan S. Marsh, and Angela Barker Jackson.
Description: Lanham : Rowman & Littlefield, 2018. | Includes bibliographical references and index.
Identifiers: LCCN 2018012461 (print) | LCCN 2018027349 (ebook) | ISBN 9781538107997 (electronic) | ISBN 9781538107973 (cloth : alk. paper) | ISBN 9781538107980 (pbk. : alk. paper)
Subjects: LCSH: Clergy–Psychology. | Clergy–Mental health. | Pastoral theology.
Classification: LCC BV4398 (ebook) | LCC BV4398 .O48 2018 (print) | DDC 248.8/92–dc23
LC record available at https://lccn.loc.gov/2018012461

By surviving passages of doubt and depression on
the vocational journey,
I have become clear about at least one thing:
self-care is never a selfish act—
it is simply good stewardship of the only gift I have,
the gift I was put on earth to offer others.

—Parker Palmer, *Let Your Life Speak*

Contents

Contents

Preface

Out of our experiences—and our frustrations—we offer you a guide to self-care that we hope is significant help for many religious leaders.

As we write, we are aware of the wide array of places where people serve and of the variety of ages and ethnicities, and therefore differing self-care issues, of people doing ministry. Furthermore, these are fast-changing and difficult times for many in ministry. Often there are diminishing numbers and shrinking resources. Self-care is much needed to strengthen and renew all who are living and serving with these many challenges.

A word about how this project came to be—for a number of years, Richard Olson (Dick) taught courses first called "Stress Management" and then "Self-Care and Stress Management" at Central Baptist Theological Seminary. In recent years he team taught with colleague Ruth Rosell out of her many gifts in this subject.

This involved searching for the best resources on this subject. Though they found many wise and helpful books, none seemed to offer the breadth of self-care, nor did they address the varied and changing milieu in which religious leaders now work. Further, they didn't find resources that described the need to rethink these things in a changing world, changing religion, and evolving ministry.

Clergy in their varied ministries and students for ministry would benefit from a wider approach. And so Dick took this on as an early retirement project—to imagine a broad vision of clergy self-care, develop an outline, and find an interested publisher. He recruited his colleague Ruth to write a few chapters where her practice and teaching were particularly strong.

A bit later, we invited two doctor of ministry students, Angela Jackson (Angie) and Nathan Marsh (Nate), to join our writing team by contributing out of their doctoral work. Nate did his research on the issues in early ministry, and Angie's dissertation topic was on financial self-care. Nate completed his doctoral work in 2017, and Angie finished hers in 2018.

Here is how we proceeded: One of us would write a draft of a chapter. Then the rest of us would read it and offer suggestions. The author would then revise, change, and add. Therefore the chapters at times will speak in the first-person plural—this is what "we" think on a topic. When an individual's unique point of view or experience is mentioned, that person's name will be given in parentheses.

Angie was the primary author for chapter 11, as was Ruth for chapters 4 and 8. Nate contributed from his work and research in several places. All of us and several guests wrote parts of chapter 2. Ruth and Dick shared writing chapter 9, and Dick was the primary author for the other chapters.

Working as a team helps us speak to a wide spectrum of religious leaders. Dick has been a staff member or lead pastor in urban, suburban, university city, and rural pastorates as well as a college and seminary professor. Ruth has been pastor of a small rural church, coleader and church planter in a ministry with refugees, and associate minister at a suburban church. She also has worked as a psychiatric and medical nurse. Both Ruth and Dick have been church-based pastoral counselors. Angie has served as youth/children minister, homeless shelter director, and copastor in state capital cities, as well as solo pastor in a rural farming community. She also has been program director and coach in a theological school setting. Both Ruth and Angie are bi-vocational ministers, and both are partners in clergy marriages. Nate has ten years' experience pastoring local congregations and, most recently, two years of experience as a region judicatory staff member for the American Baptist Churches of the Central Region. Our ages range from the thirties through the eighties. We represent three generations of ministers.

We hope our variety of age, gender, ministry experience, and specialties will give this book a broad scope. Still, our team has at least one limitation: all four of us are Euro-Americans. However, we have tried to fill that gap, at least a bit, by consulting with our African American and Asian American colleagues, friends, and students to learn of unique issues and common needs.

So welcome! Our prayer is that something in this book will touch your life and renew your ministry. We are in this together, and we are in it for the long haul.

Dick, Ruth, Angie, Nate

Part I

The Need for Self-Care

Chapter One

Ministering during a Rummage Sale
after a Perfect Storm

Everything nailed down is coming loose!

—Angel, *The Green Pastures* [1]

The present age is indeed filled with drastic changes and unprecedented challenges for the Christian enterprise and for those who offer ministry within it. Of course, from time immemorial, ministers have had more work and hazards than they could face in their own power. In the first century, Paul, after speaking of all the physical threats he had endured, added, "And besides other things, I am under daily pressure because of my anxiety for all the churches" (II Cor. 11:28). A few verses later, he speaks of his anxiety for the church to which he was writing—the Corinthian church, "For I fear that when I come, I may find you not as I wish. . . . I fear that there may perhaps be quarreling, jealousy, anger, selfishness, slander, gossip, conceit, and disorder" (II Cor. 12:20). With constant physical dangers and churches like this, first-century minister Paul certainly had his self-care challenges. Certainly, there have been other hard times for the church. Indeed, in the mid-twentieth century, Robert Phillips and Thomas McDill wrote, "The minister of the Christian gospel has responded to a call to one of the most exacting and stressful vocations open to human beings." [2]

While self-care for ministers has always been important, we believe it is even more so now. Though today's clergy may not face the dangers Paul did, the contemporary church, religion, and indeed all humanity are in a time of rapid and extreme change. Much of this feels like loss. Contemporary writers have suggested two metaphors to interpret our disrupted Christian world.

A RUMMAGE SALE

Jeffrey Jones and Phyllis Tickle explore a quote from Bishop Mark Dyer, "Every 500 years, the church has a rummage sale." In other words, "Everything is prone to change, and perhaps we are at one of those times!"[3] They contend we are indeed in such a time of world and church modification. Quite probably, these changes in the world are so vast and drastic that traditions that held the church together for centuries are no longer meaningful.

Jones works his way backward through church history to trace other "five-hundred-year rummage sales." Five hundred years ago was the Protestant Reformation. Five hundred years before that was the split between Eastern and Western Christianity. Going back five hundred years earlier was the development of the monastery to seek ways to survive and minister during the collapse of the Roman Empire with which the church had identified. Five hundred years before that, it was the formation of the Christian church as a way for followers to be faithful. This was paralleled by the emergence of the synagogue for Jewish people. Five hundred years before that was the exile and the return of Jews to Palestine, and five hundred years before that was the establishment of kingships in Israel.[4]

Bishop Dan Edwards finds the "five-hundred-year rummage sale" a helpful metaphor and explains, "The reason for these periodic restructurings is that the truth we proclaim is eternal but the culture to which we proclaim it keeps shifting. So we have to revamp strategies and refine our language to communicate the faith to the generation before us."[5]

However, Phyllis Tickle sees this current five-hundred-year rummage sale affecting us even more drastically. Tickle notes, "Intellectually, politically, economically, culturally, sociologically, religiously, psychologically— every part of us . . . has been reconfiguring, and these changes are now becoming a genuine maelstrom around us."[6]

Jeffrey Jones adds that the fact that we live in such a time explains a number of things; for example, why "ministerial leadership today is so difficult, why answers are so hard to come by, why hard work is not producing the results we are accustomed to, why tension and blame abound."[7] He adds, "This sorting, deciding, saving, and unloading the rummage sale involves a lot to deal with. No wonder we feel overwhelmed at times."[8]

Jones and Tickle go on to possible strategies for the church and its leaders to live faithfully and hopefully during this "rummage sale." This is well worth pursuing. However, for now we will grant a large measure of truth to their metaphor and then ask, what does this say about the place of clergy and the self-care that is needed for those of us who live through it?

A PERFECT STORM, A SHOCK, AND TWO AFTERSHOCKS

We turn now to a second set of images. These also explore what is happening to religion and to us clergy. This metaphor is from sociologists Robert Putnam and David Campbell in their book, *American Grace: How Religion Divides and Unites Us*.[9]

They noted that American interest and participation in religion had increased during the 1940s and into the 1950s. This involvement was stirred by the crisis of World War II and its aftermath. Indeed, the 1950s marked the high point in public affirmation and encouragement of religious participation.

However, this high point was followed by a shock and two aftershocks. They point out that the decade of 1960s was a "perfect storm" with great upheaval for virtually all American institutions, whether political, social, or religious. This was the age of the huge baby boomer population. It was a time of changing sexual mores and the introduction of "the pill." There was the beginning of discussion—and much religious conflict—about a number of issues in regard to the lesbian, gay, bisexual, transgender, and queer (LGBTQ) community. There was also the vast growth of the use of pot and LSD. Further, there were the tragic assassinations of the Kennedys and of King, and the changes in civil rights legislation that finally began following those killings. The vast growth of Internet media with its competition and demands had its roots in this period.

Furthermore, on the religious scene, there was Vatican II and the many changes it initiated. As theologians tried to make sense of the overwhelming changes in belief and religious practices, some wrote about the "Death of God." Sales of religious books declined by one third.

That combined set of happenings in the 1960s was the shock. They note the first aftershock came in the 1970s and 1980s. This was the rise of religious conservatism. While conservative-evangelical Christianity has always been a sturdy part of the American religious scene, it began to grow tremendously. As a reaction to all these quite sudden and bewildering changes, many people were searching and confused. People sought guidance and foundation in the face of these rapidly evolving times. Many found this in the teachings and practices of evangelical-conservative Christianity.

This was at least one influence that led to a marked growth of membership and participation in conservative churches. This included the rise of nondenominational churches. Prominent religious figures during this time included Jerry Falwell and Pat Robertson, seen as widely influential in both religion and politics.

The second aftershock was the disaffection with religion by many youth and young adults through the 1990s and 2000s. It might have been that more and more Americans were not happy about the large presence of conservative

Christian leadership and their involvement in ideological causes and support-ing political candidates. At any rate, there was growing alienation from relig-ion in all ages of Americans, but it was strongest among those under thirty. [10]

THE RISE OF THE "NONES"

Quite probably, it was this shock and two aftershocks that account at least in part for the growth of those in the religious category we now call "nones." They are called that because of what they check as to religious preference on questionnaires. Observers note that there is an additional category— "dones"—those who once were active in a church but have withdrawn and participate no longer.

While there have always been some "nones" in America, they have grown dramatically in recent decades. According to the General Social Survey, "nones" were 5 percent of the population in 1972, 7 percent in 1975, 8 percent in 1990, 14 percent in 2000, 18 percent in 2010, 20 percent in 2012, and 22.8 percent in 2015. [11] There are now more "nones" than mainline Protestants and also more than Roman Catholics. They number at least fifty million, more than a fifth of the American population, a full third of them under thirty years of age.

AFTER THE "STORM" AND "SALE"

Not surprisingly, after such massive changes, the church in North America has been on a consistent decline in the past decades as fewer and fewer people participate in congregations. Walking in the World Ministries found that 250,000 Protestant churches in America are either stagnant, with no growth, or declining. [12] This comprises nearly 80 percent of the churches in America. The trend has led to an average of four thousand churches closing their doors every year.

In a year's time, two thousand new church plants will take place in main-line denominations. Out of these new church starts, only 68 percent will continue to do ministry after three years. Furthermore, the number of churches today are half of what it was one hundred years ago, and there are one-third fewer churches now than in 1950 in the United States. [13] Why are churches closing at a rapid rate? Because nearly 3,500 people leave the church every single day.

Over the recent decades, even as many churches shrink and close, there is a surprising contrast. This is the growth of mega churches all over the coun-try, each with thousands of members and dozens of staff. The result is that among worshipping Christians, there are many more small churches than mega churches, but more people are in the mega churches than in the many small congregations.

The Impact on Clergy

Along with this, respect for clergy is decreasing. There are a number of polls that frequently survey public trust in a variety of professions. These surveys do indeed show a steady decline of trust and respect for clergy, from about 67 percent in the 1980s to 50 percent in 2009. Clergy used to be somewhere in the "top 5" of respected professions (along with nurses, veterinarians, physicians, and teachers). That regard has now sunk a few levels to ninth, behind engineers and police.[14]

A recent extensive survey by the Barna organization reports further decline in public respect for clergy. In their survey, only one-quarter of respondents have a "very positive" opinion of pastors, and roughly the same percentage have a negative view (presumably the rest fall somewhere in between). According to David Kinnaman, president of Barna, "There is a huge amount of skepticism and indifference to today's faith leaders." Surprisingly, most of those surveyed "liked the pastors they know."[15]

Why this decline in regard for us clergy? Part of the answer has to do with the rapid growth of the "nones" who no longer receive the care of a minister. Professor Terry Rosell points out that the loss of trust goes deeper than that, however. He points to clergy misconduct as a cause. In particular, he notes four aspects—sexual misconduct, financial misconduct, plagiarism misconduct, and confidentiality misconduct.[16]

Though each of these is important, it is probably sexual misconduct that has been most prominent. While scandals and lawsuits in the Roman Catholic Church have had large public attention, the problem is much more widespread than that. A General Social Survey of 2008 contained this statement: "In any given congregation with 400 adult members, seven women on average have been victims of clergy sexual misconduct since they turned 18."[17]

I (Dick) recently visited with a group of psychotherapists—some of whom have numbers of clergy among their clients. They note a growth among clergy in heavy use, perhaps addiction, of online pornography. They also hear a good bit about ministers having affairs. This is a tiny sampling, but it is indicative that these problems of clergy with sexuality have not gone away. Online pornography may have added another form of sexual temptation. A number of surveys report similar conclusions.

Still Another Aspect

As we visit with ministers and other church leaders, they speak of another aspect, also not fully accounted for in the two metaphors explored. They speak of polarization, fragility, and brittleness. While there have always been tensions over one's highest loyalty—whether to country or political party or faith perspective—these tensions have grown greater and more explosive.

One anecdote we heard was this: a minister told a political joke to a friend at church. Another member—long-term and up to then faithful—overheard the joke and was so upset that he withdrew his membership. We heard of another church that experienced much tension and disapproval by some when one of their ministers expressed despair over the presidential election from the pulpit.

IMPLICATIONS FOR CLERGY AND THEIR SELF-CARE

It is possible that our analysis so far is too negative. The previous pages do indeed contain much hard news about religion and ministry. Of course that is only part of the story. There are many ministers doing effective work in a variety of settings, making their impact on community and world, and finding joy in doing it. And there are also a good number of seminarians enthusiastically preparing for a call to serve in this changing world, which they know well. As we celebrate that, the purpose of this book is to guide clergy into self-care practices so that this enthusiasm is sustained and supported as well as to offer care and guidance for those feeling the strains.

Still, call this change what you will—shrinkage, exodus, withdrawal—its impact is vast. This impact varies with denomination and parts of the country, but all are affected. There are less people to participate, lead, contribute, or volunteer. Churches and agencies may need to reduce staffs but still be expected to provide all the services they did before the dismissals. If you experience this, it's not your fault! Rather, there are vast changes happening that affect us all.

Implications for Clergy in Their First Five Years of Service

Some of the harshest impact of this rummage sale and perfect storm falls upon those who are recent seminary graduates, ready to be engaged in ministry. In her study, "Factors Shaping Clergy Careers," Patricia Chang observes that an average of 35 percent of seminary graduates will be unable to find suitable parish work within the first two years after graduation, with a higher percentage for woman graduates. Some of these will eventually move into churches, but a third of those who go into secular work remain there. [18]

The recent graduates who are called to a ministry position have in turn many challenges to face. Quite probably, the most critical time in a minister's tenure is within these first five years. In this season, more than any other, the chances are higher for clergy leaving the vocational ministry.

There is a wide and confusing range of studies that speak of the rate of attrition in these first years of ministry. For example, in a 2009 publication, K. Meek and associates wrote, "According to studies by the Alban Institute and Fuller Seminary, 50 percent, fully one out of every two pastors drop out of ministry within the first five years, and many never go back to the church again."[19] By contrast, a careful study by the Nazarene denomination among their ministers found an attrition rate slightly higher than 3 percent a year for the first five years of ministry and slightly over 2 percent for the next five. Thus, there was 16 percent dropout at five years and 26 percent dropout after ten years of ministry. The studies also noted that this attrition rate was less for those who attended their denominational colleges and seminary.[20]

Another broad survey yielded a quite different view. In 2005, the Center for the Study of Theological Education at Auburn Theological Seminary and the Association of Theological Schools (ATS) sent a survey questionnaire to all the 1995 and 2000 graduates of all the schools affiliated with ATS (Catholic, Protestant, Evangelical, Denominational, and Nondenominational) and three rabbinic schools—some ten thousand clergy in their first five or ten years. The return rate was approximately 23 percent. One of their surprising findings was about clergy attrition in their first ten years: "The class of 1995 had been in the field ten years by the time of the 2005 survey. Over this decade . . . the percentage in ministry had dropped by about 10 percent. For the class of 2000, the attrition rate was about 5 percent. . . . These rates—on average about 1 percent per year—are not high."[21] It may be that the attrition rate was higher among those who did not respond to their questionnaire. Still, this careful study deserves attention when exploring how newer clergy are doing.

Thus, though conclusive research about clergy attrition rates is lacking, it is safe to say that early years in ministry are challenging and fragile. These ministers beginning their careers deserve caring attention and support. In chapter 2, we will consider what makes these years so difficult and hazardous.

There is a related concern. Lovett H. Weems Jr. and Ann A. Michel view with alarm the dearth of ministerial candidates under thirty-five years of age. This is partly because of the exodus of many young adults to join the ranks of the "nones," but it goes beyond that. The shrinking ratio of young ministers to the clergy pool and to church population points to a future crisis—the lack of clergy needed to serve churches, denominations, and agencies in coming decades. They advocate stronger efforts with young adults, inviting them to consider a call to ministry, and caring supportive services for those who respond.[22]

In a survey of American Baptist ministers, the question was asked, "What advice would you give a new seminary graduate about life in pastoral ministry?" The following is a small representative sample of their responses. "It's hard work and ill-paid, so be sure you love it. . . . Be certain of your calling, its costs, and your willingness to pay the price. . . . Seminary gives you some tools but is often isolated from the reality of the church. . . . Be tender hearted but thick skinned. . . Plan to be bi-vocational like the Apostle Paul, so you don't have to be dependent on the church."[23]

Impact throughout the Ministerial Lifetime

In preparing for the profession of ministry, there is a reasonable expectation. The expectation is this: if one discerns a call from God, confirmed by the community in which one is called, and if one prepares carefully and works responsibly, there should be reliable opportunities to serve and be compensated fairly. For many, those assumptions may be frustrated.

While ministry has long been considered a profession along with law, medicine, and education, the expectation for compensation fitting a profession may fall short. The National Association of Church Business Administration found in 2012 that the average pastor's salary was $28,000 a year.[24] That seems very low and perhaps includes part-time and bi-vocational clergy. Another study citing the Department of Labor Bureau of Labor Statistics indicates the median salary for ministers in 2013 was $43,800.[25] Wherever it is in this range, this compensation makes ministry one of the lowest-paid careers in the United States. Of course, salaries differ greatly from denomination to denomination. A similar study completed by the Barna Research Institute stated that nearly 70 percent of pastors felt grossly underpaid for their duties.[26] Nevertheless, this often underpaid calling comes with pressure to help congregations and other entities renew themselves, achieve a greater degree of health, and counteract the declining membership trends.

Another aspect of difficulty is the time investment expected of clergy. London and Wiseman report a survey that found "ninety percent of pastors work more than forty-six hours a week. Fifty percent found themselves unable to meet the demands of the job."[27] Likely in the years since, these hours of expected work for clergy have grown even more. This can be addressed only when all in the church family realize that all are called to minister and share ministry and maintenance tasks with their pastor.

The austere salary prospects point to another growing reality in today's religious world. The number of congregations that can afford even a minimal full-time salary will continue to shrink. Bi-vocational and multi-vocational ministry will extend even further than it has in recent years when nearly 40 percent of mainline Protestant congregations had no full-time paid clergy.[28] The minister will need to have a way to earn income in another way or perhaps provide more household and child care functions in support of a spouse's employment. This in turn means that congregants will need to make a larger time investment, undertaking responsibilities that earlier it was assumed would be provided by the minister. This is in a time when there are fewer persons available for volunteerism in the church. Further, many of the laity have heavy time pressures of their own.

The survey of American Baptist clergy mentioned earlier had a fascinating question, "What are the five adjectives you would use to describe your experience in your current/most recent ministry position?" While some persons responded with all positive or all negative adjectives, the largest number included both.

Here are a few of their responses: "stressful, challenging, rewarding, low-paying, frustrating"; "meaningful, hopeful, disappointing, discouraging, lonely"; "exciting, challenging, fulfilling, exasperating, deadly"; "joyful, painful, intense, confusing, fruitful."[29] Their responses suggest that any who enter ministry should be prepared for both types of experiences and emotions.

This survey also asked, "How has your experience in ministry affected people close to you such as your family?" While about half of the responses indicated positive, supportive, or little impact, the other half described a negative affect. Some of their responses: "Family always gets the short end of the stick. When we can spend time with them we are exhausted." "Weekends are brutal on pastors." "Children hostile to church, wife avoids." "A lot of pain in my family. My family is now largely unchurched."[30]

Another question asked on such questionaires is "How often do you think about leaving ministry?" On the questionnaire we have been reporting, 28 percent answered either every week or at least once a month. That's serious enough, but another survey received an even more somber response.

In 2006, the Francis A. Schaeffer Institute of Church Leadership Development circulated a questionnaire, a follow-up to an earlier survey. They gave this survey to 1,050 pastors who attended one of their two conferences. This study revealed that 100 percent of pastors said they had a close associate or seminary colleague who left the ministry indefinitely. Ninety percent stated that they are frequently fatigued. Eighty-nine percent considered at one time leaving the vocation, and only 23 percent shared they felt happy in their relationship with Christ.[31] Fortunately, their follow-up surveys reveal some improvement in the morale and contentment of clergy.

Another type of clergy hazard is experiencing a forced termination of a ministry position. Joe Roos and Cheri Herrboldt, both of whom have experienced such a termination, report studies that say 28.3 percent of ministers have experienced a forced termination, and 23.6 percent of those had at least two experiences. They quote Peter Chinn, who also wrote about such an experience. His chilling conclusion: "The truth is that the lives and hearts of so many pastors are being wrecked by the poisonous opinions cultivated by cliques. The church must address the fact that often what is destroying pastors are not the arrows that come from outside its walls but those that originate inside."[32]

While we don't know whether the various statistics we cite are accurate, they do point to the fact that clergy experiencing these various strains are not alone. At the same time, there are rewards and joys in ministry. Three members of your writing team are active in varied ministries and loving it. The fourth (Dick) recently retired from a much-enjoyed ministry of seminary teaching into his eighties. We also experience that there are rewards and hazards in doing ministry. Sometimes the hazards outweigh the rewards, and a minister withdraws. How are we to understand this and draw wisdom for our present and future?

It might be helpful to consider a study conducted by Michael Weise and funded by the Louisville Institute. He examined investigations on this subject and then wrote a *Comparative Report on Six Studies of Pastoral Attrition*. The careful examination and comparison of these reports did not point to one basic cause for ministers leaving their profession. Rather, there were several factors, and some or all may have figured in the minister's decision. These factors are:

1. "We were ill prepared."
2. "We were not well connected."
3. "We did not see to matters of self care and self discipline."
4. "We accepted or were assigned to a congregation that was too dysfunctional to be pastored well."
5. "We could not afford the personal cost to continue to pastor."
6. "We were not able to manage or resolve conflict."
7. "We lost our way."[33]

AND SO?

We report all this for a specific reason. Clearly, to live one's calling, a strategy of self-care, mutual support, renewal, and growth is needed. We are convinced that the need for thoughtful and intentional self-care should be a part of negotiating a covenant with an employing community, and that self-care needs to be reviewed, reconsidered, maybe even expanded throughout one's lifetime of ministry.

Our purpose in this book is to guide you into a multi-dimensional practice of self-care that renews and sustains you. To that end, we will explore the variety of self-care needs, consider how threats to well-being are experienced, and then present a broad range of self-care strategies. So, welcome to the search. The gifts of ministry entrusted to you are far too valuable to be lost or diverted. Together, let us find a way on the Way.

FOR YOUR REFLECTION AND CONVERSATION

1. What are your earliest memories of church and Christianity? In what year did that memory occur? What changes to church and faith have you seen since then?
2. What insights do the opening metaphors of "a rummage sale" and "a perfect storm, with a shock and two aftershocks" suggest to you about what is happening to church and ministry? How apt are they? What other metaphors come to mind?
3. Think about the most serene persons in ministry that you know. What makes them that way? What self-care secrets do they have? If you don't know, ask them!
4. What are your greatest joys in your practice of ministry? What are your biggest frustrations and disappointments in your life of service? How are you addressing them?
5. What cautions are there for you from the conclusions of the Weise summary of studies on pastoral attrition? What do you hope for yourself, your family, your ministry out of this exploration?

Chapter Two

Self-Care in a Variety of Ministries

> But each of us was given grace according to the measure of Christ's gift. . . .
> The gifts he gave were that some would be apostles, some prophets, some
> evangelists, some pastors and teachers, to equip the saints for the work of
> ministry, for building up the body of Christ.
>
> —Ephesians 4:7, 11–12

We hope this book speaks to clergy in all areas of ministry, for the drastic changes described in chapter 1 touch ministers whatever their situation. Reading this chapter will help you better understand the particular stresses and self-care needs of clergy in a diversity of these situations, and therefore it is of value in helping us be mutually supportive of one another. However, if your time is short, you may choose to turn to those sections that pertain especially to you before moving on to the next chapter. In the chapters after this one, we explore burnout, compassion fatigue, and stress. Then we go on to speak of varied strategies of self-care.

How widely are ministers placed in today's world? According to Jo Ann Deasy, reporting on an Association of Theological Schools survey of the 2016 seminary graduates, about 55 percent of that year's graduates entered parish ministry in some form, 11 percent were undecided, and the other 34 percent had a wide variety of ministry goals—education, chaplaincy, counseling, social service, missions, and more.[1] So we offer a quick overview of self-care needs in a variety of ministry situations.

MINISTERS IN THE LIFE STAGES OF MINISTRY

The First Five Years of Ministry

In a book for professional caregivers, Thomas Skovholt and Michelle Trot-ter-Mathison discuss the dilemmas of the novice caregiver. They offer a quote attributed to Minna Antrim, "Experience is a good teacher, but she sends in terrific bills," and go on to say, "The novice enters practice as a new canoeist enters white water—with anxiety, some instruction, a crude map, and some previous life experience."[2] New ministers share these hazards. These first five years can be some of the most trying in a minister's vocation. In this season, more than any other, the chances are higher for clergy leaving the vocational ministry.

I (Nate) did not know this when I started on this journey very young, at the age of eighteen, pastoring two small rural churches while also working as an adaptive physical education teacher of students with special needs. Further, I was attending seminary online and taking between eighteen to twenty-one credit hours each semester. All this led to poor self-care practices. I was able to sustain this pace for a while, but one day it all came to a head. I was exhausted, frustrated, angry for no apparent reason, unhappy in my call, and out of shape—spiritually, emotionally, and physically. This progressed for quite some time, but on one particular day, I knew that something had to change. Otherwise, I could easily have been one of those dropout statistics!

The terms "clergy burnout" and "pastoral attrition" were new to me. I started to spend time in prayer and God's Word, sought the counsel of people I trusted, and also reread through some of the self-care books I previously skimmed. What did I learn? The importance of boundaries, Sabbath, time management, spiritual disciplines, clergy coaches, and more.

During this season, my ministry began to change. I realized that I am a better minister to the people I serve if I am willing to take care of myself. This became a mantra of mine so much that I decided to conduct my doctor of ministry research on this topic.

Presently, the median age of a seminary student is the mid-thirties. The first years of ministry may occur in one's twenties, thirties, forties, fifties, or sixties. If one begins ministry practice while in one's twenties or thirties, there are extra hazards. For one thing, as we earlier noted, the extremely small number of ministers in their twenties or thirties may lead to loneliness and a longing for supportive peers of similar age. There may also be added pressure for this small cohort. Daniel Mejia, a young pastor, comments, "The church has very high expectations of young clergy. They expect us to save a declining church, but we are given a very short leash if what we are propos-ing has never been done before."[3]

From my (Nate's) research, these are the primary ways that new pastors are susceptible to pastoral attrition: insufficient time for non-church-related matters (family or leisure), feelings of isolation, and discouragement or depression. Clergy who want to continue long-term in ministry will need to learn how to set and maintain intentional boundaries. This conversation on boundaries and expectations for clergy can range over many topics—for example: office hours, the parsonage or other housing, days off, your expectations of those in the ministry, and the faith community's expectation of you. Nonparish ministers might construct a slightly different list based on their place of service.

A significant way to reduce pastoral attrition is to either begin or continue healthy spiritual disciplines and practices from the outset of one's ministry. Also, be sure to maintain overall good physical health by eating healthy foods and getting regular exercise. And don't forget emotional health that is so essential to whole person well-being. Another good idea is to seek out a mentor, clergy coach, counselor, or spiritual director in the early days. Such persons may be especially helpful as one navigates the transitions, loneliness, and demands of postseminary life.

Midlife Challenges

Bruce and Katherine Epperly speak of midlife as the "autumn of ministry" and suggest that renewal and transformation in midministry involves at least six tasks and thus self-care challenges.

The first is confronting grief and loss in ministry. This may involve being in touch with the feelings aroused by the periodic moving from a community, deaths of beloved friends, and loss of members. It also means coming to grips with one's own limitations in ministry as well as recognizing the limitation of rewarding opportunities in these days of upheaval and change.

The second is cultivating novelty in ministry. This can be challenging. They note that after thirty years, a preaching pastor using the three-year lectionary will have engaged those texts ten times! Other forms of ministry have similar challenges.

The third is letting go of perfectionism and indispensability. These seeming virtues in a conscientious minister can lead to overly dependent communities and overly burdened pastors. Acknowledging one's gifts and limitations is an essential process.

The fourth is taking responsibility for one's own health and well-being. In midlife, whether forty, fifty, or later, one becomes aware of one's own mortality. It is important to take fitting steps in physical health care to claim the abundant life we offer to others.

The fifth ingredient for midlife ministers is "finding harvest in midlife." Interestingly, they then discuss wilderness experiences in midlife, of "vocational and spiritual dry spells."[4] As with others before us, we need to find our way "through a combination of patience, endurance, and commitment to personal transformation."[5]

Their sixth ingredient is rediscovering your first love in ministry. It is a time to ask, "Where is your current passion? What is your first love? Are you living out of your deepest vocational and spiritual gifts?"[6]

Pre-retirement and Retirement

The Epperlys also tell about one of their friends—"As he prepared for retirement, Gordon [Forbes] recognized that retirement is a spiritual crisis, fraught with many dangers as well as opportunities."[7] As I (Dick) prepared to retire from a congregation I had served for twelve years, I found myself recalling and applying what I had once heard at a hospice seminar are the essential tasks of the dying. These tasks are to communicate these things: I forgive you; please forgive me; thank you; I love you; and good-bye. Those are also important tasks for retiring or leaving a ministry.

If there has been pain and hurt in a ministry, forgiving and seeking forgiveness may be necessary. Only then can one move to stating thank you and expressing love with those served. Saying "good-bye" in a thoughtful way is important for the ones leaving and for the community who is being left. How does one end and—as much as possible—completely let go of a ministry? Elnora Huyck, once the dean of one of the colleges within a large state university, said it well: "You have to put your ladder against a different wall."

When the retiree does that exploring, there are a number of fitting ways to do it. Some may want to utilize the wisdom of a lifetime of ministry and be available as interim leaders or consultants. Others may enjoy membership in a congregation and choosing what they do or do not want to agree to do. Still others may have a beloved artistry, craft, or subject they want to pursue without limits. And others may love the freedom of travel and living in places of their choice. All are good.

Of course there are two other realities retired people must consider. One is finances. Typically, available income at retirement will grow very little while costs of living will increase. The other is health and any limitations that may come with health issues.

MINISTERS IN BI-VOCATIONAL OR
MULTI-VOCATIONAL SITUATIONS

Bi-vocational and multi-vocational ministry is on the rise. Whether due to personal choice or unfortunate circumstance, these ministry models present particular challenges for the ministers in those contexts. While each situation is unique, certainly there are some strategies for self-care and life balance that will resonate with clergy living these realities.

I (Angie) work as a bi-vocational minister. Not only do I serve a local church as half-time pastor, but I also work as half-time program director for a graduate theological school. To complicate matters more, my husband works similarly as quarter-time pastor and full-time retirement community chaplain. Ours is a household of two persons with three ministries.

Working bi-vocationally has granted us tremendous creative, intellectual, and relational freedom to pursue ministry interests and passions outside the church. Though we both love our congregation and church work, I thrive in an educational setting, the world of books and ideas, while my husband excels at pastoral care, the world of people and feelings. We are overjoyed to work in specialized areas that would not otherwise be possible.

Adopting a bi-vocational work style frees us from significant financial stress. Our multiple income streams also afford us freedom to be generous with others and ourselves in ways we never experienced while living on a single income. We have always been faithful, disciplined givers, but now we practice even greater generosity in planned giving and special giving without hesitation. In addition to the ability to give so much more to the church and the world, we enjoy giving ourselves travel experiences that we never dreamed were possible.

On the flip side, bi-vocational ministry life is exceedingly messy. As a person who prizes order, this is the most challenging for me. Though we share a pastorate, we keep opposite schedules. Because of that, we serve together only on Sundays, and if we need to work together on something, we must do that during evenings at home. While we prioritize self-care and Sabbath, the only way to keep necessary appointments in some cases is to utilize evenings or days dedicated to rest. On top of that, we occasionally forget each other's schedule, so doing a calendar together about once a month is absolutely necessary for calming the chaos.

The learning curve is steep for bi-vocational ministers. We are learning to set boundaries and say no for our own sake, each other's sake, and the sake of healthy working relationships. We are learning just how imperative it is to communicate clearly with our employers and with each other. We are learning to balance, not only maintaining the delicate and familiar work-family-home balance but also juggling the vocational expectations of multiple employers. Likewise, we are learning to divide the labor at home in equitable ways. If you are living and ministering in a bi-/multi-vocational reality, striving for balance will contribute to your health and the well-being of those who love you.

As a judicatory employee, I (Nate) see another dimension of bi-vocational ministry in my work with churches that are calling bi-vocational ministers due to diminishing membership and resources. Finances for these churches and ministers are often more austere than Angie's experience. While people think the pattern for their minister may be half-time employment elsewhere and half-time service to church, more frequently it is full-time employment elsewhere, and what time left is available for the church. Churches may state a need for twenty hours from their minister, but even the most efficient minister and a small low-demand church often find that more hours are needed. On the other hand, this can be a growing time for all as congregants learn to take responsibility for some ministerial tasks.

Just as we were completing this manuscript, our team received a research piece from *Faith and Leadership* of Duke Divinity School titled "A Move to Part-time Clergy Sparks Innovation in Congregations." After studying churches with part-time clergy, they noted three models: pastor as equipper, pastor as ambassador, and pastor as team member. [8]

MINISTERS IN ETHNIC COMMUNITIES, EACH WITH UNIQUE ISSUES FOR SELF-CARE

African American

At our request, colleague Dr. Terrell Carter shared the unique stresses for African American clergy. He mentioned that a very large proportion of African American pastors are bi-vocational or multi-vocational with all of the previously mentioned stresses. In spite of this, he commented, "Historically, in the Black church tradition, the pastor is the end all and be all of church life. They are expected to be the smartest and strongest person in the congregation. They are held to a different standard than anyone else. They are also typically expected to have substantial amounts of energy. This can lead to pastors regularly experiencing burnout or stress. That stress is then transferred to the congregations they serve."

When Carter was a younger unpaid associate in a church in Texas, he recalls, "There were five associate ministers who were very active in the church, yet our pastor felt that he had to be the primary leader of everything. After having a health-related scare, he began to delegate responsibilities among the associate ministers." The authoritative source of guidance and wisdom for many African American clergy is *The Baptist Standard Church Directory and Busy Pastor's Guide*.[9] Pastors access it for much guidance, such as how to conduct a church business meeting, but there is not a single word about self-care within its pages.

This may lead to difficulty claiming and practicing self-care, Terrell notes. "Clergy face the stigma of being called weak and not 'led/empowered by God' if they show signs of burnout or determine to take a step back from responsibilities to practice self-care. In general, congregation members expect their leaders to be strong and able to withstand the 'trials of the devil and flesh,' or they run the risk of not being viewed as a good pastor or leader." Beyond rendering pastoral services and being bi-vocational, some pastors also serve as unpaid volunteer chaplains with police or fire departments or hospitals.

He also notes the flip side; many pastors do not want other people in their business or to see them as being vulnerable. This is because they understand that it will affect how congregation members view them and how the dynamics of power within their congregation may change. In addition, these pastors live with all the challenges of technology, possibly making them even more accessible.

Carter notes that he has been describing traditional roles. This will vary with the generation and the education of the pastor. "Younger ministers . . . have been exposed to multiple ways of thinking and can imagine the kingdom of God being built through multiple intertwined opportunities."[10]

Korean American and Other Asian Recent Residents

Dr. Samuel Park, our Korean colleague, responded to our inquiries and also provided guidance to doctoral dissertations that address Korean clergy self-care.

Young Sun Jin notes that part of the reason for the vast growth of Korean churches in America is the church's role in responding to persons' religious, social, and emotional needs in interrelated ways. The Sunday worship is a time when persons are "sustained, encouraged, and empowered through worship experience. Further, virtually all Korean-American churches use their mother language in worship services. They do not have to feel stressed with language barriers, but only feel at home in worship."[11] Another unique feature of Korean worship is that very early in the morning, prayer meetings with singing, prayer, and preaching are held every day of the week or perhaps every morning on the weekends.

The church also meets a social need. In the absence of other effective community organizations, the church is the place where social opportunities are shared and mutual support is provided. Much information about business, social activities, children's education, and more is shared at church.[12]

The church is helpful in the face of emotional needs. Many first-generation persons struggle "with language barriers, culture shock, racial prejudice, underemployment, role and status reversal, trans-generational family conflicts, and the lack of a community support system."[13] Often, the first person called in response is the pastor.

These many functions and needs place great demand on their ministers. For one thing, the minister may need to preach anywhere from two to twelve sermons a week! Probably, the average falls in the range of four to seven. Many churches are small with meager resources to pay their pastor. The small-church pastor may be bi-vocational, or the spouse may be employed so he or she can afford to minister.

Many ministers don't feel they should even take one day a week off, much less be encouraged by their congregation to do so. Taking off two Sundays in a row is rare, unless it is for a mission trip or to preach in other churches. Indeed, there seem to be cultural assumptions that it is OK for them to be in hardship, and they should not complain about their situation.[14] In his dissertation, Young Sun Jin found a moderately high level of stress and burnout among the Korean Presbyterian pastors in the Washington, D.C., area. For these reasons, Dr. Park tries to instill reasonable self-care practices in students for ministry as part of their stewardship.

Space does not permit detailed discussion of other ethnic groups, but we will briefly note hearing similar experiences from our Burmese American students. For example, Lian Lalpek, a Burmese-Chin pastor serving a church in America, shared that he was surprised how much better and energetic he felt when he rested a little more and occasionally took time off to play tennis with his young adult congregants. But he also had a major task in educating his congregation that he still loved the Lord and was doing this to be an even better minister.

All this is confounded by the needs of the various generations in one's faith community. Even a few generations can present challenges to the minister serving an immigrant population. The youngest in each family are likely to become "Americanized" most quickly—mastering the language, going to school, entering social groups, engaging media. Mediating and interpreting the contrasts between the generations can make a minister's life even more complicated.

WOMEN IN MINISTRY AND CLERGY COUPLES

In recent decades, women have entered professional ministry in increasing numbers. However, they still remain very much in the minority. A 2012 National Congregations Study survey found that 11 percent of American congregations were being led by women.[15] Of course, this varies widely among denominations, but it indicates that most often women clergy are working within male-dominated religious structures and with models for ministry shaped by men.

Women ministering in congregations and contexts that have not before experienced women pastors may encounter outright sexism and resistance based on biblical interpretations that question their legitimacy. They may experience a lack of respect in ways that question and undermine their pastoral leadership. Sexual harassment, including from ecclesiastical leaders and male ministry colleagues, may sometimes occur. Such challenges may be especially acute in cultural and ethnic contexts in which women are generally viewed as subservient to men.

As is true for other minorities, women ministers may feel the pressure of having to prove they can do the job well and of being looked upon as representing all women and their worthiness for ministry positions. They may have a dearth of adequate role models and feel very much alone. Internalized high expectations for themselves, along with feelings of self-doubt, can exert significant pressure on emotional well-being, especially when there is no one with whom these can be shared.

Having a strong sense of self, or being well-differentiated to use systems theory, is therefore critical for a female minister's self-care. On many occasions, I (Angie) have experienced firsthand expressions of surprise when I performed excellently, either by leading a meaningful funeral or memorable wedding or by preaching an intelligent sermon. Why are people so surprised? Is it because I am a woman? Fortunately, I am confident in my ability and calling to do these very things and to do them excellently and honorably. Admittedly, the remarks do sting sometimes, and I must continually cultivate my sense of confidence and my commitment to being my best self.

Working within a traditionally male profession may entail other stressors for women, as a result of differences in ministry and leadership style between men and women. Some studies have suggested that women pastors tend to be more nurturing and relational and more collaborative in decision making, while men tend to use power over laity more and value rational criteria most highly in decision making.[16] Of course, specific men and women may differ widely. But to the extent that this may be true, women ministers have wonderful gifts to offer in building a more caring faith community. However, there is also the strain of functioning in ways that are different from traditional expectations and yet retaining respect in the process.

In the traditional model of ministry, the male pastor often had a spouse who considered it her primary role as "pastor's wife" to be supportive of his ministry. This is rarely the experience of women clergy, whose spouses often have their own professional lives, along with expectations of spousal support and flexibility. Furthermore, the demands of ministry that require working long hours, frequently on evenings and weekends, can put significant strain on the marriage relationship, undermining it as a source of support.

Being part of a clergy couple can mitigate some of this strain. When both are ministers and share a position, there is the possibility of sharing much of life together, being supportive of each other's endeavors, talking over decisions and dilemmas, and thereby feeling far less isolated and alone in ministry. There are also increased challenges to ever getting away from work, as one's partner is available night and day to discuss ministry concerns. Furthermore, tensions within the ministry setting may be brought into the marriage.

More traditional congregations may treat the male partner as if he is the real pastor or in other ways prefer one partner over the other. On numerous occasions, I (Angie) have been introduced as the "pastor's wife." This is so disheartening! Again, cultivating self-confidence and attending to one's own sense of call is important. In those situations, emotional self-management is critical for me so that I do not overreact in the moment or dwell on it indefinitely.

I (Ruth) have shared several positions with my husband and overall have experienced sharing ministry together as supportive and strengthening. We have found that clearly defining the areas over which we each had primary leadership and responsibility assisted in our working well together and increased our satisfaction. Furthermore, we found that sharing a ministry position enabled both of us to carve out more time for parenting children.

One of the greatest challenges repeatedly mentioned in the research on women in ministry is the challenge of balancing family life and ministry, particularly congregational ministry when one has young children. Women pastors tend to put a very high priority on parenting their children and experience it as a calling of equal importance to that of pastoral ministry. This was certainly my (Ruth's) experience.

There is much about pastoral ministry that fits with parenting, such as having considerable flexibility in scheduling and being able to take along one's children to various aspects of one's work. But the ideals for fulfilling callings both to pastoring and mothering may also come in conflict, and the daily choices between them can be very difficult. What may easily result is women giving too much of themselves to parishioners and children, having too little to give to their spouses, and having no time for themselves or for the nurturing of friendships. The challenges for self-care are obvious. Without attentiveness, the self can be depleted.

Although high expectations for oneself as both minister and mother can be overwhelming, being committed to both gives me (Angie) an opportunity to model for my congregation that a woman can indeed be excellent at her work and still prioritize her family. By setting boundaries around dedicated family time and attending children's school events, I demonstrate healthy work-life balance that many in my congregation also need to practice. When given opportunities to dialogue about these struggles, it is a learning experience for me as a leader and for others whom I serve.

Along with the challenges, many pastors who are mothers also express that it is a profound blessing.[17] Such has been my (Ruth's) experience. I have felt the strain of juggling ministry and mothering, more so with the birth of each child, until I finally took a leave of absence from ministry for a while. But I have also experienced the great joy of children making my life fuller and connecting me with others in deep and natural ways. In retrospect, I realize that coming home to children provided a form of self-care by giving me space in which I was out of the pastoral role—to be silly, play, hug, laugh, and not think about ministry for a while.

Of course, women not only care for their children, but typically they are caregivers for elderly parents. Daughters give more than twice as much time caring for their aging parents than sons do.[18] My youngest child was only partway through high school, when I (Ruth) started providing significant levels of care for my elderly parents, one with Parkinson's disease and the other with Alzheimer's disease. I treasure the years of having more time with them, but once again it required juggling responsibilities.

And then there is being a grandmother. Kathy Pickett is a senior minister in her midfifties that we know well. She is a grandmother of four young grandchildren who live near her. Along with heavy pastoral responsibilities, she is also on call for her daughters and their children. When babies are born or grandchildren are hospitalized, she is there. This past year, her day off each week was spent caring for her newest grandbaby. Sometimes she comes to church with four grandchildren in tow. To me (Ruth), she fulfills well the ideals of being a grandmother while being a senior minister. The benefits are obvious in her connections with and understanding of the daily lives of children, parents, and grandparents. Surely, she must at times experience it as demanding, and the challenge to carve out time for herself must be significant. Once again, attentiveness to intentional self-care is essential.

LGBTQ CLERGY

Clergy who identify as lesbian, gay, bisexual, transgender, and queer (LGBTQ) are likely to experience greater self-care needs than their straight counterparts. After all, only in recent years have some religious bodies begun to develop theologies that care for the LGBTQ people in their midst rather than condemning them as sinners in need of judgment, condemnation, and punishment.[19] Though gender and sexuality issues have threatened many religious bodies with division, LGBTQ individuals and the LGBTQ community are increasingly out of the closet, proud, and vocal as they publicly wrestle with their own personal faith and the faith community's response to their identity. Although numbers of welcoming and affirming churches are on the rise and cultural stigmas are on the decline, queer clergy may still find that self-care is particularly challenging and critically essential.

Our writing team enjoys the friendship and collegiality of several LGBTQ ministers, and we share some of their thoughts with you here. While each voice and ministry context is unique, our interviews yielded some common themes when we asked honestly, "What are the particular challenges of self-care for LGBTQ clergy?" We are grateful for their willingness to share the following self-care wisdom.

Rev. Bethany Meier is an ordained minister in the United Church of Christ (UCC). She shares that one of the greatest challenges for her lies in discerning with whom she can be her authentic self. Citing interfaith group work as an example, Bethany knows that not everyone in those settings accepts her; so she is cautious when she first gets involved in ecumenical efforts. Because of the need to move slowly in establishing new professional and personal relationships, she expresses insistence that queer clergy find support groups and networks where they can be who they are without fear or hesitation. Bethany suggests seeking out Facebook groups and recommends the Gay Christian Network as helpful and meaningful. [20]

Dionne Boyice, a same-gender-loving African American minister, launched a ministry, WHOSOEVER: Community of F.A.I.T.H. (Finding Answers in the Hurt), that offers all people, particularly those who've been hurt by the church, safe space to nurture their faith in God. Her advice is to find the right community that can be a safe place for living one's truth. Dionne says, "If you're not living your truth, then you can't speak the truth to others." [21] According to her, it is imperative to connect with others who not only understand but also support one's true identity.

Rev. Sean Weston is a recently ordained minister in the UCC tradition. He spoke of two layers of relational connectedness. First, Sean emphasizes the absolute necessity of having other queer clergy (especially seasoned ones) in his network—people who know, love, and respect him as a leader. Second, he encourages a connection to the beautiful diversity of the queer community out in the world—people and places where he can simply be a quiet participant. Speaking of his search for a call last year, Sean says, "I deserve a context that accepts me for who I am." [22]

For LGBTQ clergy and straight allies interested in additional resources, check out the Center for Lesbian and Gay Studies in Religion and Ministry, [23] Institute for Welcoming Resources, [24] and Association of Welcoming and Affirming Baptists. [25]

MINISTERS WITH RESPONSIBILITIES OTHER THAN PARISH SETTING

Institutional Chaplains and Pastoral Counselors

Granted the wide variety in chaplaincy-counseling positions (hospital, hospice, mental health facilities, corporations, colleges and educational institutions), we will report and reflect on an interview with Rev. Denise Hill (certified educator and supervisor with ACPE, Inc.) who supervises clinical pastoral education at Saint Luke's Hospital in Kansas City, Missouri. She notes that hospital chaplaincy is not shrinking, but it is changing in focus in a number of ways. In many settings, chaplains are now seen as part of the healing-caring team. Medicare policies, for example, require focus on the physical, emotional, and spiritual aspects of care.

Further, chaplains are transitioning from representatives of their own faith heritage to interfaith caregivers, helping each patient access and claim that patient's faith heritage or none. Hospital literature speaks of a "ministry of presence," which includes self-awareness, compassionate listening, assessment of spiritual distress and resources, and appropriate religious and spiritual interventions. Such a ministry is very demanding. Chaplains are available to patients and their families in times of crisis, emergency, illness, injury, suffering, death, and bereavement. Often the chaplain conversation is a brief encounter, perhaps an interaction or two, and one may not know of how these persons in crisis fared. So establishing healthy boundaries and effectively communicating patient needs to the next chaplain on call is essential.

Further, patients are not the only individuals for whom chaplains care. These clergy provide emotional and spiritual care to the hospital staff in consolation, debriefing, and more. Staff retention is important to a hospital's effectiveness, and so support that helps fellow employees cope and persist is a valuable contribution. In fact, staff may be "regular members" of a chaplain's responsibility while patients are "visitors."

Another change in chaplaincy is the need to know and conform to both governmental (HIPAA) and corporate requirements. Confidentiality, conformity to policies, and record keeping are expected, and one can anticipate submitting regular reports of hours on the job and number of contacts made. Chaplaincy is part of the media revolution as well. Technological applications like Zoom are being utilized to provide pastoral support, and professional continuing education using such media to reach remote locations is becoming more widespread. Simple phone calls or computer correspondence may sometimes be used for pastoral care.

Being on the staff of an institution created to respond to the ill, the suffering, those at life's end, and emergencies is demanding and draining. Hopefully, settings allow reasonable time expectations and collegial support, as well as encourage self-care wisdom. Denise strongly recommends preparation that includes a full residency consisting of four units of clinical pastoral education, certification by a professional board, and membership and collegiality found in professional organizations.

Chaplains in Military Service

Captain Jose R. Martinez, Chaplain 139th Airlift Wing, Air National Guard, responded to our query about self-care challenges for military chaplains.[26] Joint Publication 1-05 says in part, "The Services maintain chaplaincies to accommodate religious needs, to provide religious and pastoral care, and to advise commanders on the complexities of religion with regard to personnel and mission, as appropriate." Chaplains operate out of their religious heritage but are available to military personnel of all religions or none. From early training, they learn to be "pastor to some, chaplain to all."

Each of the military branches has a resiliency program that includes a spiritual pillar. The chaplain is often charged with the responsibility of providing training in this regard. Chaplains are noncombatants, and they do not carry weapons. However, they are officers in a fighting organization and are responsible for the care of those who carry on the activities of war.

Chaplain Martinez identifies three primary unique self-care needs for military chaplains. The first is compassion fatigue. He notes, "Chaplains are constantly on the move within the military. . . . There are not enough chaplains in the active duty to maintain the requirements [both] at home station and in deployed settings." And there are the additional responsibilities in providing the spiritual resiliency training for military personnel and their families. The overwhelming demands can wear one down.

The second self-care challenge is concern about the topic of moral injury, a relatively new concept. However, many breakthroughs have been achieved since its inception as a topic for military members. Moral injury goes beyond the combat field. The Department of Veterans Affairs notes, "The key precondition for moral injury is an act of transgression, which shatters moral and ethical expectations that are rooted in religious or spiritual beliefs, or culture-based, organizational, and group-based rules about fairness, the value of life, and so forth."[27] This can affect the chaplain in at least two ways. For one, the chaplain may experience moral injury if, when advising a commander, the chaplain does not speak up about ethically questionable aspects of a strategy. This may occasion moral injury as the chaplain looks back.

For another, the chaplain may have self-care issues in counseling persons who may be suffering from moral injury. Martinez observes, "Chaplains are the only profession in the military that have one hundred percent confidential counseling. What this means is that in the confines of the military structure, they are not mandatory reporters. By military regulation they are prohibited to say anything about a counseling session of an individual." This means that, due to this military regulation, chaplains cannot provide information to a commander about a counselee's mental state, thus leaving an even greater burden on the chaplain.

The third self-care issue for military chaplains is difficulty or failure at reintegration into the back-home rhythms of family, community, and work life upon returning from duty. The constant mobility of military personnel involves their families as well, so the adjustment is all the more difficult. And of course, events have happened in family, community, and work during the chaplain's absence, which require adjustment as well.

Those Serving in Judicatory, Denominational, and Ecumenical Settings

I (Nate) confess that, prior to becoming a judicatory employee, I had minimal understanding about the complexity of the work. After I came on staff, I realized that the job was varied in ministry duties and could be twenty-four hours a day seven days a week if a person would let it. Granted, now my ministry is with churches and organizations and their employees while my parish ministry was more with individuals and families. My "high-demand" times and "low-demand" times are just the opposite of the local pastor. I receive few calls during Lent–Easter and Advent–Christmas but experience heavy demands the rest of the year.

Now, rather than being minister to those in one community and congregation, I (and other staff members) minister to more than two hundred congregations. The calls for leadership, guidance, counsel, resourcing, and conflict transformation come from leaders in those congregations. There are important considerations for doing this well while still doing self-care effectively.

When serving in judicatory positions, one needs to realize that the overall system is not always about you. Those in denominational leadership often are blamed for what has been said or done by other congregations, pastors, ministries, or institutions. This added stress on an elevated level can cause a breakdown on the holistic self of the judicatory minister.

When these attacks happen, it is important to step back in order to gain what Ronald Heifetz and Marty Linsky term "the balcony perspective."[28] In ministry we tend to spend most of our time on the dance floor, metaphorically, but at that level it becomes difficult to see the full picture; it is easier, however, to see only what is right in front of us. If ministers can attain balcony perspective, we soon realize that there are other systems, emotions, and outlying struggles at play. There may be places for our intervention, but through the process, it is important to remember that it is not always about us.

Those in judicatory leadership positions also need to be aware of the danger of cynicism about the church. Denomination leaders are often called to deal with pastoral misconduct, conflict, financial embezzlement, and churches with declining resources. These and other situations can cause ministers in this field to become deeply discouraged. When this happens, it is important to spend time writing down the "bright spots" within their jurisdiction. As denominational leaders encounter difficult situations, it is important to remember that God is still in control and that God is still doing amazing work among your other constituents.

As it is with other ministry settings, it is important to set intentional boundaries. In regional ministry, there is always work to be done, and it is essential to remember that most of the situations we encounter did not develop overnight. Therefore, some of these situations can wait. Ensure your own self-care so you are fully prepared to minister in these difficult situations.

OTHER RELIGIOUS LEADERS WITH SELF-CARE NEEDS

There are many other ministers whose life and ministry situations have unique self-care challenges. For example, there are clergy who would like a supportive relationship or group but are isolated for a variety of reasons. One may have very few people of one's ethnic or racial group where he or she is situated. Persons who have been mostly urban dwellers may find themselves lonely and confused serving in rural settings and vice versa. One may feel theologically or ethically isolated from other religious people and leaders in the community.

This isolation may be even more difficult if the clergy person is unmarried. Self-care, including finding a community of support, is an especially urgent challenge for those of us who are single. Ingenuity may be required to make those connections. Electronic media like Skype, Zoom, and FaceTime can aid long-distance supportive relationships, and it is worth time and effort to develop those connections.

Some religious leaders have family members with disabilities. Giving the extra care that may be needed for this family member, as well as finding and securing the services needed, can be very time consuming. Further, it may mean that moving to a new position is complicated by changes that could upset this family member's routine and care; plus, needed services may not be available in the new community. There is the further challenge that sometimes the stress and extra care that must be provided can strain a marriage. Doing ministry and responsible care for a person with a disability multiplies the self-care challenges we mention in this book.

AND SO—

Your writing team will keep this diverse community of ministry in mind as we write about threats to well-being and specific self-care strategies. We invite each reader to use creativity in selecting and adapting our suggestions to your own setting.

FOR YOUR REFLECTION AND CONVERSATION

1. As you see it, what self-care needs are common to all clergy and religious leaders? What are the unique self-care issues in your present ministry and life circumstance? What most urgently needs your attention?

2. Have you ever had feelings of being isolated? What were the most creative and effective ways you found to address that feeling? How are you doing now?
3. As you think of clergy in some other form of ministry than yours, what support can you offer? What support would you like?

Chapter Three

Burnout and Compassion Fatigue

The expectation that we can be immersed in suffering and loss daily and not be touched by it is as unrealistic as expecting to walk through the water and not get wet.

—Rachel Remen[1]

In his 1990s book, *Clergy Self-Care*, Roy Oswald wisely distinguished between two challenges to clergy equilibrium: stress (in a word, too much change) and burnout (too many demands).[2] To explore this, he created basic diagnostic tools to help clergy and spouse recognize which malady threatened and suggested ways to act on the need discovered. Since then, these topics have grown even more complex. In this chapter, we will explore the challenge of burnout and the more recent discussions of compassion fatigue and secondary stress and in the next chapter consider the many and changing dimensions of stress.

The term "burnout" has been around for at least forty years, but its meaning has evolved and expanded. Herbert Freudenberger was one of the first to write about it. He was working in an agency for persons with drug abuse problems. At that time, drug users were called "burnouts." As Freudenberger noted the strain and deterioration on his staff from engaging in this difficult and demanding work, he identified "staff burnout" and began to describe it for a wider public. In this connection, "burnout" was first used about the impact of many pressures on persons who were in caregiving occupations.

However, researchers Christina Maslach and Michael Leiter have been investigating how much more widespread burnout has become. They describe how the workplace has changed—and not for the better as regards worker well-being. They note that all too frequently corporations engage in a number of practices that negatively impact workers, such as these:

- cashing in on a corporation's intrinsic worth, both product and employees. That is to say, rather than providing a foundation for research and long-term growth, these assets—both persons and corporate knowledge—are used for short term stock and profit performance;
- engaging global economics, including moving, downsizing, closing places of employment;
- replacing/reducing jobs by use of technology;
- tight human resource management, including the reduction of worker power once available through unions and other means; and
- failing corporate citizenship. Often there are huge rewards for top executives but little loyalty or reward to the gifted employees below.

Out of this changed work environment, they note "burnout is thriving." The comments they hear throughout the workplace include these: "We feel overloaded. . . . We lack control over what we do. . . . We are not rewarded for our work. . . . We experience a breakdown in community. . . . We aren't treated fairly. . . . We're dealing with conflicting values."[3]

This means that clergy and other caregivers need not only pay attention to their own tendencies to burn out but also be aware that a growing part of their constituency might need help with this very same issue.

WHAT IS BURNOUT?

It will be helpful to look at a few definitions and then to note the dimensions of burnout that researchers have identified. Here is a definition from the Merriam-Webster Dictionary: "exhaustion of physical or emotional strength or motivation usually as a result of prolonged stress or frustration."[4] Pioneering researcher Herbert Freudenberger defined burnout as "a state of fatigue or frustration brought about by devotion to a cause, way of life, or relationship that failed to produce the expected reward."[5]

In their definition, Maslach and Leiter start with the source of burnout and go on to describe its development. They write, "Burnout is the index of the dislocation between what people are and what they have to do. It represents an erosion in values, dignity, spirit, and will—an erosion of the human soul. It is a malady that spreads gradually and continuously over time, putting people into a downward spiral from which it's hard to recover."[6]

WHAT IS COMPASSION FATIGUE? SECONDARY STRESS?

As we consider definitions, there is a question on which some of the most sensitive students of this subject do not agree. When we speak of burnout and of compassion fatigue, are we using interchangeable terms for the same thing? There are some who think so, including respected clinician Robert Wicks.[7]

On the other hand, there are some who say compassion fatigue, while similar, is quite different in cause though it may be similar in affect. For example, the American Institute of Stress website offers this distinction. Their definition of compassion fatigue is "the emotional residue or strain of exposure to working with those suffering from the consequences of traumatic events. It differs from burn-out, but it can co-exist. Compassion fatigue can occur due to exposure on one case or can be due to a 'cumulative' level of trauma." They contend that burnout has other causes and is not trauma related.[8]

Chris Marchand, who studied the origin of the term "compassion fatigue," concluded with his definition:

> Compassion Fatigue is the natural behaviors and emotions resulting from Secondary Traumatic Stress, which can be defined as: the stress associated with helping or wanting to help a traumatized or suffering person, resulting in a reduced capacity or interest in being empathic. Although it may lead to burnout, it can emerge suddenly and without warning.[9]

His definition includes another term that we need to understand, "Secondary Traumatic Stress" or "Acute Secondary Distress." This refers to the strain on a caregiver that comes from involvement and emotional identification with a person or series of persons who have gone through tragic and traumatic experiences.

Robert Wicks speaks of the "destabilization of one's own personality as a result of constant treatment of the severe psychological, physical, and sexual trauma experienced by others."[10] He also connects "Acute Secondary Stress" to another term, "Vicarious Post Traumatic Stress Disorder."[11] The combination of these terms expresses some of the pain, disruption, and disorientation that can be the experience of one providing care and aid to those who have experienced catastrophes and grief.

Denise Hill and associates note these distinctions among others: compassion fatigue can occur quickly, while burnout tends to be cumulative. Compassion fatigue connects to empathy, while burnout connects to heavy demands of daily living.[12]

Our sense is that, sometimes in a life of ministry, it is important to keep these terms as distinct from each other while at other times they come together in one's experience. A clergy may have heavy leadership duties and then be asked to minister in deaths of two or three persons from church families in a short time. At such times, the two terms may be used interchangeably as same or similar. However, when we speak of the various types of ministry, the dangers of compassion fatigue may be greatest for some (counselors, chaplains, persons responding to disasters) and dangers of burnout greater for others (those with heavy parish leadership and administrative issues). The rest of this chapter is offered with all three of these topics—burnout, compassion fatigue, and acute secondary stress—in mind.

WHAT IS THE IMPACT OF BURNOUT/COMPASSION FATIGUE?

In what ways does one experience burnout? Compassion fatigue? What is its impact? Various writers identify different effects of these issues. These classifications are overlapping. We consider each of these in turn to become aware of how drastic the effect and how diverse and pervasive the pain of burnout or compassion fatigue can be.

This malaise touches us at many levels. Maslach and Leiter note three aspects of a person's life that are impacted: energy/exhaustion, involvement/cynicism, and efficacy/ineffectiveness.[13] Similarly, Dennis Portnoy notes that symptoms of compassion fatigue/burnout may affect the whole person, manifesting in a variety of the body's systems:

- cognitive—lowered concentration, apathy, rigidity, disorientation . . .
- emotional—powerlessness, anxiety, guilt, anger, numbness, fear, helplessness . . .
- behavioral—irritable, withdrawn, moody, poor sleep, nightmares . . .
- spiritual—questioning life's meaning . . . hopelessness . . . loss of purpose . . .
- somatic—sweating, rapid heartbeat, breathing difficulty, aches and pains, dizziness.[14]

Further, burnout can impact one's personal and professional boundaries. A person may be less effective in counseling. One may have decreased discretion about the distinction between professional behavior and personal behavior. There may be less attention to one's appropriate dress for work. Also, weakening commitment to one's professional code of ethics may result. In other words, a person in burnout is a hazard—to others, to oneself, to one's employment, even to one's professional survival.

Meaning and Caring Burnout

Skovholt and Trotter-Mathison distinguish between *meaning* burnout and *caring* burnout. Meaning burnout happens when the purpose or significance of the work has been lost and the idealism that led one to the work seems like an illusion. Caring burnout happens when there is too frequent experience of loss of clients to whom one was attached, ambiguous endings, or insufficient time to offer the depth of caring needed.[15] Though they wrote for the broad caregiving community, this distinction between meaning and caring burnout seems particularly relevant for us clergy. As resources, volunteers, and respect diminish and as demands and expectations expand, clergy may not need to ask if they are suffering from meaning or caring burnout—it may be both!

While burnout has been acknowledged as widespread, it has never been a category in the diagnostic tools such as the DSM (*Diagnostic and Statistical Manual of Mental Disorders*) manuals. This is probably because burnout has a marked resemblance to depression, which is included in these diagnostic guides. Or, indeed, it may be a subset of the malady of depression.

Degrees/Levels of Burnout

Not only are there dimensions of burnout, there are also degrees or levels. J. Gill has offered a common sense description of these levels.

> The first level is characterized by signs (capable of being observed) and symptoms (subjectively experienced) that are relatively mild, short in duration, and occur only occasionally. . . . The second level is reached when signs and symptoms have become more stable, last longer, and are tougher to get rid of. . . . The third is experienced when signs and symptoms have become chronic, and a physical and psychological illness has developed. [16]

Gill notes that all of us experience level one, and most caregivers experience level two. However, in intense high-demand settings, professionals need to take fitting steps to prevent falling into level three and to seek qualified help if they do.

WHAT CAUSES BURNOUT?

Our next question is: why is there burnout? What causes it? There are two broad explanations: the social environment or the individual. (We have already mentioned the causes of compassion fatigue.)

Out of their extensive research, Maslach and Leiter argue emphatically it is the social atmosphere, the structure and functioning of the workplace, that is the most basic cause of burnout. We have reported above on their analysis of what is happening to the workplace. They contend that when the place of employment does not recognize the human side of work, the risk of burnout grows. [17]

While acknowledging the threat to well-being in the workplace, many others look to a variety of personal causes of burnout. For example, some caregivers are not prepared for the attacks and criticism that, from time to time, come the way of those who serve the public. The rhythm of work may be disrupted by criticism or by fear and avoidance of it.

For others, the need for Sabbath may be a source. Many clergy work on Sunday and may fail to make provision for other ways to meet their deep human need for spiritual sustenance, emotional renewal, and rest. We will speak of this more in chapter 6.

For some, isolation of the minister is the key element in burnout. The isolation may be geographical. Others may lack accessible persons with commonality in gender, age, ethnicity, sexual orientation, or relationship status (single, married, childless, with children). Still others may feel isolated theologically or spiritually. Some may fear revealing their vulnerability to others. In turn, Judith Schwanz, with clear awareness of the danger of isolation, suggests a systematic relational way to approach clergy burnout. Her book addresses relationships: with self, with other people, and with God.[18]

Lloyd Rediger, who devoted his career to counseling clergy and who pioneered in writing about burnout within our particular profession, reflected on his experience and came up with his own list of reasons that ministers burn out. He brings together a number of elements to which we have alluded, but he also adds a take on them. We offer Lloyd's list below, together with some of our reflections on these items. Clergy may burn out for any or all of the following reasons:

1. *The gap between expectations and reality.* Milestone events—graduation, ordination—are so exciting. A goal has been reached after years of effort. But then comes an entry-level placement, perhaps with low wages, limited resources, tradition-bound constituency, and little chance of "success," whatever that is.

2. *Double binds.* Depending on what aspect of ministry, the double binds may vary. For example, it may be the bind between what the minister feels is important and what one's supervising board does. Or the tension between wanting to take prophetic stands and the fear of losing influential members over those stands.

3. *High-intensity living.* The bi-vocational minister, the counselor in an underfunded agency, the minister trying to be all things to all people, each and all experience high-intensity living. Further, it has been noted that for the first time in history, churches and agencies are trying to minister to seven generations at the same time. That can make for high-intensity living!

4. *The something-to-prove agenda.* If one comes to this profession with the need to show someone (parents, professors, siblings, or peers) that one is more talented, capable, or effective than they thought, extra pressure is created.

5. *Energy drainers*. There are many energy drainers in every ministry. These may include do-nothing committees, required paperwork, or other bureaucratic expectations. Or it may be people—the person who has all the time in the world to talk about nothing, the overly needy, the critic, or the complainer.

6. *Lack of affirmation*. If one came to ministry out of being a volunteer, the appreciation and affirmation may have come freely back then. In a professional paid position, that is not so much now, perhaps not at all.

7. *Role pressures*. Some parts of ministry and some communities have role expectations that go with the clergy person everywhere. It may seem that some parts of a person need to be let go—teasing, flirting, some kinds of humor, or some kinds of dress, for example.

8. *The loner lifestyle*, sometimes imposed by circumstances, sometimes chosen by the clergy person.

9. *Life formulas*. One may have a need to be acknowledged and praised. Another may expect more services from an employing organization than it intends to provide. Or a person may be more relaxed about keeping current on finances and credit than one's employer expects.

10. *Attitude*. One may be too dependent and trusting (the church/agency is my family; it will take care of me) or hostile (the church/agency is a mess, and I will straighten it out). Either attitude can accelerate burnout.[19]

Another Perspective—Self-Violence

There are two other perspectives worthy of note as we attempt to understand what causes burnout/compassion fatigue in clergy. One comes from Kirk Byron Jones and his book *Rest in the Storm*. Jones writes out of his own experience and self-discovery. He was a husband, father of two children, pastor of a church, PhD candidate, community leader, and frequent preacher at revivals. He lived with all this, as he says, the only way he knew how.

One evening, while preaching at a classmate's church, midway through the sermon, he turned to the host pastor and said, "I can't go on." He had come to his limit with an overwhelming sense of fatigue, anxiety, and physical disturbances. Then he sought medical help. One question from his doctor stopped him short: "What do you do to relax?" He had no good answer; in fact, he had no answer at all.

Sometime later, he came upon a quote attributed to Thomas Merton: "There is a pervasive form of contemporary violence . . . [and that is] activism and overwork. The rush and pressure of modern life are a form, perhaps a most common form, of its innate violence."

After that, he was asked to prepare lectures for a conference on the theme of violence. As he prepared, a realization hit him: "I was led to focus on a form of violence we rarely address: the self-violence that committed clergy and caregivers unleash inadvertently on themselves in caring for others."[20] This led to Jones's perspective, unique as far as we know, of the actions that lead to burnout as "self-violence," admittedly unintended but self-violence nonetheless.

The antidote to this? Jones responds with a scripture passage that serves as his master metaphor. The scripture is Mark 4:25–31. This is the story of Jesus and his disciples in a boat on the Sea of Galilee. A storm comes up, but Jesus is asleep on a cushion in the back of the boat. Frightened, the disciples awaken him, and he speaks peace to the storm; the wind ceases and is followed by a great calm. The "back of the boat" becomes Jones's metaphor for living life at a "savoring pace." With this metaphor, Jones explores what keeps one from the back of the boat and how to get there.[21]

Incidentally, this book launched a new direction in Kirk Jones's career. With an eager response to the vision he holds forth, persons have invited him to conduct seminars all over the country. He has written a number of sequels on the quality of life he discovered.

Another Perspective—Codependence

The second perspective in understanding the cause of burnout is Fred Lehr's concept of burnout as "codependence." It is probably more accurate to speak of "codependence" as the cause of burnout rather than burnout itself, but we won't quibble. In his book *Clergy Burnout: Recovering from the 70-Hour Work Week and Other Self-Defeating Practices*, he explains this view. What is codependence? Lehr offers this definition:

> A set of maladaptive behaviors that a person learns to survive in an experience of great emotional pain and stress and that are passed on from generation to generation. These behaviors and their accompanying attitudes are self-defeating and result in diminished capacity. Codependents do not take adequate care of themselves and are far too controlled by (or controlling of) other persons' behaviors and attitudes.[22]

The term "codependence" is usually associated with a person in an addict's life. The codependent person acts in dysfunctional ways that allow the person to continue with the addictions. They are sometimes referred to as "enablers." For example, this person might make excuses for, cover for, or minimize the addict's behavior, thus protecting the addicted person from facing the consequences of his or her behavior and considering the need to make changes.

Lehr suggests the indicator that both church/agency and clergy are addicted and/or codependent is the seventy-hour work week. And if not seventy, it is devoting far more than a human being can reasonably give and still be creative with a love of life and work. When this happens, Lehr contends, there is codependence in the picture. The congregation/institution has an impossibly long list of needs and expectations that they firmly believe only the minister can fulfill. The clergy in turn accepts this whole list of expectations along with the assumption that only he or she can handle them and plunges in on the—in Lehr's terms—seventy-hour work week.

It is far easier to prevent such a codependent pattern than to extract oneself from it once it has developed. This is done by negotiating a reasonable contract and job description in advance and monitoring it periodically. At times this agreement will be stretched but hopefully won't break.

However, if clergy and employer are caught up in this pattern, someone is going to have to interrupt it if this pattern is ever going to change. The one who initiates this change will need to be ready for some upset and unrest in the community. Change is almost always uncomfortable. Further, no employer ever asks an employee to work less!

Once a clergy has initiated this change, she or he will need to explore two questions: First, where do I find the greatest satisfaction in what I do? What parts of my work do I love most? What energizes and what drains me? How can I do more of what I love to do and do well and less of what I dislike and/ or do poorly? What is a healthy balance, and how do we get there?

I (Dick) once discovered the power of these questions. Tired, nearly burned out, thinking of withdrawing from ministry, I took part in a two-week training on life/career planning with Richard Bolles based on his books *What Color Is Your Parachute?* and *The Three Boxes of Life.*[23] Out of my discoveries in that exciting time of self-exploration, I came back and spoke with my church board. I told them, "I want to do more for you, and I want to do less for you. I want to do more pastoral counseling and more leadership of retreats, educational events, and creative worship designs. I want to do less administering building, budgeting, and fund-raising."

Almost too easily the board responded, "Why, Dick, those former things are what we appreciate about your ministry. As to the others, you never were very good at those. We can handle them." And we had a few more good years together.

Second, what is the amount of time I can reasonably invest in my work, still love it, and be fair to the important people to me and to myself? This question is so delicate. It is important to be as clear as we can, for rarely do many of us have good balance on this.

Earlier, we noted two perspectives on what causes burnout: the work setting or personal decisions and practices. Gradually, we become aware it is both. The workplace may have unreasonable or unfair expectations, and the individual may accept these patterns too easily.

Those in various ministry positions have reason to hope that their workplace is not as impersonal and harsh as those that Maslach and Leiter described. Still, there is ambiguity about what a minister does, how much time is needed for it, and what priorities should be applied when all cannot be reasonably done. Therefore, clergy also need to negotiate workplace expectations and issues.

Each of us will be wise to ask, "Where do I see myself from the descriptions of the various authors? What hints am I hearing for living well and working well? How can burnout and compassion fatigue be prevented, reduced, or treated in my life?"

THEOLOGICAL AMNESIA

There is another aspect of the cause of burnout, a most basic one. A/the cause of burnout may be "theological amnesia." That is to say, burnout may come from forgetting or ignoring why we are doing what we do—theologically speaking. We may also forget or ignore the theological resources accessible to us to renew us to do the difficult work we are called to do.

There are stories in the Bible of leaders who struggled with this at times. Perhaps they had theological amnesia as well. For example, the great prophet Moses, sick of the weeping and complaining of the people in the wilderness, cries out to God, "Why have you treated your servant so badly? Why have I not found favor in your sight, that you lay the burden of all this people on me? Did I conceive all this people . . . that you should say to me 'Carry them in your bosom as a nurse carries as a suckling child?'" (Numbers 11:11–12). Moses was wearing out under all the whining, and there was more to come!

We might consider Elijah, who one day was standing fearlessly against all the false prophets of his land, defeating and destroying them. Shortly after this, he was under threat, fleeing into the desert for fear of his life. While in the desert, "There came a voice to him that said, 'What are you doing here, Elijah?' He answered, 'I have been very zealous for the Lord, the God of hosts, for the Israelites have forsaken your covenant, thrown down your altars, and killed your prophets with the sword. I alone am left, and they are seeking my life to take it away'" (I Kings 19:13b–14). But the Lord told him to return, anoint a new king, and behold, he was not alone, but there were seven thousand in Israel who had not bowed their knee to a false god.

Or, centuries later, the Apostle Paul speaks time and again of the dangers, threats, and responsibilities that nearly overwhelmed him. For example, in II Corinthians 1:8–10, he wrote, "We do not want you to be unaware, brothers and sisters, of the affliction we experienced in Asia, for we were so unbearably crushed that we despaired of life itself. Indeed we felt that we had received the sentence of death."

When we think about Jesus in this regard, there is virtually no evidence of burnout in his life. However, there may be one brief incident of possible burnout. Of all things, he was coming down from a mystical time of spiritual communion. In divine transcendent brilliance, he had communed with Moses and Elijah in the stunned presence of his three closest disciples. When he and his companions came down the mountain, they encountered a distressed man with his son who suffered from epileptic seizures. The other disciples had been no help. The desperate father cried out for help. Jesus began with these words: "You faithless and perverse generation, how much longer must I be with you? How much longer must I put up with you?" Perhaps that is the brief glimpse into a momentary lapse into burnout or compassion fatigue. (Of course, other interpretations are possible.) But then he added, "Bring him here to me" (Matthew 17:17–18). And he responded healingly to the father and son's desperate need.

Burnout may come not only from *theological* amnesia but also from *ecclesiastical* amnesia, which is forgetfulness about what the nature of the church is, what it is called to be, and how it is to do its ministry. We may have ignored Paul's word to all the members of the church at Corinth: "To each is given a manifestation of the spirit [that is a spiritual gift for the ministry of the church] for the common good" (I Corinthians 12:7).

When such amnesia occurs, the spiritual gifts—and responsibilities—of the laity are missed or forgotten—by clergy and by congregation/agency. More demands fall on the minister's shoulders, less on lay leadership. The loss of creativity and the increase of clergy fatigue result.

ON THIS WE STAND

We see that some of God's greatest servants from the pages of the Bible suffered burnout at times in their lives. Further, as we noted earlier, all of us will experience at least stages 1 and 2 of burnout. In face of this threat, what theological resources are available to us? How do we overcome our theological and ecclesiastical amnesia? While we will further explore these resources in later chapters, for now, we consider foundational affirmations that are there to undergird us.

Paul, whose struggle with burnout we already mentioned, also describes how he was theologically sustained. He writes, "But we have this treasure in clay jars [or, as the King James Version translates so vividly, "We have this treasure in earthen vessels"], so that it may be made clear that this extraordinary power belongs to God and does not come from us. We are afflicted in every way but not crushed; perplexed, but not driven to despair, persecuted, but not forsaken, struck down but not destroyed. . . . We are given up to death for Jesus' sake, so that the life of Jesus may be made visible in our mortal flesh" (II Corinthians 4:7–11, portions).

We are in a calling we believe to be from God with important responsibilities, sometimes more than we can handle. And we operate in partnership with a community that also has a calling, gifts, and responsibilities for our mission. In that setting, how do we operate in a theologically fitting way?

We begin with the awareness that God is God and we are human. We are called to a life of faithfulness. However, the whole responsibility and the whole destiny are not in our hands.

There is a delightful story that Dick Sheppard, a beloved English minister of an earlier generation, told. He felt himself becoming sick, and as he fell asleep he was thinking that he could not get sick because of the many things he had to do. During the night, he had a dream. In that dream, God was pacing back in forth in heaven asking, "What am I going to do? Dick Sheppard is sick." Sheppard woke up, smiling sheepishly. He decided that God could handle his being sick and unavailable for a time, and so could he. That is theological awareness!

And so, we covenant and commit to a high but reasonable workload, no different than we would ask of a person under our supervision. Roy Oswald identified that as a fifty-hours-or-fewer work week.[24] That guideline is a starting place, but personal energy and other aspects may cause this to vary from person to person.

We (Ruth and Dick) once had a student who was an employee of a denomination. When her department was forced to make staff cuts, they gave her the portfolios and responsibilities for two positions. She tried so hard to perform all the services for both positions that she reported to us she was sleeping four hours a night! We, her professors, tried to intervene, warning her that she was tampering with her health. This dedicated minister heeded our advice as best she could and cut back so she could sleep six hours a night. She reported to us how much better and more efficient she felt when she did so!

DIAGNOSIS OF BURNOUT AND COMPASSION FATIGUE

If one is not sure, how can one gain clarity about whether there is burnout or compassion fatigue in one's life, and if so, how severe? There are at least two sets of instruments that can be used to learn about this. For one, the Compassion Fatigue Awareness Project offers three inventories: (a) Professional Quality of Life, an instrument to identify three aspects of professional quality of life—compassion satisfaction, burnout-fatigue, and secondary traumatic stress; (b) Compassion Fatigue Self-Test; and (c) Life Stress Self-Test (which might fit the next chapter even better). Each of these inventories is available on the website provided in the following endnote. These inventories are free of charge on the condition that the inventory is not altered, that credit is given to the author, and that there is no charge for its use.[25]

Another is the Maslach Burnout Inventory (MBI), considered the definitive measure of burnout. It has been used by many organizations and researchers to yield important discoveries and insight. This inventory is available in three versions, one more related to human services, one for educators, and a general survey that is applicable to persons in a wide range of occupations. In accordance with the authors' conviction that burnout results from social and work setting, this survey is often used in conjunction with another instrument they designed, the Staff Survey.[26]

These instruments may be helpful for a beginning awareness of one's situation and need. They will be even more helpful if discussed with a counselor or a caring friend, family member, or colleague whose perspective you trust. Professional—psychological, medical, or pastoral counselor—consultation may well be an important next step.

SO WHAT? WHAT DOES THIS SAY TO ME?

While this is the beginning of our book conversation about self-care, there are a few initial takeaways from this chapter.

One is that it is much easier, wiser, and better to prevent or reduce burnout than to try to heal from an advanced stage of it. And so, a careful reading to raise awareness and suggest healthy alterations is a wise use of this chapter. Further, we will never be far from this topic as we move through the rest of this book. All of the areas of self-care that we explore in the book's second portion are both good ends in themselves and important means to help one deal with the threat and impact of burnout or compassion fatigue.

If one senses that burnout is already taking its toll, what might be a first step to getting out of that rut? It will, of course, vary from individual to individual, but it just might be something like a group of nurses that Ayala Malakh Pines and associates described. These nurses had volunteered to work with terminally ill cancer patients. They were persons of high ideals who cared about their patients and wanted to help.

However, a number of factors combined to dampen their enthusiasm. The work was hard and discouraging. Further, it was painful to become close to patients and then lose them. Further still, very sick patients and their frightened families are often not grateful but demanding and even emotionally abusive.

Unconsciously, they began to do things to protect themselves such as a little more detachment, gallows humor, beginning to resent the very people they were there to help. When these feelings came, they felt guilt and shame. Some would try to hide such emotions as they looked about at the other nurses who seemed to be doing OK. They were beginning to have severe problems of staff morale and burnout.

A team of researchers-interventionists was called in to work with the nurses. The way this team started was fascinating. They called a group of them together and instructed each one to take a piece of paper and write their five greatest points of stress in their work. Then they were told to turn to each other and tell the others what they had written.

There was an electric atmosphere in the room as they did this. Emotions of laughter, tears, and relief were expressed. Each had felt alone in this struggle. When each discovered that colleagues were all contending with similar emotions, there was relief beyond words. They could give support to each other and strengthen their caring community. They were on their way back to being able to serve longer and well.[27]

We have summarized insights from some of the wisest students of burnout and compassion fatigue. This is offered to you for your thought and consideration with the hope that there are the seeds of discovery for effective and sustained ministry. Next, we will explore the corresponding threat of stress. Later, we shall go on to consider a variety of topics and practices that wise professionals have found renewing and life giving.

FOR YOUR REFLECTION AND CONVERSATION

1. Where do you see yourself as regards the balance of the demands on you and your ways of resting and recovering? Do important other people in your life agree with your assessment?

2. As you look back on your life, can you identify times when you were burned out? When you suffered from compassion fatigue? From secondary traumatic stress? Tell another about them. Also tell how you dealt with that crisis and recovered (if you have).

3. We have mentioned a few Bible passages that point to our theological resources for addressing these threats. Which spoke to you most deeply? What other Bible passages come to your mind? What do you take from these biblical passages as far as addressing your possible burnout and compassion fatigue?

4. What are your hopes, your questions, and your needs as you begin this journey with us?

Chapter Four

Stress

The greatest weapon against stress is our ability to choose one thought over another.

—William James[1]

In the previous chapter, we explored burnout and compassion fatigue. We now turn our attention to addressing the subject of stress. We have already noted that those in ministry encounter much stress as part of fulfilling their vocation. The dynamics and expectations of the pastoral role have always entailed this. With the many societal shifts described earlier and the rapid pace of change, the continual need to adapt only increases that strain. Thriving in ministry requires the capacity to manage stress well, and in this chapter, we will deal with that challenge.

Since people talk of feeling stressed in regard to many different experiences, we will seek first to define more clearly the meaning of stress. We will explore the various aspects of our "stress response," noting both its benefits for short-term acute stressors and its potentially negative effects when stress is ongoing and chronic. From there we will look at the new science of stress for further insight into the importance of our mindset and explore the potential benefits of stress. Finally, we will offer beginning suggestions for handling ministry's stressful aspects.

SO WHAT EXACTLY IS STRESS?

Hans Selye began researching what he would coin "stress" in 1936, later defining it as "the nonspecific response of the body to any demand."[2] His early work involved subjecting rats to various noxious situations and noting the similarity of bodily responses elicited. These early observations kicked off a tremendous amount of research into what we now refer to as "the stress response."

Among the many definitions of stress, here are two that will help us better understand it. Dr. Herbert Benson and Eileen Stuart put forward this definition in *The Wellness Book*: "Stress is the *perception* of a threat to one's physical or psychological well-being and the *perception* that one is unable to cope with the threat" (italics theirs).[3] This helpfully points out the importance of how we view stress. What may be very stressful to one person may result in very little stress for another. Stress is therefore a highly individual matter. And much of this relates to how each person has assessed both the level of threat and their capacity to cope.

Carnegie Mellon University researchers Tracy Herbert and Sheldon Cohen also emphasize the importance of perception in their understanding of stress. They write, "Stress arises when a person appraises a situation as threatening or otherwise demanding, perceives that it is important to respond, and does not have an appropriate coping response immediately available."[4] It is those times in ministry—when we are confronted with demanding situations that we know require a response but that seem to outstrip our coping capabilities—that we experience significant stress. The prominent role that perception plays in the experience of stress is important because it helps to explain why individuals vary widely in their levels of experienced stress to similar situations. As we shall see, it also points the way toward how to better manage stress.

It should be noted that stress is on a continuum and that a certain amount can be positive when it increases focus and enhances performance and efficiency. When a manageable deadline is looming, it is quite amazing how much better we can suddenly concentrate on completing the task at hand. So our goal is not to lead an entirely stress-free life. That would probably be boring and without much challenge and accomplishment. And for those within the vocation of ministry, it would be quite impossible. But when our ongoing stress moves beyond increasing focus and efficiency to triggering an outright stress response, it is then that it becomes problematic.

THE STRESS RESPONSE

Like other animals, we have been marvelously made to be able to respond quickly and effectively to physical danger. When confronted with a significant threat to our well-being, our brains and our bodies respond with what has been called the "fight or flight" response, which prepares us to battle or flee from imminent peril. This complex physiological response works well in cases when we are suddenly confronted with a physical threat, such as an attacking bear or an armed intruder, and it helped to assure our ancient ancestors' survival. But ministry demands, marital conflict, or constant criticisms are threats to our well-being that are not effectively resolved with a fight or flight response. They remain as ongoing stressors for such long periods of time that the physiological effects of the stress response can be detrimental. To understand this, it is helpful to consider this response in more depth.

The amygdala is a small part of the brain that acts as its alarm center. Upon receiving sensory information from our seeing, hearing, smelling, or feeling something that indicates danger, it sets off the alarm to respond immediately. Because it receives information directly and can interpret and act more quickly than those parts of our brain that process thoughts, it can start a response even before one is consciously aware of the danger. This happened to me (Ruth) recently when I was taking a walk close to dusk. Suddenly I startled and jumped over a snake in the road before it had really come to my conscious thought that it was even there.

The amygdala sets off the fight or flight response by sending a distress signal to the hypothalamus of the brain, which functions as a command center and arouses the body to danger. By activating the sympathetic nervous system, it gets the body ready for action. The adrenal glands secrete the stress hormones adrenaline and noradrenaline into the bloodstream. This energizes the body, causing the heart to beat faster, increasing the blood pressure, and sending blood to muscles, heart, and other vital organs that will need to do extra work. Breathing becomes more rapid to take in more oxygen for exertion and to increase alertness. Glucose and fats are released into the bloodstream to provide more energy to run or fight.

If it is appraised that the danger continues after this initial surge of adrenaline subsides, the hypothalamus activates what is known as the HPA (hypothalamus, pituitary gland, and adrenal glands) axis—the second aspect of the stress response. The result is that cortisol is released into the bloodstream, which then keeps the sympathetic nervous system active and the body revved up and alert to respond to the threat. When the danger is past, often indicated by the body having exerted a large amount of energy in fighting or fleeing, then the parasympathetic nervous system of the body dampens the response, and cortisol levels fall. The body can then rebalance and return to its previous more relaxed state.[5]

A couple years ago, while just finishing up extended renovations on a recently bought home, we smelled smoke and soon discovered a roof fire. With great speed and strength, my husband and a friend put up ladders, pulled up garden hoses, jumped on the roof, and sprayed as much water as they could on the fire. I (Ruth) grabbed the phone to call 911, raced to shut off the electricity, and then ran into the house several times to grab important documents and photo albums. We were fortunate. By the time the fire engines got to our country home about twenty minutes later, the fire was out, and the damage was contained and easily repaired. We all experienced the energizing effects of the stress response that day. Although it took a while for us to quit talking about it and calm down, eventually we were again back to normal.

The fight or flight stress response is a rapid and well-orchestrated bodily response that helps us survive physical danger through extra energy and focus. And there certainly remain occasions when we may still encounter sudden threatening physical danger that requires this kind of response. However, most of the stress we experience in contemporary society and, more specifically, within ministry is of an ongoing and chronic nature. It is fed by our capacity to think and worry about problems, such that the stress response remains activated and the stress hormones continue circulating throughout our bodies. Although life-saving during times of acute physical danger, the fight or flight stress response can cause bodily damage if chronically activated by ongoing psychological stress.

DETRIMENTAL EFFECTS OF CHRONIC STRESS

With this understanding of the fight or flight stress response, it will now be easier to grasp the potential negative consequences of ongoing stress. We will look briefly at some of the physical and mental health problems that can be triggered or exacerbated and then factors that affect the perception of stress.

Effects of Stress on Physical Health

Prolonged stress can insidiously affect our cardiovascular system because sustained high levels of the stress hormones (adrenaline, noradrenaline, and cortisol) may cause increased inflammation of our blood vessels. With such irritation, it is more likely that a chronic and progressive disease process called atherosclerosis develops, in which deposits of cholesterol, lipids, calcium, and cells form plaques in the walls of arteries.[6] As these plaques progress, they may obstruct blood flow or they may weaken the artery wall so it balloons out as an aneurysm, with the potential for rupture. Alternately, pieces of plaque may suddenly break loose to form a blood clot. If this occurs in heart vessels, it may result in a blockage that causes a heart attack. If this happens in brain vessels, the consequence may be a stroke. And renal disease may be the outcome if it occurs in the blood vessels of the kidneys. Because this type of damage to blood vessels can cause so many problems throughout the body, Dr. Richard N. Fogoros has written, "In the United States, atherosclerosis causes more death and disability than any other disease."[7]

The experience of ongoing stress often increases cardiac risk factors in other ways. When feeling overly stressed, people may often overeat or eat more poorly, choosing junk foods and those high in fats, salts, and sugars. They may take less time to exercise, gain weight, and smoke more. These behaviors increase the risk of a cardiac event and can affect blood vessels throughout the body.

I (Dick) learned about stress the hard way and had a "face to face" encounter with these health hazards. Shouldering the stresses of a demanding senior pastorate, I went to what I thought was a routine doctor appointment. While there, I mentioned a slight chest pain and was immediately referred to a cardiologist, who detected a blockage in my left anterior descending artery. He administered a heart catheterization and placed stents. I was told that, before this procedure was available, this blockage was known as "the widow maker." While recovering, I went to cardiovascular rehabilitation sessions for twelve weeks. There I discovered that mine was a "lifestyle disease" and that there were steps to improve lifestyle—exercise, diet, and meditative practices, among others. Recently, at my annual appointment, I thanked my cardiologist for twenty years of good life. He told me that I had been a good patient and that was a significant part of my successful and sustained recovery.

Prolonged stress also has a negative effect on the immune system. The stress response that arouses those parts of the body needed to fight or flee at the same time suppresses functions that are not essential in such an emergency, including the immune system. The released adrenaline and cortisol interfere with the proper functioning of the immune cells. Since these are the very cells that defend against bacteria and viruses and that produce antibodies, this then results in a lessened capacity to defend against a wide range of diseases, from colds to cancer.[8] So the common experience of getting a cold or sick during a particularly stressful time is quite probably no coincidence.

Effects of Stress on Mental Health

Chronic stress contributes to the development of depression in several ways. Dr. Paul Gilbert, who is a professor of clinical psychology at the University of Derby and authored the book *Overcoming Depression*, wrote, "Stress is probably the most common influence on our mood chemicals. Many depressions are triggered and maintained by stress."[9]

The release of cortisol during a prolonged stress response affects the brain. In fact, ongoing and significantly elevated levels of cortisol are toxic to the brain because they cause inflammation and suppress the growth hormone factor that repairs brain tissues. Furthermore, they cause the neurotransmitters related to depression, such as serotonin, to become depleted.[10]

In addition, we know that disrupted sleep can trigger depression, and stress can cause sleep disruption. When the brain's stress circuits are engaged, there is a steady disappearance of slow-wave sleep, the deep, restful form of sleep the brain needs to keep brain hormones and chemicals in balance and to coordinate tissue repair. Many of the core symptoms of depression emerge with the disappearance of slow sleep—depressed mood, negative thoughts, erratic appetite, diminished concentration, and less social interest. [11]

Probably many of us have had the experience of waking up at night during especially stressful times and being unable to sleep because our anxious minds are going over and over that about which we are worried. Then when we get up, we still feel tired and inadequately rested to face the stresses of the day. If this goes on for a prolonged period, it increases our vulnerability to depression. University of Kansas psychology professor and researcher Dr. Steve Ilardi writes, "Disrupted sleep is one of the most potent triggers of depression, and there's evidence that most episodes of mood disorder are preceded by at least several weeks of subpar sleep." [12]

Factors Affecting the Perception of Stress

We must point out again that perception plays a crucial role as to whether a particular stressor results in the experience of a full fight or flight stress response, with the resulting negative consequences that we have just explored. For example, when people undergo stressful experiences over which they feel they have no control, they are far more likely to become depressed than when they feel there is something they can do to change things. [13]

Difficult early life experiences, such as abuse, neglect, or parental loss, can make one more susceptible to depression. Such stressful experiences at a time when the young brain is developing increase the sensitivity of the stress response system, such that it is triggered more easily and more fully. [14] Furthermore, our life experiences, especially during childhood, help us develop our core beliefs about ourselves and our world, which then function as the lens through which we interpret what happens to us. These interpretations of our experience generate automatic thoughts that powerfully influence our emotions, stress levels, and hormones because our brains accept these thoughts as the reality to which they need to respond. [15] For example, a core belief from childhood that one is unlovable can escalate a relationship breakup or divorce into an experience of despair. With such a core belief, a breakup is easily viewed as confirming that one is unlovable and will never find lasting love. It thus becomes a stressful situation indeed.

The role of perception in the experience of stress and its bodily consequences has been shown by several other findings. Those who struggle with low self-esteem tend to feel overwhelmed and stressed more quickly by a difficult situation because they more easily appraise themselves as not having the personal capacity to meet the challenge. Those with high self-esteem, on the other hand, generally feel more capable of dealing with the same potentially stressful event and thereby view it as much less stressful.

Much research has been done on the relationship between having a Type A personality and the likelihood of stress-related coronary disease. People with a Type A behavior pattern have very high expectations of themselves to accomplish more and more in less time. As such, they live under the constant pressure of time and trying to achieve more and thus can be tense and impatient. Such people tend to appraise situations as more stressful, react with a stronger stress response, and experience heightened levels of stress hormones. This then makes them more vulnerable to develop atherosclerosis and other related diseases.[16]

THEN ENTERS THE NEW SCIENCE OF STRESS

Dr. Kelly McGonigal, a health psychologist at Stanford University, starts her book *The Upside of Stress* with a research study that changed her mind about stress. Using information similar to what has been written above about the "fight or flight" response and the detrimental effects of prolonged stress, she had spent the early part of her career warning people of the dangers of stress and encouraging them to reduce stress for their health and well-being. Then she ran across a research study in which thirty thousand adults were asked how much stress they experienced and whether they believed it was harmful to their health. Eight years later, it was determined which of these research participants had died.

The study found that the risk of dying was increased by 43 percent among those with high levels of stress *but only* if they also believed that stress was harmful to their health. Those who did not believe stress was harmful had no increased risk of death, even if their reported stress levels were just as high. In fact, their risk of death was even lower than those who reported low levels of stress. These puzzling results caused the researchers to conclude "that it wasn't stress alone that was killing people. It was the combination of stress and the *belief* that stress is harmful."[17]

This led McGonigal to dig deeper into the research that had been done on stress over the past thirty years. While finding evidence for the harmful effects already cited, she also found benefits to stress that were less widely known. These benefits included facilitating learning and growth; becoming stronger, smarter, and more successful; and growing more compassionate and courageous. Instead of teaching people to manage their stress by reducing or avoiding it, she now indicates that the best way to deal with stress is by shifting the way they think about it and even embracing it. Since clergy often do not have the option of radically reducing stress if they are to remain

within their ministry positions, this new science of stress may offer considerable assistance to our efforts to manage stress and care for ourselves.

More Than One Stress Response

McGonigal indicates that two concepts are important for this new understanding of stress. The first is that there is not just one uniform stress response for all stressful occasions. That is, the human response to every
stressful situation is not a full-blown "fight or flight" response, which is most
often mismatched to the stresses of contemporary life. Rather, there are several different stress responses, each differing in the ratio of hormones released, cardiovascular changes involved, and other bodily aspects altered. As
we have already seen, the "fight or flight" response, or what she calls the
"threat response," is activated during times of severe threat and danger. But
McGonigal indicates there are two other stress responses—the "challenge
response" and the "tend-and-befriend response."

The challenge response occurs when the situation is stressful but less life
threatening. One's stress system is still activated, such that adrenaline is
released, the heart rate increases, more energy is available for muscles and
brain, and alertness increases, but it is for the purpose of helping one perform
well under pressure. Musicians and athletes often experience this challenge
response. It enables peak performance by enhancing concentration and confidence and by giving them access to physical and mental resources. Pastors
may experience this challenge response in relation to the pressure of preaching. We, your writing team, experienced stress as challenge while working to
complete this book by the date we had promised.

The challenge response is different from the "fight or flight" response
because a different ratio of stress hormones is released. Among these are
higher levels of DHEA, a neurosteroid that helps the brain grow, learn, and
become stronger from stressful experiences. It also counteracts some of the
negative effects of cortisol. Ongoing high levels of cortisol in a prolonged
"fight or flight" response can cause the cardiac, immune, and depression
problems mentioned above. However, when high levels of DHEA are also
released in the "challenge" response, its ratio to cortisol is changed, and there
is a reduced risk of these health difficulties.

The "tend-and-befriend response" is facilitated by the release of yet another hormone from the pituitary gland in response to the stress. This hormone is oxytocin, which creates the desire to connect with others, enhances
empathy and intuition, and encourages trust and care for others. By turning
down the fear response and suppressing the instinct to flee or freeze, oxytocin gives courage, such that one is motivated to protect loved ones who are
being threatened. Oxytocin also enhances cardiovascular health, by helping
heart cells to repair and regenerate.

Stress Mindsets

The second major concept McGonigal talks about is that of mindsets, which she says are "beliefs that shape your reality."[18] A mindset is like a filter through which everything is seen, and therefore it affects how one thinks, feels, and acts. It shapes how one interprets experience and therefore how one responds to it. As a fundamental belief, it reflects one's philosophy of life. Mindsets include such beliefs as: "money will make you happy" or "people cannot change."[19] We each also have a mindset in regard to how we view stress. It may be a mindset that views stress as negative and harmful and therefore something that should be avoided. Or it may be a mindset that sees stress positively, as enhancing performance, health, and growth, and therefore to be utilized. This stress mindset affects our biochemistry and thus shapes our emotions and response to stress.

Research shows that a mindset that views stress positively and sees it as a challenge, rather than as an unmanageable problem, leads to more beneficial results. McGonigal writes, "People who believe stress is enhancing are less depressed and more satisfied with their lives than those who believe stress is harmful. They have more energy and fewer health problems. They're happier and more productive at work. . . . They have greater confidence in their ability to cope with those challenges, and they are better able to find meaning in difficult circumstances."[20]

It appears that one's stress mindset affects what kind of stress response is elicited. For those who view stress as harmful, the experience of feeling stress leads to being stressed out over being stressed, which then leads more easily to a "fight or flight" type of response, with its attendant problems, if the situation is prolonged. Those with a more positive stress mindset may activate instead the "challenge" or "tend-and-befriend" response, both of which lead to more favorable outcomes and help people thrive under stress.

This leads us to consider how it is that we may change our mindset about stress. McGonigal suggests, first of all, that we need to become aware of our current stress mindset, something she calls developing "mindset mindfulness."[21] This is done simply by noticing what it is that we are thinking and saying to ourselves about the stress we encounter on a regular basis, along with the feelings and actions such thoughts elicit. When we start to experience the physiological effects of a stress response—such as anxiety, increased heart rate, or tenseness—we need to take note, embrace it, and tell ourselves that something meaningful to us is at stake. Then we can proceed to use that extra energy to do something that will address the problem at hand, rather than use it to try avoid the problem or suppress the stress response.

She further suggests that the best time to practice new responses to stress is when we are right in the middle of a stressful situation. The brain's neuroplasticity enables it to change and grow, and that capacity to learn is heightened by hormones released during the stress response. Learning from stressful experiences increases our capacity to handle well such situations in the future. In time, it also increases our confidence, so that similar challenges become less stressful.

Astronaut Scott Kelly spent almost a year in space—340 consecutive days—which is more time in space than any other American. He was manning the space station, doing technically demanding and risky work, and being himself the subject of research as to how the human body is affected by so long a time in space. During an interview on NPR, he reflected on the reality that there was the real possibility at any point that things could go very wrong, such that he and others would not survive. But he did not let his mind go wandering down the road of catastrophizing. His strategy for handling this intense pressure was to focus on those things he could control and to ignore what he couldn't. Using the energy naturally elicited by a stress response to address the problem at hand and disciplining his thoughts in this way resulted in his being able to manage well the highly stressful situations he encountered. The title of his book *Endurance: A Year in Space, a Lifetime of Discovery* expresses something of his view of stress.[22]

McGonigal defines stress simply as "what arises when something you care about is at stake."[23] She encourages us to realize that a meaningful life will, in fact, be a stressful life. If we are engaged with life and pursuing that which makes life meaningful, such as personal relationships, parenting, and a pastoral vocation, we will inevitably experience stress. But she encourages us to focus on its benefits. When we notice our heart pounding and our restless anxiety, we can consider how stress is helping us rise to the challenge of doing something important by focusing our attention, increasing our energy, and enhancing our motivation. When we find ourselves wanting to be near family and friends and feeling the desire to protect them, we can consider how stress is helping us connect with others and increase our courage. And when after a particularly stressful time, we find ourselves still mentally charged, going over the situation repeatedly in our minds or talking about it time and time again with others to make sense of it, we can appreciate that stress is helping us learn and grow as it pushes us to process and integrate the experience while our nervous system returns to its previous balance. Furthermore, in the midst of stress, it is helpful to remind ourselves that what we are going through is connected to what is important and meaningful to us and try to respond in ways that fit with our values.

SELF-CARE AND STRESS MANAGEMENT

With this fuller understanding of our responses to stress and the effects that stress has on us, let us consider the initial implications this carries for stress management and self-care. The first thing to note is that the activation of our sympathetic nervous system and the release of stress hormones, such as adrenaline and cortisol, are crucially important for an effective response to life-threatening situations. However, these bodily responses can cause harm if prolonged because of ongoing psychological stress. It is therefore important that we pay attention to how we typically respond to stress and become aware of the warning signals we tend to have that indicate that our stress level is becoming problematic.

We may experience physical symptoms such as headaches, indigestion, sleep problems, back or neck pain, or tiredness. Or we may notice behaviors that indicate excessive stress, such as overeating or being bossy and critical of others. It may be that emotions, such as feeling overwhelmed, easily upset, crying, or anger, emerge when stress is high. Or we may notice cognitive symptoms of stress, such as difficulty making decisions, memory problems, lack of creativity, and loss of humor. Each individual has different warning signals that the stress is getting to be too much, and it is good to be self-aware enough to recognize them. Many of these stress warning symptoms are caused by the extra adrenaline and cortisol that the stress response has dumped into our bodily system, which keeps the body tense and activated.

During a life-threatening situation in which one survives by fighting or fleeing, a great deal of this extra energy is used up, so that when the danger is over, the body is able to relax again. But when the stress response is related to ongoing psychologically stressful situations, we may wonder how we can help ourselves release this extra stress energy, reduce stress hormones, and rebalance our nervous system so that we are in a more relaxed and healthy state.

This leads us directly to realizing the importance of physical self-care and, in particular, that of exercising. Aerobic exercise is comparable to the energy exertion of fighting or fleeing, and thus can greatly assist our stress response system to rebalance rather than remain in an aroused stress state.

Slow diaphragmatic breathing also counteracts the stress response by eliciting the relaxation response. It helps to turn off the sympathetic nervous system and enhances the parasympathetic system, so our bodies and brains get back into balance, release the stress, and relax. Diaphragmatic breathing is breathing so that the air taken in causes the belly, not the chest, to expand. Twenty minutes of such breathing has been shown to turn down the stress response, lower blood pressure, improve mood by increasing serotonin, and heighten attention and higher-level processing due to more oxygen going to the brain.[24] Furthermore, meditative practices that elicit the relaxation response also assist the body and mind to move to a more relaxed and balanced place. We will look more closely at these aspects of self-care later.

One thing that will not be helpful is to ruminate negatively about the stressful situation we are facing. To think repeatedly about our problems, troubling emotions, defects of character, and mistakes only makes us feel worse. It deepens our negative mood and decreases our motivation, concentration, and capacity to problem-solve. In fact, social psychologist Sonja Lyubomirsky, who we will meet later, tells us it is toxic and a bad habit that must be broken. It's far better to distract ourselves from such thinking and do something to address the concern. [25]

When I (Ruth) begin to feel overstretched and stressed by too much work and pending deadlines, it is easy for me to start feeling overwhelmed and more emotionally upset. Negatively ruminating about the situation comes easily but only makes things worse. What I have found to be helpful at such times is to get myself organized and tackle the task of getting something done. The extra energy and focus of stress enables me to make some progress on what seemed like unsurmountable tasks, and as some work is accomplished, my sense of being stressed out lessens. I also find it is very beneficial to take a break and go for a brisk walk in the outdoors.

Research has, in fact, shown that spending time in nature can reduce feelings of stress, improve mood, and contribute to physical well-being. One study on the effect of spending time in nature found that 95 percent of people reported that their mood changed from being depressed, anxious, and stressed to being more balanced and calm after spending time outside. Not only does it contribute to emotional well-being, being in nature also reduces blood pressure, muscle tension, and the production of stress hormones. [26] It draws us out of focusing on ourselves and pulls us into the natural world filled with beauty. Evidence for the benefits of being in nature is strong enough that there are now ecotherapists, who use nature as an aspect of therapy and who consider many of us who live in high-tech societies as suffering from a "nature deficit disorder." [27] I (Ruth) find immersion in nature to be a wonderful way to release stress and regain calmness. Even looking out the window at trees and water is internally calming to me. As I do so, Psalm 23 comes to mind, "[God] leads me beside the still waters; [God] restores my soul" (vv. 2–3, adapted for inclusive language).

From our discussion of stress, it is obvious how important a role perception plays in determining how stressful a situation is experienced to be. It is when we assess that we do not have adequate coping resources or capacity to respond adequately to what we view as a threat that we begin to feel significant stress. Spiritual practices that nurture our relationship with God, such that we more fully trust God as a source of strength and wisdom, can greatly increase our sense of adequacy in dealing with the stresses of ministry. Social support also enables us to view ourselves as better able to cope with difficult situations. Chapters on spiritual self-care and relational self-care will delve further into these areas.

Finally, McGonigal's work shows that how we think about stress, that is, our mindset regarding stress, is of crucial importance. A positive mindset that sees the benefits of stress can elicit the resources of the challenge or tend-and-befriend stress responses, instead of the more problematic threat response. But there is still more to explore in future chapters regarding how we can nurture a positive thought life and develop wisdom, such that we can better cope with the challenges of ministry. We will now turn to explore more fully the various aspects of self-care.

FOR YOUR REFLECTION AND CONVERSATION

1. What aspects of your ministry and life do you experience as being particularly stressful? What causes them to be so stressful for you? How well are you handling it all?
2. What do you experience when you feeling overly stressed? What physical, emotional, psychological, and relational signs do you have?
3. What did you learn about the body's responses to stress that you find helpful in better understanding your own experience of facing stress?
4. When have you experienced the "fight or flight" stress response? How about the "challenge" or "tend-and-befriend" stress responses?
5. What did you learn from this chapter that will help you begin to better handle the stress in your life and increase your physical and mental health and well-being?

Part II

Strategies of Self-Care

Chapter Five

A Starting Place

Resilience

Our habit is to view challenging situations as if something is wrong; that we are a victim and we have a problem. What if instead of a problem we perceive stress as a signal to call on our resourcefulness, our intelligence, care, and courage? Resilience grows when we become intentional about bringing our best to difficult life seasons.

—Tara Brach[1]

Now that we have viewed the changes and hazards of ministry in the twenty-first century and have described burnout, compassion fatigue, and stress, our next question is: how do we survive and thrive in the face of it all? A beginning answer may be found in an important concept that has been discovered and developed in recent years. This concept is resilience.

WHAT IS RESILIENCE?

A focus on resilience is part of a shift in psychology from considering what is wrong to what is right, from psychopathology to positive psychology. So what is resilience? "It is . . . *the ability to bounce back*. The word comes from the Latin word *resilire*, 'to leap back.'"[2]

Martin Seligman, a pioneer in conceptualizing and applying resilience, views it within an understanding of well-being. He identifies five elements in well-being. One is *positive emotion*—happiness, life satisfaction. Another is *engagement*—taking part in totally absorbing challenging activities. Still another is *meaning*—belonging to and serving something that is greater than the individual. Then there is *accomplishment*—succeeding, mastering chosen ac-

tivities for the satisfaction of the achievement itself. The last element is
positive relationships—finding and relating to the people who participate in
well-being and encourage it for the others.[3]

Seligman has been instrumental in helping develop educational experiences for children and youth to help them grow in well-being and resilience.
He has also participated in the U.S. Army program of training in resilience to
prepare soldiers who are not only physically fit but psychologically fit. It is
worth asking what this positive psychology concept says to clergy in this
time of five-hundred-year rummage sales and perfect storms.

Pauline Boss offers a nuanced definition: "I define resiliency as the ability to stretch (like elastic) or flex (like a suspension bridge) in response to the
pressures and strains of life." She expands on the bridge analogy: "Stress
means the bridge has pressure on it, strain means the bridge is shaking but
holding, crisis means the bridge is collapsing, and resiliency means the
bridge is bending in response to the stress on it but can absorb this pressure
[and perform what it was created for] without incurring damage."[4]

Al Siebert further fills in this definition by suggesting that resilience
includes the following abilities to:

- cope well with high levels of ongoing disruptive change;
- sustain good health and energy when under constant pressure;
- bounce back easily from setbacks;
- overcome adversities;
- change to a new way of working and living when an old way is no longer
  possible; and
- do all this without acting in dysfunctional or harmful ways.[5]

Siebert points out furthermore that there is a verb form for resilience,
"resile," as well as an adverb form, "resiling." These grammar possibilities
remind us that resiliency is more something one does than something one
has. Indeed, it is a process with constant room to grow and fresh challenges
in which to be resilient. As Sheryl Sandberg and Adam Grant note, "Resilience is not a fixed personality trait. It's a lifelong project."[6]

Siebert has also created a "Resiliency Quiz" that may be accessed through
the reference in this endnote.[7] The quiz can help you discover not only your
overall resiliency but also where you are, where you are not, and where you
have grown or regressed. The creators of this quiz are careful to say this is for
insight and reflection; it is not a clinically verified instrument.

While there have been persons who have overcome adversities over the
centuries, the specific observation and study of resilience is quite recent.
Such studies began in the past sixty to seventy-five years. The understanding
of how to experience and teach well-being and resilience has been developed
in the past twenty years or so.

One of these pioneers in studying resilience is Emmy Werner, who with her colleagues began a research project in 1954 with 698 children in Kauai, Hawaii. Some 210 of these children were born and raised in poverty, suffered pre- or perinatal complications, lived in families with chronic discord or psychopathology, and were reared by mothers with less than an eighth-grade education. They saw the prognosis for these children's future as very grim. And indeed, two-thirds of these children developed learning, behavioral, or mental health problems.

"However, one out of three of these children grew into competent, confident, and caring adults."[8] They grew up without learning or behavioral problems as children and adolescents. They managed home life well and reached reasonable educational and vocational goals. In their longitudinal study of these children, Werner and associates could report, "By the time they reached age 40, not one of these individuals was unemployed, none had been in trouble with the law, and none had to rely on social services."[9]

Werner and her team asked what contributed to the resilience of these children and identified three clusters of factors. The first was individual temperamental characteristics. Throughout infancy and childhood, they were seen as active, affectionate, good natured, cheerful, friendly, and sociable. In their older childhood years, they demonstrated problem-solving skills, higher reading skills, and, perhaps, a special talent.

Second, there were protective factors in the family. There might have been a close bond with "at least one emotionally stable person who was sensitive to their needs," perhaps a grandparent or aunt, a substitute caregiver. Resilient boys often came from homes with structure and rules and perhaps an adult male role model.

Third were the helpful factors in the community. Elders and peers in the community enriched their lives. Perhaps a favorite teacher, caring neighbor, friends among their associates, youth leaders, ministers, or church groups influenced them positively.[10]

Still, we are led to ponder, what contributed to these children's resilience against the odds? What can be learned from this? And how can these discoveries be brought to bear other places where such resiliency might be needed?

HOW DOES ONE BECOME RESILIENT?

What do these studies mean to us clergy? How can we access resilience and become more adept at it, when reverses, difficulties, and crises come our way?

We might start with the recognition of how important this topic is. As Dean Becker, president of Adaptive Learning Systems, has stated, "More than education, more than experience, more than training, a person's level of resilience will determine who succeeds and who fails. That's true in the cancer ward, it's true in the Olympics, and it's true in the boardroom."[11]

This leads us to a basic question—are resilient persons born that way? Is resilience in one's genes? We can probably think of a person who, time and again, faces reverses and crises and not only survives but comes out stronger.

Those who have studied this question carefully acknowledge that there are a few people born with abundant and obvious resilient gifts (as Werner and associates noted in that pioneering study). They see resilience as a characteristic possessed by some and not by others. For example, the Strength-scope organization lists twenty-four strengths in four categories—Emotional, Relational, Thinking, and Execution skills. They list resilience as a relational strength and define it: "You deal effectively with setbacks and enjoy overcoming difficult challenges."[12] They seem to see it as a strength possessed by some but not by all.

However, others note that all of us have some potential. Resilience can be learned. New methods and skills can be mastered. It is well worth the effort! As Sheryl Sandberg and Adam Grant note, "Resilience is the strength and speed of our response to adversity—and we can build it. It isn't about having a backbone. It's about strengthening the muscles around our backbone."[13]

Nan Henderson compares gaining resilience to learning to ride a bicycle. Everyone can learn. However, for some it comes naturally, seemingly automatically. Others may have a much slower learning process. But, with time and effort, all can learn.[14]

Seligman lists five elements in the journey into becoming more resilient. The first has to do with how we regard the problem confronting us. When an unexpected and unwanted event occurs, all of us have feelings of fear, uncertainty, perhaps numbness—resilient or not. Where we go with those feelings is the place to start. Most basically, we need to be aware of a "victim reaction" or "learned helplessness." This reaction can take a number of forms. It may be blaming others—this happened because of the government or "the system" or fate or something else. One may conclude: "It is all out of my control and there is nothing I can do."

Or a victim response may be a mantra such as "Life isn't fair, and it's happened again." Joan Borysenko speaks of three poisons of pessimistic thinking: taking things personally, seeing the problem as pervasive of all the other areas of life, and believing that problems are permanent.[15] Such feelings are normal initially. But it is important not to stay there.

Clearly a basic step in becoming more resilient is to identify any victim thinking and to shed it as much as one can, so that other problem-solving thinking can begin. Granted, this is easier said than done. Still, at least being aware of the presence of victim thinking is an important first step. It is important to understand that these shattered beliefs and feelings are normal.

The second element is to reduce anxiety by learning to control intrusive thoughts and images. This step is to resolve to face the reality of the situation. It's all too easy to rationalize, to deny, to engage in wishful thinking, but those evasive thoughts are self-defeating. It is important to acknowledge the situation and to take at least an initial step to address it.

There may be many hurts and feelings that come with the upsetting situation. Some of us may be of the temperament that wants to live in those feelings, explore them, and express them, and this has been useful for us in the past. However, the practical wisdom in these moments of upset and crisis is to "control their emotional reactions in a crisis, engage the problems, and then process their feelings afterward."[16]

A third element is to engage in constructive self-disclosure. One can turn to a trusted individual—friend, family, or professional—to tell some of the feelings inside, those we can't seem to ignore, and begin to think and talk about a different way. Quite possibly a beginning perspective and some possible responses will begin to emerge.

The fourth element is to create a narrative in which one can see the stressful event in a new light. It might be helpful to take this step with a sense of curiosity. Siebert suggests that a helpful response is "a sort of 'open-brainedness' [that] does not distort new information with preexisting assumptions or beliefs. Active curiosity lets you orient yourself to new developments."[17]

Seligman speaks of seeing the frustrating event as a "fork in the road" in which one senses paradox, "loss and gain, grief and gratitude, vulnerability and strength."[18] Following this narrative, one can see what personal strengths were engaged, what relationships came out of this, and how one's spiritual life was enhanced. Similarly, Borysenko quotes an adage from William Arthur Ward, "The pessimist complains about the wind; the optimist expects it to change; the realist adjusts the sails."[19] An African proverb suggests, "Calm seas do not make skillful sailors."[20]

The fifth element is to articulate what life principles were experienced and are still needed to live with openness to the future. One of these life principles may be a trust in the meaningfulness of one's life and in the opportunity to discern meaning within the crisis one is facing. In this connection, many speak of Viktor Frankl, the Austrian psychiatrist who, along with his wife and family, was arrested and imprisoned in the Holocaust of World War II.

Frankl survived, at least in part, through his remarkable thinking and strategy in the midst of the most intense suffering and direst of circumstances. He concluded that to survive, one needed some hope for the future; the ability to transcend one's environment, sometimes through humor; and a belief in the meaningfulness of one's life. He would often quote the philosopher Friedrich Nietzsche: "Those who have a 'why' to live for can bear with almost any 'how.'"

After the war, Frankl constructed a new theory and method of therapy that he called logotherapy—therapy through assisting one to find meaning. He pointed to three kinds of values where one might find meaning. There are creative values—finding meaning by doing worthwhile work of some kind. Further there are experiential values—experiencing beauty, truth, compassion, kindliness, saintliness, for example. And finally there are attitudinal values. Even when faced with uncontrollable suffering or death, one has the opportunity to find meaning in the attitude with which one endures it. [21]

This subject of meaningfulness has particular significance for us clergy. It might be said that we are in a "meaning profession." We are those who interpret foundational beliefs that we believe are basic to the meaning of life. It can be reasonably expected that we have something to offer here.

At the same time, while we search for our own resilience, we may discern that our crisis is a crisis of meaning. We may reflect on all the changes mentioned in chapter 1 that impact clergy and often diminish our role. Perhaps beloved colleagues give up and withdraw. The crisis we face may be to ask if there is meaning left in doing this work, and if so, where is it? We won't tarry at this point any longer for now. However, if this resonates with you, it may be wise to bookmark this topic and see if anything in the rest of this book offers further wisdom for your questions.

Another life principle that is important to develop in being resilient is the ability to adapt, to improvise. We can learn from children who devise all sorts of play scenarios from a few boxes, newspapers, or pots and pans. Some writers use the French term for this, "bricolage," which means some sort of construction or creation from a diverse range of available things.

Resilient people learn how to be innovators, tinkerers, or improvisers. When confronted with events that have closed doors and changed possibilities, resilient persons talk, dream, and invent new possibilities. They do so with the resources at hand.

Sheryl Sandberg combines these insights as she reflects on the shock of the sudden death of her husband and living that loss with her children.

> Resilience comes from deep within us and from support outside us. It comes from gratitude for what's good in our lives and from leaning into the suck [that is, acknowledging how hard the loss is]. It comes from analyzing how we process grief and from simply accepting that grief. Sometimes we have less control than we think. Other times we have more. I learned that when life pulls you under, you can kick against the bottom, break the surface, and breathe again. [22]

Further, resilience is not just an individual trait. There are groups that strengthen their members through "collective resilience." There are resilient communities with strong social ties among persons so that both the community and the persons within it can flex, change, and thrive when crises come.[23]

AN IMPORTANT CAUTION

As we explore resilience, there is this caution—persons may have practiced a helpful repertoire of strategies, but when a new crisis comes, these may not work. New or different ones are needed.

This may be because different types of crises need different coping strategies. Mostly, this failure can happen in either of two circumstances. It can happen when responding to good news and events or when experiencing deeper pain and tragedy than previously experienced.

An example of seeming good news not being that good is what happens to many people when they win the lottery and have more finances than they ever dreamed possible. One tragic example is Billie Bob Harell Jr., a Texan who squandered his $31 million jackpot. He provided handouts to many friends and family and made poor financial decisions. Soon he was broke again and eventually committed suicide. Sadly, he is not the only one whose good news of a lottery win turned sour. Struggles in personal relationships, unwise and uncontrolled spending, legal problems, and tax issues may harass a person's world and cause them to long for their previous simpler life.[24] However these lottery winners handled previous life challenges didn't seem to help them deal with the crisis of a financial windfall.

Diane Coutu tells a story of a similar challenge to resilience. She writes of the great Russian author Aleksandr Solzhenitsyn who lived through—and wrote movingly—of war against the Nazis, being imprisoned in the gulag, and enduring cancer. But when he moved into a farm in isolated and safe rural Vermont, he found it impossible to cope with what he termed the "infantile west." He questioned and criticized what he saw as "the destructive and irresponsible freedom of the West." Upset with the disagreement and criticism of his views, he withdrew into his farmstead and stayed behind a locked fence. He was seldom seen in public, and in 1994, bitter and disillusioned, he moved back to Russia.[25] Resilience is not easy, even when the news appears to be good!

But more frequently the challenge to resilient practices comes when one must face harsher events than previously experienced. I (Dick) recall a number of times when I was willingly overextending myself to respond to the many needs at hand. When near exhausted, I would hear one more demand or criticism of my efforts or one more refusal, and I would collapse. Perhaps I would give up on the multiple tasks, feel sorry for myself, read the want ads, search for a different line of work—for at least a day or two. Or it might happen that while giving lavish ministry, one experiences hurtful family issues or a health crisis or the death of a loved family member or friend.

In Skovholt and Trotter-Mathison's words, how do we search for resiliency during "these disequilibrium periods, these times of exhaustion, pain, despair, and disquiet"? These authors illumine the hard claims on many caring professions. However, they acknowledge they have just a bit to suggest: "A short answer to a difficult question is that we must continue self-care but do so at an accelerated pace."[26] Self-care at an accelerated pace!

Such times call us back to the basics—face the issue squarely without victim mentality; trust in the meaning of life; seek help and strength from the many resources at hand. And be just as caring to yourself as you would to any client-patient-parishioner who was in as dire pain as you are.

RESILIENCE AND THE CLERGY'S DILEMMAS

We have been discussing specific steps to take and strengths to engage to be resilient in times of upset. At the same time, there is a kindred question to explore: with all the changes, what specifically can we do to be strong, healthy persons, as prepared as possible for these emergencies? That is the question that inspired us to write this book.

Robert Wicks speaks of "A Self-Care Protocol" as absolutely essential for caregivers who want to be resilient.[27] In the next seven chapters, we offer such a protocol of possibilities for your self-care. These are the best answers we are capable of giving. To give a brief preview, we believe we will be most resilient, stress hardy, and healthy when we consider, explore, and practice these:

- being aware and growing in the spiritual practices and disciplines that will strengthen and enrich our lives and ministry;
- finding supportive relationships—friends, pals, support groups, family, coaches, mentors, counselors, and spiritual directors, to name a few possibilities;
- attending to our physical health, including nutrition, exercise, and rest;
- tending to, exploring, and seeking healing from our inner messages from our past and present, and listening for the joy and affirmation in the present and future;
- nurturing our playful selves with humor, jokes, things we do just for fun that bring us joy and help us to relax;
- having a wise strategy as to finances including past debts, present management of income and expense, and future goals and needs; and
- developing a plan and method for the growth of our minds throughout our lifetimes.

We hope to explore this with you in a way that is supportive and helpful. Each of these, we believe, is worthy in itself and useful in increasing one's stress hardiness and resilience. And at the same time, even with our best intentions and efforts, we certainly have not discovered all the ways that may help strengthen one. Pauline Boss notes, "There are multiple and sometimes unexpected pathways to resilience."[28] What is helpful for one may not be so for another. Trust in one's own and another's journey is important.

While each will need to pick and choose, we cannot overemphasize the importance of having an intentional strategy. Skovholt and Trotter-Mathison warn persons in caring professions, "We need to lose our innocence about the need for assertive self-care. . . . We must take care of ourselves if our self, the healing agent, is to thrive for the decades of our work."[29]

They go on to suggest a continual self-monitoring of one's self-care and other-care balance. They further call for what various persons have described with such terms as "altruistic egotism" (Hans Selye) or "holy selfishness and self-attentiveness" (J. Buchanan).[30]

FAITH AND RESILIENCE

The researchers and writers in resilience informing our discussion did not speak of any specific faith perspective. However, as we reflected on their wisdom, we felt at home, receiving a fresh word and strategies for claiming some of the healing aspects in our faith heritage.

The connection comes from the prefix re-. The most basic meanings of this prefix are these: "again, or again and again" and "return to a previous condition." So resilience is in a family of words that includes these—renewal, revival, resurrection, and rebirth. And this is where it connects to the Scriptures and faith perspectives that we treasure and that uphold us in this demanding work.

We will mention just a couple Bible passages where we hear resilience included within the promises and assurance that are there. These will undoubtedly remind you of many more.

In Psalm 71, a prayer for lifetime protection and help, the Psalmist makes this statement:

> You who have made me see many troubles and calamities
> will revive me again;
> from the depths of the earth
> you will bring me up again
> you will increase my honor,
> and comfort me once again. (Psalm 71:20–21)

This Psalmist expresses the trust that after much stress, God's care will be such that richness of life will be experienced once more.

And Paul, in his correspondence with his beloved Philippian church, speaks of his resilience even while thanking them for a gift. He writes:

> Not that I am referring to being in need; for I have learned to be content with whatever I have. I know what it is to have little, and I know what it is to have plenty. In any and all circumstances, I have learned the secret of being well-fed and of going hungry, of having plenty and of being in need. I can do all things through [the one] who strengthens me. (Philippians 4:11–13 adapted)

He concludes his words of thanks with a promise, "And my God will satisfy every need of yours according to God's riches in glory in Christ Jesus" (Philippians 4:19 adapted)—truly a resilient minister and a resilient community!

These witnesses from within our sacred Scriptures offer an additional important perspective. We can be grateful to the pioneers and teachers about human resilience who have informed this chapter. As persons of faith, we nod our heads in acceptance yet with recognition that the God of our faith is touching our lives, providing renewal time and again and, yes, leading us to resilience for the tasks that remain.

FOR YOUR REFLECTION AND CONVERSATION

1. What have been the times in your life where you faced the need for great change? A move, a marriage, a birth, a job loss, a death? How did you find the strength to go on?

2. Recall a time in your life or ministry when a crisis happened or when you felt overloaded. How did you work your way out of that? What helped? What did not help?

3. What did you learn about yourself from the Siebert Resilience Scale? What from this chapter helps you recall how you have grown in this regard? What other helpful thoughts for further growth do you have?

4. While writing this chapter, we struggled with overuse of the word "resilience." Write or say as many words as you can that talk about this word in one way or another. What are your favorite terms for this quality, resilience?

5. As you anticipate the discussions of the next chapters, where are you strongest in self-care to enrich life and support your ministry? Where are you the weakest? What changes would you like to make?

Chapter Six

Spiritual Self-Care

Henri Nouwen told of a reunion with his friend, Borys, a fellow priest who had been on a month long retreat at the Ukrainian Monastery in California. Nouwen commented, "Borys, who often looks exhausted and overworked now looks rested and relaxed. It was clear that this retreat had given him a new focus, a new perspective, and a new energy." Borys reflected, "Somehow I nearly lost God in my busy life for God. I am so glad to have refound my first love."[1]

Your writing team has a daunting task in this chapter as we look at spiritual self-care strategies. Likely, these practices are well known to you. Yet, these reminders are important, for like Borys, we may become so busy for God that our relationship with God becomes rusty.

PRELIMINARY CONSIDERATIONS FOR THE SPIRITUAL EXPLORATION

How do we develop an authentic and renewing spirituality? First, we are wise to practice humility and transparency. Many people hold either of two erroneous views of ministers' spirituality. On the one hand, there are some who think ministers don't struggle with the same questions, doubts, and meanderings others have. On the other hand, large numbers of people think that a church or minister is the last place to go for guidance on the spiritual quest. And so we suggest humility. Even Barbara Brown Taylor, who has written so helpfully on the Bible, faith, and spiritual practices, confesses, "I am a failure at prayer,"[2] and then digs deeper into dimensions of prayer and enriching an anemic prayer life.

Perhaps we can be transparent—"I also walk a road of spiritual discovery and have moments of doubt and searching as well as dark nights of the soul.

But I will be present to your questions. I will share what I have found and will grow with you."

Second, avoid the twin traps of perfectionism and guilt. If this is the way you think, "disciplines/practices = oughts = guilt," we suggest you replace it with "disciplines/practices = self-care, a means of healing and renewal." Many of us aspire to more than we are able to do. Then we discover that we can't (or don't) give the time to spiritual growth we intended. Our spiritual self-care may feel meager or nonexistent. The temptation is to give up and then feel guilty. Rather, begin with self-acceptance and self-forgiveness. In balancing the responsibilities of ministry, care for a family, and spiritual reflection, there will always be a tug of war. We aim for the "good enough" way of life—doing our best in response to the many claims upon us.

Third, our spiritual journey should fit who we are. Many find the Myers-Briggs inventory a helpful way of identifying important clues about oneself and one's spiritual path. Here is a brief synopsis. The Myers-Briggs inventory helps one identify four aspects of oneself.

- Where do you find the source of your energy? If with public events and large groups of people, you are an Extravert; if with one person or a small intimate group or alone, you are an Introvert.
- How do you perceive or focus on information? If you respond to the outer world, you are Sensing. If you rely more on internal thought and imaginative world, you are iNtuiting.
- How do you make decisions? With logic and consistency? Then you are Thinking. If emotion, both yours and those affected by your decision, influences you, you are Feeling.
- As you think about how you process the information you received, do you like to stay open ended, improvise, explore other options? Then you are Perceiving. Do you organize what you know, stick to your plan, and usually meet deadlines? Then you are Judging.

None of these qualities are right or wrong, good or bad. They just are. The combinations of these four qualities—E/I, S/N, T/F, J/P—lead to sixteen different personality types, and the differences among us are vaster than that. If this is new to you, there are a number of simple inventories and explanations available online to learn more about yourself.[3]

This may provide some clues as to what spiritual practices attract and nourish and which do not. For example, clergy couple Bruce and Katherine Gould Epperly describe how each engages spiritual practices that fit the individual. Bruce, an INFJ, rises before sunrise with an affirmation from the Psalms. Each day he practices centering prayer learned long ago and then goes for a solitary two- to four-mile walk, devoting part of the walk to petitionary prayers.

Katherine, an ENFP, dislikes rigid schedules but engages in journaling to chronicle her journey and discoveries. She has added contemplative knitting as part of her church's prayer shawl ministry—the knitting focuses her mind and stirs prayers for the person who will receive the shawl and for others in her concern. Her favorite prayer times are while working in the garden or walking with colleagues. She prefers spontaneity rather than repeated habits in her spiritual journey.[4] Discovering who we are and who we are not—with or without knowing our Myers-Briggs initials—is an important step in claiming helpful spiritual practices.

Fourth, our spiritual practices need to develop in harmony and dialogue with our theology—both the foundational affirmations and the emerging challenges and changes of one's life. For example, I (Dick) have been on a journey of developing deeper dialogue, friendship, and advocacy in regard to the other Abrahamic religions—Judaism and Islam. And so in addition to my prayer times of gratitude for the joy of knowing Christ and intercession for the church, I need to learn how to integrate what I have learned about the spiritual practices of Jewish and Muslim friends. How do I view them, and for what should I pray in regard to them?

As you consider the theological vision that informs your spiritual practices, the Epperlys suggest three related aspects: "(1) your theological perspective and understanding of prayer, (2) the role your body plays in spiritual formation, and (3) the interplay between action and contemplations in your life of faith."[5] Their questions might stimulate one's own thoughts and questions to ponder in stating a theology of spirituality.

LIFE JOURNEYS AND SPIRITUAL GROWTH

It is wise to be open to the likelihood that some of your spiritual practices will change. This may be for any number of reasons. A practice may become routine and stale. Or a spiritual practice may become so much a part of you that you are free to consider still more ways. Some spiritual growth opportunities are by definition onetime experiences—a conference, a retreat, a sabbatical, a pilgrimage, a mission trip, for example—but may provide discovery and awareness that leads one's spiritual exploration in new and different directions.

Or it may happen that changes in your life experiences or world events demand changes in your spirituality and theology as well. Six such persons tell their stories. Each one is a story of theological challenge and spiritual change.

Jason's Difficult Discovery

Jason Micheli, a thirty-seven-year-old United Methodist minister, experienced pains that led to the diagnosis of mantel cell lymphoma, a rare and virulent form of cancer usually found only in older men. This is an aggressive cancer. He was to consider himself in "stage-serious."

Over the next several months, he underwent eight cycles of nine chemo drugs (he called them "chemo-poison"). He suffered the full range of side effects that included loss of body hair, strength, muscular structure, and sexual vitality and the strong possibility of imminent death. At the end of all this, he received the best news a cancer patient can get—that for the present he was symptom free, though he would need constant monitoring and monthly chemo treatments.

In telling this story, Jason speaks of his spiritual journey during treatment. Before cancer, he said he was "cool and detached . . . feigning self-sufficiency and self-reliance."[6] When first diagnosed, he wrote to his church, "I don't believe there's any mysterious 'reason' other than the chromosomal one that cancer—however rare—is happening to me,"[7]—a bravado "that later made me cringe."

In the course of his treatment and long hospital stays, he met many fellow patients that touched his heart, among them children and a young mother with a two-week-old child. He heard their tears in the night, their agony, fears, and grief. At this point cancer didn't make him wonder "Why me, God?" but rather "Why them, God?"

By the sixth round of treatment, however, "I couldn't help but wonder why God was doing this to me."[8] Up to then, both for others and himself, he had been "exonerating God"—saying God did not do this. But that view was not working. He reread the Bible with fresh and naked eyes and heard the Bible with new ears. He saw the constant complaints of the Israelites in the Exodus, the preponderance of laments/complaints in the Psalms, the rejection of Jesus and his cry on the cross.

He found himself moving from "God didn't do this" to "God damn you, God." As he discovered, "A God at whom you're royally POed is not yet a God you don't believe in."[9] After rereading the Psalms "with eyes that never really dried," he came to something of a thesis: "You only get a Bible like ours when you do not feel the need to get God off the hook."[10]

In the light of this harsh yearlong experience, Jason titled his book *Cancer Is Funny*, but not what many people mean by funny. "No, when I say cancer is funny, I mean that your every pretense falls away, right along with your pubic hair."[11] The laughter in cancer comes from "feeling not well or strong but free—genuinely free—to be myself, with others and before God." He concludes, "Cancer is funny, then, because the suffering occasioned by cancer draws you nearer to God, and the closer you get to God, the louder laughter becomes."[12]

Wesley's Anchor

Wesley Granberg-Michaelson recalls that the results of the 2016 election "plummeted me into such a mood of disbelief, emotional reactivity and political angst that I was in danger of losing my spiritual center."[13] As he visited with friends on how to live with this pain, his wife, Karin, suggested that, rather than react to each statement and story, "we have to find safe spaces to support proactively the things we are called to do."[14] He responded to her wisdom by identifying five new-old practices that became particularly important as an "anchor in the storm."

The first is memory. Continually, in scripture, the people of God are called to memory of what God has done, including Jesus's word at that final meal, "Do this in remembrance of me." Theologian Scott Hahn has noted, "Memory is more than just a psychological exercise of data retrieval, but the faculty that tells us who we are."[15] It is religious memory that keeps us grounded in the face of other competing narratives.

The second practice-dimension is truth. He notes that truth is firmly commanded again and again in scripture because "truthfulness is essential for sustaining community." Further, in biblical faith, what one understands to be truth is influenced by the perspective of those who seek it. Scripture, including the life of Jesus, calls on the faithful to see truth about any social order through the eyes of the poor and the marginalized.

The third practice-dimension is community. Granberg-Michaelson recalls Dietrich Bonhoeffer's response when he witnessed the rise of the Third Reich with accommodation from the state Lutheran church. Bonhoeffer's response was to seek to create a community that learned to confess sin, meditate on scripture, and identify with the weak and powerless. "The habits of thinking, practices of living, disciplines of praying, celebrations of worship, and clarity of calling can only happen with one another."[16]

The fourth practice-dimension is suffering. Suffering comes from the inability to control devastating and unwanted events in our lives. However, the experience of suffering as lack of control can be the place where God's spirit breaks through with the power of new life. Our suffering can make us even more aware of those more vulnerable than we—those "lacking protection of wealth, class, or race and therefore less able to protect themselves."[17]

This leads to the fifth practice-dimension, solidarity. Solidarity is the way we live the truth of Ephesians 4:25, that we are all "members of one another." As we recognize our solidarity in the face of human suffering, we are particularly led to solidarity with young black men and women, with the immigrant and those hoping to be, and with Muslims. Solidarity does not end there, but the times call for these particular expressions.

Granberg-Michaelson concludes by recalling the anchorites of the Middle Ages. These were persons who entered a radical form of solitary life, seeking God and interceding for the world. His leading is that we need to gather in committed groups and engage in these practices-dimensions that we might be anchorites—anchors in a time of storm—for such a time as this.[18]

Tabatha and Joy's Painful Growing Edge

In 2003, Tabatha Johnson joyfully began her first ministry position as director of children's ministries for a congregation. Sadly, harsh realities were coming. "In my twenty sixth year, I had two miscarriages, a cancer diagnosis, radiation therapy, and a fairly steep learning curve for a new ministry position."[19] Though outwardly she hid her feelings about the miscarriages, "I truly believed it was all my fault. . . . I believed if only I were a better Christian, minister, wife, mother (especially mother) and had a stronger, more mature faith none of it would have happened."[20]

She relates that she would go through many months of denial of the deep grief she felt, the death of a mother's hopes and dreams for her children. At the same time she felt a guilt and shame that she had not been good enough, disciplined enough, Christian enough to bear and raise these children. Though she would have counseled any woman who had the same pain that it was not her fault, Tabatha could not tell that to herself.

And these feelings were followed by anger.

> Anger with God for allowing my suffering. Anger with God for not allowing my children to breathe and laugh and grow. Anger with God for allowing my husband to reach the point past exhaustion while having to take care of a two-year-old son and a sick wife. Anger with God for forming an existence and creative system in which terrible things happened to good people. The anger grew until God and I were no longer on speaking terms.[21]

Even in the worst of the loneliness, "somehow hope clung to the edges of my anger," and very, slowly, the anger began to recede and hope began to grow. She was comforted by persons who had lived through cancer, and she held out the prospect that she would survive, too. At the same time, she wondered why there had not been similar support from others who had miscarriages.

Looking back, she discerns where God was more present than she thought, speaking to her woundedness, guiding her into her "nuanced call into ministry-pastoral care."[22] And she has a particular compassion and giftedness with those who experienced the loss she did.

In the third month of pregnancy for their second child, Joy Freeman—wife, mother, ordained minister, and hospital chaplain—underwent a sonogram that indicated possible complications. Subsequent tests revealed that the baby's intestines and liver had grown outside the abdominal cavity. This meant "that the likelihood of our baby surviving to birth was very slim and if the baby did survive, he or she would require immediate surgery, probably several. . . . If the baby did survive this, the baby would be in pain for the rest of his or her life."[23]

Though Joy and her husband had never thought about ending a pregnancy, "in those few seconds . . . my whole ethical view shifted."[24] They could not ask their baby to endure that kind of pain and so sadly made arrangements for the pregnancy to be terminated. Joy and her husband, Collin, experienced firsthand the many shades of gray in having to face such a decision.

Before saying good-bye, they gave their baby a name—Hope. There was also a time of ritual. Joy gave her baby a Celtic Christian blessing, as she had done for her first child, CJ. One of their pastors came to their home and conducted a brief child blessing service for this much loved child that would not be born. In this ritual the pastor brought a red rose (this church puts a rose on the organ to announce a birth) and a candle (this church has a service in Advent where candles are lighted to remember those who died).

Joy and Collin affirm that they were surrounded and supported by wonderfully caring church, ministers, and parents. All of these could care and support, and this would soften but not take away the pain. However, one conversation with her mother stands out. Her mother "told me, in no uncertain terms, that this was not my fault. I was not a failure as a mother. I needed to hear that affirmation from her, the one whom I hold as my model of motherhood and all I aspire to be as a mother myself."[25]

As she lived with this pain, she tried to practice what she told the patients with whom she ministered, that "it was okay to feel whatever it was that I felt. It was ok, in my time with God, to let it all hang out, because God's shoulders are big."[26] Eventually, the time came to return to work as a hospital chaplain, which included serving on the maternity ward. There were times when she felt jealousy for those with healthy births and anguish of her own spirit when needing to be with couples who suffered some neonatal tragedy.

There was another step in grieving for and memorializing Hope. Joy has used labyrinths in her own spiritual walk and has guided others in this spiritual aid. She had long wanted to build a labyrinth in their back yard. Now she would do it in memory of Hope. The stepping stone at the entrance to "Hope's Labyrinth" is Hope's memorial stone.

Both Joy and Tabatha told their stories in various small group settings to deep response and encouragement to tell their stories more widely. They responded by editing-authoring a book, entitled *Still a Mother: Journeys through Perinatal Bereavement*, to offer support for the grieving and guidance to those who care for them.

Peter's Iceberg

Peter Scazzero had given up on church at age thirteen but was drawn back to enthusiastic faith in Christ at age nineteen by means of a sacred concert and a university Bible study group. He recalls, "For the next seventeen years, I plunged headfirst into my newfound evangelical/charismatic tradition, absorbing every drop of discipleship and spirituality made available. I prayed and read Scripture. I consumed Christian books. I participated in small groups and attended church regularly. I learned about spiritual disciplines. I served eagerly with my gifts. I gave money away freely. I shared my faith with anyone who would listen."[27]

However, "the emotional aspects or areas of my humanity remained largely untouched."[28] With later insight, he sees that his vital Christian faith was affecting only a small part of his life. His analogy is that his spirituality was as the tip of the iceberg.

He went on to seminary and founded a multi-ethnic church in Brooklyn, New York. With all this, he began to sense something was wrong. He was not experiencing joy or contentment but instead was "angry, bitter, and disappointed." His wife, Geri, felt something wrong before he did and one day confronted him, telling him that she loved him but might be happier single. Further, she was leaving his church and concluded, "Oh, yes, by the way, the church you pastor? I quit. Your leadership isn't worth following."[29]

While his first response was anger and then shame, he later realized this was the most loving thing Geri could have done—"she realized something vital: emotional health and spiritual maturity are inseparable."[30] This led them to marriage counseling. The use of genograms, a deep look at their deeply dysfunctional families of origin, led to ways of living better with this awareness. The fascination of this subject led Peter to explore it deeply, take courses on it, and bring this perspective into the teaching ministry of his church.

And so a journey began to discover how spiritual maturity and emotional maturity are closely intertwined. Studies of emotional intelligence lent insight to what might be blocking spiritual growing and how this growing might be enhanced. Scazzero relates that the lessons he was learning were slowly brought into the life of the church he led.

Peter also discovered that a second strand is essential to spiritual wholeness, and that is contemplative spirituality. His book is punctuated with many quotes from the spiritual fathers and mothers through the centuries. He tells of exploring the spiritual practice of the Daily Office in a one-week visit with Trappist monks. This led to many other explorations to Roman Catholic, Protestant, and Orthodox monastic communities in addition to such spiritual renewal places as Taize, France, and the Celtic Northumbrian community in England.[31]

He concludes, "The combination of emotional health and contemplative spirituality addresses what I believe to be the missing piece in contemporary Christianity. Together they unleash the Holy Spirit inside us in order that we might know experientially the power of an authentic life in Christ."[32]

Laura's Ride

Laura Everett's car died, and she needed an inexpensive way to get to work and move around Boston. Her Bible study group suggested biking, which, though she didn't consider herself very athletic, she decided to try. "What she found was that riding a bike was more than just transportation. It transformed her relationship with her adopted home, and it opened her eyes to people and communities she never would have seen through the window of a car."[33]

As she continued this practice, she perceived her bicycling as a spiritual discipline. One aspect is the daily discipline of a cyclist—being intentional, preparing, and providing what will be needed for the day's journey. The second is being open to a cyclist's vulnerability "to the weather, to the people around you in a way that being encased in a giant metal car, separated from the world around, you are not."[34]

This led to availability to the community of cyclists. "These cyclists that I'm connected to build community and support one another and practice a way of living that's deliberate and intentional, with a kind of faithfulness that any good pastor would give her right arm for. But it's like we don't know how to recognize it as devout, because it's not religious the way we are."[35]

In turn, this led to the discovery of an urban spirituality "to find the transcendent in the frenetic, sometimes chaotic motion of cities."[36] She has told of her experience and discoveries in a book, fittingly named *Holy Spokes: The Search for Urban Spirituality on Two Wheels*.[37]

SOME SPECIFICS

We now turn to specific spiritual disciplines/practices. After considering a few we consider basic, we will summarize some of the vast array of choices and resources where they can be explored.

Sabbath, A Neglected Essential

When I (Dick) take seminary classes to Friday evening Sabbath Prayer times at a local Reformed synagogue, the first greeting at the door is " Shabbat Shalom" (Sabbath Peace), a theme that is echoed through the time of "bissela nosh" (little bites) as we gather, conversations, the lighting of Sabbath candles, and the prayer service that follows. Whatever the theme of the rabbi's teaching that night, the master theme throughout is God's delightful gift of Sabbath, not just for Jews but for all humankind, indeed for all creation.

Many thoughtful persons call on us to regain this neglected topic. For one, Wayne Muller has written a beautiful book, *Sabbath: Finding Rest, Renewal and Delight in our Busy Lives*. He notes that Sabbath is both a specific practice and larger metaphor that points to the "forgotten necessity of rest."[38] Muller points out that in the creation story in Genesis, there is a fascinating phrase: "And on the seventh day, God finished the work that he had done and [God] rested" (Genesis 2:2 adapted). What did God create on Sabbath, completing the work? Muller points out ancient rabbis respond, "God created *menuha*—tranquility, serenity, peace, and repose—rest, in the deepest possible sense of fertile healing stillness."[39]

Wayne recalls a time when he was near death, infected with streptococcal pneumonia. He was hospitalized, treated medically, undergirded with the prayer and love of many friends. He concludes, "I owe my life to the simple act of rest."[40]

Arden Mahlberg, group facilitator for the Sabbath Renewal Project at Princeton Theological Seminary, points out that scriptural teaching on Sabbath is freeing because it doesn't tell us what to do but only what not to do. He goes on to point out that there are three scriptural clues:

- "Remember that God rested; it is a special day to the Lord
- Keep it holy, and
- Rest from our work."[41]

Out of this guidance, he and the Princeton group discovered "Sabbath reorients us, helping us to get our bearings both to the world, and to God."[42] Sabbath rest needs to occur on many levels: physically, mentally, emotionally, and spiritually.

Without rest, our hearing is impaired, and we will probably get things wrong. "Only at rest can we hear what we have not heard before, and be led to what is most deeply beautiful, necessary, and true."[43] Therefore, "Sabbath is an incubator for wisdom."[44]

While we clergy may grant the possible richness of true Sabbath, we have difficulty to find a way to observe it. Religious gatherings and worship, where we are responsible, are not Sabbath rest for us. Where can we find the combination of worship, rest, and relaxation-enjoyment?

Muller describes how Eugene Peterson, when a church pastor, observed his Sabbath. He and his wife would pack a lunch and drive to some trailhead. As they prepared for their hike, they would share scripture, usually a Psalm, and prayer. They would then hike in complete silence for hours. Only at lunch would they would break the silence with a prayer of thanksgiving for the food and what they had seen and heard. Then they would talk about "their bird sightings, observations, feelings, and thoughts."[45] Many of us ministers long for, but rarely find, such a total experience of Sabbath.

More often we may have to fill in the various parts of our Sabbath on different days, places, or times. Mahlberg speaks of "Mini-Sabbaths" and "Sabbath moments." His example is of being put on hold when making a phone call—a time to relax, reflect, and pray. This is well worth pursuing, for Muller points out the result may be "we become Sabbath for one another. We are the emptiness, the day of rest. We become space, that our loved ones, the lost and sorrowful, may find rest in us."[46]

A New Old Spiritual Practice—Meditation

I (Dick) discovered an important spiritual practice when studying to teach a course on stress management. In the late 1960s, Dr. Herbert Benson of Harvard Medical School was searching for causes and effects of hypertension. He was amazed that practitioners of transcendental meditation could lower their blood pressure. Transcendental meditation is a popular secular simplification of ancient Buddhist and Hindu meditation practices.

Dr. Benson sensed he was on to an important insight into mind-body healing, and in time he discovered that practicing the "relaxation response" (the term he chose for this practice) was an effective means of relieving and healing all sorts of stress-related maladies.

He described the steps in the "relaxation response."

> Step 1: Pick a focus word, a phrase, [a mantra]. . . . Step 2: Sit quietly in a comfortable position. . . . Step 3: Close your eyes. Step 4: Relax your muscles. . . . Step 5: Breathe slowly and naturally . . . repeat your [mantra] as you exhale. Step 6: Assume a passive attitude. Don't worry about how well you are doing. Step 7: Continue for ten to twenty minutes. Step 8: Practice the technique once or twice daily.[47]

Benson changed one thing. Rather than meditating on a "mantra," an assigned word with no known meaning, he changed the term to "focus word" and allowed persons to pick their own focus word for their meditation. He was surprised that religious people almost always picked a phrase from their faith: the Lord's Prayer, the Twenty-third Psalm, "God is love," or "Lord, have mercy." He noted how readily people of faith took to this and that 80 percent of them chose a prayer from their own religious tradition. Without realizing it, he was guiding persons to faith-filled meditation and centering prayer.

Benson's awareness of the spiritual dimension can be seen in the title of his book *Timeless Healing: The Power and Biology of Belief* (1996).[48] He is careful to say he's a medical person, not a theologian, who sometimes finds himself in the unusual position of teaching religious people how to pray! A modern scientific researcher accidentally discovered how health giving is the biblical call to "be still and know that I am God" (Psalm 46:10).

Becoming Intentional

How do we put the various aspects of a spiritual life into action? Marjorie Thompson suggests we each develop our unique "rule of life." This is an intentional plan of spiritual disciplines/practices that gives structure and direction for one's spiritual growth.[49] This is so we can move in the direction of what we discern we are called to be. There may be a corporate rule of life for a group of people, or there may be a personal one.

Thompson suggests we start with three basic questions: "What am I deeply attracted to and why? Where do I feel God is calling me to stretch and grow? What kind of balance do I need in my life?"[50] She points out that this should fit one's personality as well as one's life situation—for example, heavy work demands or retired status, chronic illness or disability, or other circumstances.

When you have answered those three questions, it is important to write down a plan. One should do this with the awareness that this is not a decision for the rest of your life but rather what fits this chapter of your life. Once it is written down, keep a copy of this rule of life in a place where you will frequently see and read it.

Then find one person you love and trust and share your rule of life with that person. Ask her or him to pray for you and to help hold you accountable for working on it. The support of one's faith community is important as well. These steps can help one clarify where spiritual hunger is leading and where you are being guided in this journey of faith.

A GLIMPSE AT OTHER MEANS

Here are brief descriptions of spiritual growth methods many have found helpful along with references for accessing more information.

Dorothy Bass, Craig Dykstra, and Others—Spiritual Practices

"Practice" can simply mean what we do, or it can mean to work at something in order to improve. But it also has a deeper and more specific meaning. This is the term that Craig Dykstra, Dorothy Bass, and those in the *Practicing Our Faith* project selected and redefined for an important perspective on what leads to and supports the growth to which we aspire. They write, "Practices are those shared activities that address fundamental human needs and that, woven together, form a way of life"[51] and "*things Christian people do to-*

gether over time in response to and in the light of God's active presence for the life of the world."[52]

These practices arise from listening to the wisdom of the Christian tradition and those in the present who can guide us in living it—from the "communion of saints." Practices are ordinary activities, things people may do every day. There is additional power when a combination of such practices are discovered and woven together. Quite possibly living this way will create openings in our lives where the grace, mercy, and presence of God may be experienced. Each practice addresses one area of fundamental human need.

This group of religious leaders selected the following twelve practices:

- honoring the body;
- hospitality;
- household economics;
- saying yes and saying no;
- keeping Sabbath;
- testimony;
- discernment;
- shaping communities;
- forgiveness;
- healing;
- dying well; and
- singing our lives.

Bass's edited book, *Practicing Our Faith*, features a chapter on each practice. Bass and associates also prepared a book on spiritual practices for teenagers and included such practices for that time of life as stuff, creativity, play, justice, and truth[53] and a guide for persons in their twenties, where they add such practices as study, discerning God's will, friendship and intimacy, loving neighbors of other faiths, and peacemaking-nonviolence.[54]

Richard Foster and *Celebration of Discipline*

Before Dykstra, Bass, and the Practicing our Faith group developed this concept, a widespread term to describe committed exploration into Christian growth was "discipline." This term is closely related to "disciple," meaning student, follower, or devotee. The road to deeper discipleship involves disciplines of the spirit, and those disciplines have been described by many writers. One of the most influential and well-known developments of this theme is *Celebration of Discipline* by Richard Foster.[55]

In the introduction of this book, Foster tells of how he came to write it. Many factors came together including his own sense of spiritual bankruptcy early in his ministry, the needy people with whom he ministered, and the mentoring of several vital Christian leaders.

Out of his experience, he identified twelve disciplines necessary for Christian growth and wrote a chapter about each. He spoke of them as follows:

- inward disciplines (meditation, prayer, fasting, study);
- outward disciplines (simplicity, solitude, submission, service); and
- corporate disciplines (confession, worship, guidance, celebration).

His book has long touched a widespread hunger. It is still helpful to many.

More Possibilities

But the ways to engage in spiritual enrichment and renewal are even wider and richer. Susan Roth enhances our search in her book *Spiritual Exercises: Joining Body and Spirit in Prayer.*[56] She expands the possibilities of things that can be spiritual exercises with the body and through the body. These may be particularly appealing for us who have long been refreshed by physical activities. Here are a few samples: prayer or meditative walking; "walk, look, and listen"; pilgrimage or labyrinth walking; Hatha Yoga; Tai Chi; Pilates; aerobic exercise; relaxation and massage. She may well open the window of devotion to some for whom traditional observances don't appeal.

While we cannot speak of all that might enrich, a few other opportunities for spiritual enrichment should be at least mentioned. *Music*—singing, chanting, listening, or playing an instrument alone or with others opens some to God's beautiful presence. *Planned retreats*, perhaps silent retreats, maybe with a guide, maybe alone, are also enriching for others. *Reflecting and meditating on the Christian Year*[57] even as one leads the faith community may be reviving. We will speak the vital role of *spiritual directors and friends* in the next chapter.

A fitting conclusion to this discussion comes from Barbara Brown Taylor. As longtime admirers of Taylor, we read her book *Leaving Church*[58] with great sadness. Brown wrote about frustration and pain in a church she loved so that she abruptly resigned and accepted a college teaching position. How we welcomed her next book, *An Altar in the World,* a few years later! She describes what sustained her in that painful time. In this book, she recalls an invitation to come to a church and speak, "telling us what is saving your life right now."[59] To which she responds, "What is saving my life right now is . . . engaging the most ordinary physical activities with the most exquisite attention I can give them . . . becoming more fully human, trusting there is no way to God apart from real life in the real world."[60]

As she develops her report of this discovery, she writes of some well-known spiritual practices—pilgrimage, fasting, and prayer. She also writes of surprising places for an "altar in the world"—eating, working, walking, feeling pain, and wilderness (getting lost). We particularly appreciate a passage from her chapter on getting lost. "I know that this is a stretch to call this a spiritual practice, but perhaps that is the point. *Anything can become a spiritual practice* once you are willing to approach it that way—once you let it bring you to your knees and show you what is real, including who you really are, who other people are, and how near God can be when you have lost your way."[61]

"Anything can become a spiritual practice . . ." So as we conclude the chapter on renewal through spiritual practices, we go on to other roads to renewal and resilience. We believe spiritual practices are there as well, renewing each of us to vibrancy in life and ministry.

FOR YOUR REFLECTION AND CONVERSATION

1. What in this chapter stirred recognition of what has enriched your life? Where did you experience longings or invitations?

2. As you reflect on who you are (with or without the Myers-Briggs inventory), to what spiritual practices are you drawn as rich and fulfilling? To which are you not drawn?

3. How do you respond to the thoughts on Sabbath? Do you have a way of doing Sabbath or a longing for Sabbath? What helps and what hinders?

4. If you follow the suggestion to write a "rule of life," whom will you ask to be your companion and hold you accountable?

5. What suggestions and resources in this chapter stirred your interest and curiosity? What would you add to a chapter on self-care through spiritual resources?

Chapter Seven

Relational Self-Care

After working with hundreds of beginning pastors in Lilly Foundation's "Transition into Ministry" program, David Wood commented, "We have become convinced that one of the best predictors of success in ministry is . . . 'the relational system of the minister's life.'"[1]

Our own experience confirms what so many in helping professions tell us—that a range of deep and satisfying relationships is needed for a rich and meaningful life, not to mention cushioning the impacts of burnout, compassion fatigue, and stress. So we pause to think about our relationships. Which are helpful? Which are not? What is missing? What needs to change?

PRIMARY RELATIONSHIPS

We start with relationships in our own families: the family from which we came and the family to which we now belong. We need care from family as well as needing to offer support to them. At the same time, we must also be aware how our families are impacting our ministries and our ministries impacting them.

There is infinite variety in the families of origin from which we came. How many children were there? Where are you in the birth order? What was the emotional atmosphere? The cultural imprint? What was the relational and spiritual climate of that family?

There are likely many other variations more subtle. It may be helpful to reflect on relationships with parents and siblings in the present. Families may vary in their feelings about a child entering ministry. As one looks at family of origin, one may see gifts that family gives you for ministry and possibly pain and unresolved issues. In chapter 9, family of origin will be explored further. Mutual care with this most basic of relationships is so important to flourishing.

As we move through the seasons of life, we may discover that we are sandwiched between caregiving needs for frail parents or grandparents and care for children. We have a vital link with those who shared our lives from birth on. Again, mutual caregiving and support is vital, and so is as much family health as we can achieve.

It is also important to be compassionate about the family where one is presently involved. Married ministers may have a spouse who is a staff member or lively volunteer, or their partner may be deeply engaged in his or her own career. They may have a spouse of another denomination or faith. As previously mentioned, female clergy often have less spousal support than their male clergy colleagues.

A minister's children may be a source of delight or disapproval in the community. Ministers in congregations may discover that strong influences—for good or ill—are offered by some church members on their children. Young women pastors may have challenging seasons of bearing and raising children while providing ministry.

No matter our marital and family setting, ministers need to give priority to these primary relationships. We've reported clergy comments that the heavy tasks of ministering had a negative impact on their family life. Tragically, statistics reveal that the divorce rate for ministers is about the same as for others.

Whatever it takes, working to achieve a caring, supportive, enduring marriage is well worth the effort. Being spouse is a covenant relationship and equal to the ministry claims. Relational self-care involves giving priority to this commitment. Care for one's family, including establishing boundaries between reasonable and unreasonable expectations of an employing community, is an important step in self-care.

Gary Chapman has offered a helpful checklist in his best-selling book, *The 5 Love Languages: The Secret to Love that Lasts*. The five love languages of which he speaks are as follows: Words of Affirmation, Quality Time (and enough of it), Receiving Gifts, Acts of Service, and Physical Touch.[2] He points out that marriage partners may vary in what they see as expressing love. The wise person discovers a partner's "love language" (which might be quite different from one's own) and offers those gifts to one's life partner. It is so important to communicate how treasured and loved those bonds of marriage and parenthood are.

Those who are single also have family. They have another set of topics to negotiate with an employing community, including claiming time for where and however family is experienced and support is gained. Whatever our circumstance, self-care leads to identifying one's family and the ways this family needs and provides nurture and then interpreting this to and protecting it with an employing community.

FICTIVE KINSHIPS

Close family-like relationships with persons outside our birth family or marriage family are likewise significant. A term for these is "fictive kinship." Helyn Strickland focused on these relationships for her doctor of ministry project. Specifically, she wrote about the impact of fictive kinships on longevity among long-term employees at the minimum security psychiatric hospital where she is employed.

She defines it thus: "Fictive kinship/fictive family: any non-blood/non-consanguineous kinship through association whose members identify themselves as family or family unit. Fictive kin can, but do not necessarily, replace blood kin and may be situational and of varying duration."[3]

Any number of terms can designate fictive kin connections—"team, posse, gang, [pal, buddy,] special interest group . . . club, work family, church family, clique."[4] A variety of studies reveal the importance of fictive kinships among various populations—athletic teams, fire fighters, law enforcement officers, minority or geriatric populations, for example.

Strickland noted fictive kinships throughout the Bible. In the Hebrew Bible, there was Moses raised in the family of the Pharaoh, and there was Ruth, a Moabite widow, telling her Israelite mother-in-law, "Your people shall be my people and your God my God" (Ruth 1:16).

In the New Testament, Strickland suggests Matthew 12:46 is a key passage. When told his family was outside waiting for him, Jesus responded, "Who is my mother, and who are my brothers?" And pointing to his disciples, he said, "Here are my mother and here are my brothers! For whoever does the will of my Father in heaven is my brother and sister and mother."

She observes, "With these five verses, Jesus not only redefined the family constellation, formerly a legal, biological, or familial unit; he also reinterpreted discipleship as an inclusive relationship of those who followed the will of God regardless of gender, gender identity, religious affiliation, race, or ethnicity. . . . In fewer than sixty seconds, Jesus gave a disparate group of people regardless of their previous family and community roles . . . an identity: membership in his family."[5] This fictive kin theme is carried forward in the New Testament, most notably where Jesus calls his followers "friends" (John 15:12–17) and in the teaching that all followers of Christ are adopted family and "members of the household of God" (Ephesians 2:19).

Fictive kin can have a dark side, just as families with biological ties can. But there is also power in deep acceptance and trust, bonds that sustain and hold one up. Some fictive kin ties may be situational and temporary, but some last a lifetime and beyond.

As Strickland did her interviews among long-term employees at the hospital, there was another discovery germane to this discussion. She wrote of the "power of one." In a few interviews, the person pointed to one other employee who was so helpful as to be the key person in sustaining the interviewee's career. Sometimes this powerful one did not reciprocate the feeling and might not even be aware of this impact on the other![6]

"Fictive kin" is a term that draws a variety of different relationships together. It also points to a vitally important self-care practice—finding, initiating, and sustaining those relationships that conquer the loneliness and empower us for the many tasks and challenges in our ministries.

FRIENDS' VOICES

Robert Wicks has found that for a person to "maintain a sense of perspective, openness, and balance,"[7] one needs four "types" of friends or "voices." These may be provided by the same friend at different times in life or may be provided by more than one friend.

The first of these is the prophet. "The true prophet's voice is often quiet and fleeting, but nonetheless strong. She or he is living an honest courageous life guided by truth and compassion."[8] This is never easy. Discomfort and pain may be a part of relating to the prophet.

The second of these is the cheerleader. These are the persons "who are ready to encourage us, see our gifts clearly and be there for us" when we may be down because of others' and our own demands upon ourselves. Far from being a luxury, "make no mistake about it—it is a necessity not to be taken lightly."[9]

The third is the harasser. Perhaps a better term might be "heckler" or "tease." Wicks comments, "'Harassers' help us to laugh at ourselves and avoid the emotional burnout resulting from the . . . expectation that people will always follow our guidance or appreciate what we do for them."[10] Their gift is perspective.

The fourth voice is the guide. These are the sensitive persons who listen to us carefully and well so that they help us recognize both what are the values and callings of our lives as well as what are the forces that make us "hesitant, anxious, fearful, and willful."[11]

As we explore such relationships as these that will enrich and sustain our self-care, there is a vast range of possibilities. We might think of two broad categories: relationships on a level plane between friends and relationships with persons who have wisdom or help to offer.

Of course, this distinction—peers and wise persons—is not entirely accurate. Friends may offer the candor, insight, and growth just described, and the relationship with a mentor may be filled with warmth and mutuality. Still it provides a beginning way of thinking about types of relationships that enrich and renew.

Probably we have friends we gained along life's journey—high school friends or friends from college, seminary, or military service. Some of these friendships are locked into the past: they mostly help to relive old times. Others may be a valued gift from the past in the present to be nourished and enjoyed.

FRIENDSHIPS WITHIN THE CHURCH, ORGANIZATION, OR AGENCY WE SERVE?

But we need new friends as well. Where do we look and how do we form them? Can friends be found within the congregation, community, or agency where we serve?

Often, the prevailing opinion says no because there are too many hazards and dangers in such friendships. For example, there may be jealousy among persons who want the pastor's attention and friendship. Also, the minister is trusted with many confidences, personal and congregational/organizational. These might be violated in close friendships with parishioners. And further still, if a congregation comes to have conflicts over the minister's performance, such friends will be put in an uncomfortable position.

These resistances seem to be based on a "therapeutic" view of ministry. The reasoning is that just as a therapist or doctor cannot socialize with patients while treating them, neither can the minister. This would be awkward at best and dangerous at worst.

A thoughtful alternate view has come from the Theological Colloquium on Sustaining Pastoral Excellence. Lillian Daniel points out, "We should acknowledge up front that friendships between clergy and laity will exist and then talk about how to behave once we are in them." She goes on to point out that all friendships in a church should be different than the world's thin definitions of friendship.

Clergy-lay friendships will be different in some ways from clergy-clergy relationships, but they are still valid. "After all, if friendships are a gift from God, they should all be treated with reverence and care." She lifts up the concept of "holy friendship" as a practice of one's faith, marked by other faith practices such as forgiveness. Within such friendships, there are clearly limits, and "limits can strengthen friendship with one another and with God."[12]

Colloquium member Bob Wells adds, "Holy friendships may not look different to the outside world. But what sets them apart is that they have a larger purpose beyond the friendship itself; they help point us toward God. Holy friendships are about truth telling, encouragement, and accountability."[13]

How does a minister initiate and define such helpful friendships? Lillian Daniel says: "In church, friendships are not chosen but discovered." Some promising candidates for such friendships may be clear to the pastor. But thought and discretion are necessary. Out of rich experience, Judith Schwanz offers these suggestions: Choose wisely—not everyone can be the minister's close friend. Share wisely—with the acknowledgment that neither confidences nor "pet peeves" will be revealed or discussed. Be sensitive at public church times not to concentrate on or favor such friends.[14]

If the story of every church or community is to be a love story, then holy friendships among the participants and between the leader and some participants will be a part of that story. Out of living in the wider community, a minister may well form friendships with lay persons from outside one's own church family. The wisdom of holy friendships applies there as well.

PEER RELATIONSHIPS WITH FELLOW CLERGY

We now go on to another aspect—friendships among those who are in some aspect of ministry. At times, this also may seem like an unlikely possibility. Many of us may have gone to clergy gatherings that seemed competitive, a time when some seemed to be eager to impress. What are the ways to helpful friendships with other clergy?

Gary Kinnaman and Alfred Ells relate that out of a need they sensed in themselves and others, they experimented with what they came to call PIC—Pastors in Covenant groups. The group they created out of their need had three basic aspects:

1. *Covenant.* They did not have rules but boundaries that would define what it meant to be in covenant. They agreed to meet once monthly for a three-hour duration and to give those meetings priority. Missing three or more meetings a year could mean a person sacrificed his place in the group.
2. *Accountability.* They identified three areas where they would be accountable to each other. These were (a) doctrine—for simplicity, their standard was the Apostles' Creed; (b) professional conduct; and (c) personal behavior. For both of these, they agreed to abide by the teachings of the Pastoral Epistles.

3. *Exclusivity*. In order maintain the trust they had worked so hard to establish, they agreed that no one could invite another to become part of the group without the agreement of the whole group.[15]

They describe how these monthly three-hour meetings go. It begins with each sharing what has been happening in his life. The facilitator may next ask, "Who needs time today?" When a person asks for time and shares what is troubling his heart, the question is asked, "Do you need counsel or prayer or both?"

The members of the group by agreement can ask any question about the presenter's personal or professional life that may be helpful to the person sharing. At times, the larger group may be divided into smaller groups to give caring attention to each group member who has requested it.[16] A member of this PIC group wrote what it meant to him: "Joining a covenant group is not about getting busy with one more project. We're there to facilitate each other's growth, health, and leading with excellence."[17]

Their book provides much more information, but perhaps this is enough to give us one model for developing growing trust and friendship among ministers. Certainly, there are many patterns for intentional group sharing among clergy. They might meet and share case studies or have each member, in turn, present something from one's growing edge or discuss a book. Modern media makes possible yet other means to supportive groups. These might be social media groups, video conferencing, and even more. This book could be a resource for such clergy sharing groups. A limited duration for the group (that can be renewed) and a commitment to confidentiality are essential for any type of group that supports and helps members grow.

From our reading of the Kinnaman and Ells book, we gather the members of their group were exclusively male clergy. We are also aware of a group of four women ministers. They all went to the same seminary at about the same time, but they are varied in age, marital status, denomination, race, and place/type of ministry. This cadre has formed a deep bond. In particular, when any of them suffers a crisis in ministry or has a decision to make, she would call her group together for support, counsel, and perhaps advice. They say that none of them would make a major decision until she had consulted with these trusted friends. We are also told those sessions last as long as they need to!

With the growth of numbers of women in ministry, male-female friendships among clergy is another possibility. Your writing team has such friendships—we are two females and two males. These need to be relationships of partnership and mutual support, not flirtation or sexual attraction. These friendships need to be guided by one's code of ethics and consideration for the spouses.

I (Dick) celebrate memories of both male and female friendships. Committed to the ecumenical community, I have expected to find helpful associates and friends wherever I have gone, and I have not been disappointed. I recall my first church in a county seat town in the rural Midwest. Four young ministers—Lutheran, Presbyterian, Methodist, Baptist (three of us in our first churches out of seminary)—met often, shared a spiritual discipline, planned interchurch events, and held each other up as we made that difficult transition.

In another community, when I was moving to a new pastorate, the last person to come to see me was Sister Michelle (from a progressive order of nuns) to give me a hug and pray for my new congregation and my family and me. During my last pastorate, three of us with churches within a couple miles (Presbyterian, United Church of Christ, American Baptist) met for lunch every two weeks for years. In my present setting, I was saddened by the retirement and move of Rabbi Alan Cohen, just as we were becoming friends in the interfaith clergy group he founded. It seems simplistic to say, but if we avoid pretense or dishonesty as we get to know each other, deeper trust and supportiveness may well develop over time, perhaps on an "as needed" schedule.

There may also be times intentionally to identify, discover, and recruit a friend. John Landgraf tells of doing just that. He accepted a new pastoral counseling position a thousand miles away from his familiar community and old friends. He was lonely.

In time, he made the acquaintance of a man he saw as wise and thoughtful but busy with many commitments. Nevertheless, John summoned his courage to ask him out for lunch and, staring down at his plate, started a conversation, "I've watched you from afar for some time. I like what I see. I am seeking a friend, and the reason for this lunch is to ask you to consider becoming my friend. I don't know how close we'd want to get or what form our friendship would take, but we could start [with an occasional luncheon like this]."

At this point, as John's voice trailed off, he looked up and saw this man crying. "He was lonely, too. No one had ever approached him this way. He was touched. We became fast friends. What a great feeling!"[18]

Friendships exist on many levels and fill various needs in life. I (Dick again) am grateful especially for two long-term, life-enriching friendships with fellow ministers. Lee and I met at a youth conference as high school kids, and then we went to the same church-related college. Lee loved excitement—someone said of him that for relaxation he went to a riot. He was outgoing and playful; he touched my "inner child" like few others. People said they saw a different side of me when I was with him. Above all, he was a faithful true friend, spending money and making efforts to keep in touch. Sadly, he died at age fifty-six—we had been friends for thirty-eight years.

Ron and I met at a seminarians' conference when we were in our twenties. We liked each other from the outset and had the good fortune to have work within a few hours' drive of each other for many years. He suggested that each year we spend a few days together at a seminary or other good library. We would study and prepare for Lent by day and relax, play, and enjoy each other in the evenings. We did that for many years and grew in trust to the point where we could tell each other anything weighing on our hearts. I should add Lee's wife, Barb, and Ron's wife, Marjorie, were supportive of our friendships and good friends too.

Sam Keen comes to the heart of things on this subject:

> Friendship, *philia*, brotherly [and sisterly] love, the affection that exists only between equals is at once the most modest and rugged of the modes of love. It is as quiet as an afternoon conversation, but strong enough to survive the acids of time. . . . It is based on simplest of the heart's syllogisms: I like you, you like me; therefore we are friends. And while we can imagine a satisfying life without the juicy overflow of sexual love, or the sweet burdens of family, we know intuitively that without a friend the best of lives would be too lonely to bear. [19]

MENTORS AND OTHER WISE FRIENDS

We also need friends whose experience, wisdom, or expertise supports and guides us. We will discuss five such possibilities. Three of them—mentor, spiritual guide, and *anam cara*—are closely interrelated and in some ways are different terms for the same deep relational gifts. The other two, coach and counselor, are quite different from this first group.

Mentor

For a start, consider mentor. A dictionary will tell you that mentor can be spelled with a capital or small m. Mentor in Homer's *Odyssey* was Ulysses' trusted friend who protected, nurtured, guided Ulysses' son Telemachus in the father's absence. Echoing that, mentor simply means a trusted advisor.

From a psychological perspective, this term "mentoring" describes nurturing, educating, and guiding another. Daniel Levinson, a pioneer in research on life stages, spoke of how important mentors often are in helping a young adult enter an occupation, develop the necessary skills and relationships, and grow into this new place in life. Mentoring often begins with friendliness, one person being a little older and more experienced.

The mentor (often an informal and developing role) may act as a teacher, a host and guide, or an exemplar to admire and emulate. The mentor may also provide counsel and moral support in some of the difficult times. This sometimes grows into a deeply rich and meaningful relationship. Sometimes the bond between mentor and mentee becomes an even closer bond than one feels with one's own family members—fictive kin, if you will.

Levinson points out that mentoring may be best understood as a love relationship. However, it is a limited-time relationship in this form. The person receiving mentoring grows, changes, matures, or discovers differences between oneself and the mentor. Levinson noted that these relationships last "perhaps two or three years on the average, eight to ten years at most."[20] Then, it seems, one must "fire" (our term) one's mentor, sometimes with hurt and pain and sometimes by moving on to a different, more mutual relationship.

Edward Sellner notes, "Everyone needs the support a mentor can provide, especially when making a transition from one psychological and social state to another."[21]

While the previous few paragraphs offer a broad description, clearly mentoring applies to us ministers, priests, and chaplains. Although often mentoring is caregiving guidance by an older person to a younger, it happens other ways as well. Inexperienced and experienced, novice and veteran, discomfort and comfort with a needed skill or practice—all of these may be occasions for mentoring. When I (Dick) needed to learn to teach seminary classes online, I was mentored by a patient, gentle colleague a third of my age, and he made it a much better experience than I had anticipated. I still regard him warmly for this gift to me.

And so as we build our "relational system," the question is this: Who may help me grow in a way I desire? Or what do I have to offer some young (or old) friend who is struggling with things I have learned?

Anam Cara

Spiritual friendship and mentoring come in a variety of forms. The Celtic tradition speaks of one of these ways, the *anam cara*. *Anam* is the Gaelic word for soul, and *cara* is the word for friend. John Donahue elaborates: "The *anam cara* was a person with whom you could reveal the hidden intimacies of your life. This friendship was an act of recognition and belonging."[22]

In the early Celtic church, this was a person who acted as a teacher, companion, or spiritual guide. Donahue says, "With the *anam cara*, you could share your inner most self, your mind, and your heart. . . . In this love, you are understood as you are without mask or pretension." Further, "love is the threshold where divine and human presence ebb and flow into each other."[23]

How does one find—or offer oneself—to explore this deep adventure of soul friendship? Edward Sellner responds that it starts with "a normal spontaneous human relationship." But as far as discerning whether this person will be a soul friend, an *anam cara*, he points to seven signs:

- maturity;
- the ability to hear what another is trying to say;
- genuine respect for the other, including one's stories and agonies;
- ability to keep things confidential;
- the willingness to be transparent, to share parts of one's journey but only when helpful;
- being "something of a scholar" continually reflecting and exploring personal questions and experiences as they illuminate our relationship with God; and
- the ability to "discern movements of the heart."[24]

So much more could be and has been said about the *anam cara* spiritual friendship. The persons we have cited can start you in that direction. But for now, we turn to another way of thinking and defining this spiritual guidance.

Spiritual Guide, Spiritual Friend, Spiritual Director

Spiritual directors were formerly mostly associated with the Roman Catholic tradition. Every student for the priesthood had a spiritual director with whom he consulted throughout his seminary years as did women in religious orders. In some ages, a spiritual director might be seen as hierarchical and authoritative. In recent years, the spiritual director-friend movement has spread to many forms in various denominations and religions. The role is now negotiable as is seen by these interchangeable terms—spiritual director, guide, companion, or friend (or *anam cara*). Some of us may have experienced spiritual guidance as part of a small covenant group or family. Sharing wisdom perspective in small groups is one form, and one-on-one is another.

There are spiritual directors-friends who have taken training for this role, and there are people without such formal training who nonetheless provide this gift, often informally, perhaps not even knowing that they are doing so. I (Dick) remember discussing this with seminary students in a spiritual formation class. I described the trained and lay, formal and informal ways that spiritual guidance is provided. I asked them what had been their experience, and they all looked blank. I inquired if there was one person to whom they could turn to talk about their Christian walk, problems, questions, searching. One woman's face lit up, "Oh, you mean my cousin Muriel," she responded. She then described that she and Muriel, an ordained minister with a leadership position, talked by phone daily, prayed together, sought God's leadership for their lives. What a gift for this midlife woman, seeking discernment about ministry as she took seminary classes!

If one is looking for a spiritual director, there are certain qualities to consider. In close kinship with Sellner's description of an *anam cara*, Marjorie Thompson advises us to note these characteristics: Seek a person with maturity of faith, but at the same time one who knows she or he is not perfect. It is important this person be a good and attentive listener, and one in whom one can trust. And most of all, look for a person who places trust in the grace of God.[25]

A potential spiritual friend/guide/director may be already among your friends. Or a nearby retreat center may have suggestions. Spiritual Directors International[26] has a directory on their website that will list anyone who requests to be considered a spiritual director. And so some caution, discernment, and exploratory interviewing is especially important when contacting someone from this source.

When we find a spiritual friend, what will happen? What will we talk about? What will a spiritual director do? Thompson responds, "A spiritual guide—listens to us, . . . helps us notice things . . . helps us respond to God with greater freedom . . . points us to practical disciplines of spiritual growth, [and] . . . will love us and pray for us."[27]

Quite probably, these are the very things that people have asked of us as clergy. It may be such a relief to be able to put ourselves in someone else's care to tend to our own growth and healing as we engage spiritual self-care for continued ministry.

While one may want to find such a spiritual director, another way is to covenant with a friend or a peer to be spiritual partners–spiritual friends and guide to each other in turn. Earlier in this chapter I spoke of my friend Ron, I think, informally, this is one of the gifts we have given each other. I know I felt renewed and strengthened from times in his presence, particular those pre-Lenten retreats and study times together.

COACHES

We now move to a different kind of helping relationship: coaching. In the past several years, coaching has been recognized as an efficient path to people development and leadership development in the corporate world. Only recently has coaching become a familiar concept in a self-care regimen for leaders of faith communities. I (Nate) have been trained and credentialed in this skill.

Mentors and coaches are both significant but are quite different in philosophy. While mentoring is primarily relational and often a long-term commitment, coaching is less about the relationship and more about tasks. Coaching facilitates growth in others through intentional conversations. A definition of coaching used by Discipleship Development Coaching is "an ongoing professional relationship that helps people produce extraordinary results in their lives, careers, businesses or organizations. Through the process of coaching, clients deepen their learning, improve their performance, and enhance their quality of life."[28] Coaches are trained to help clients work through concrete issues and situations. When a coach works with a client, it can be for an indeterminate amount of time, but often coaching relationships only require a couple of sessions to help work through particular life situations. Coaches do not tell clients how to fix or handle the problem. Rather, the client is coached on how to think critically, logically, and strategically. A foundational concept in coaching is the belief that the expertise to fix the problem or situation lies within the client. A coach helps one to understand the issues and develop a concrete methodology for moving forward.

A Typical Conversation

Every coach is a little different in style and methodology, but here is a broad overview of a traditional coaching session. These sessions usually last between forty-five minutes to an hour and a half. In the coaching conversation, the coach begins by asking an open-ended question to figure out the course of the conversation. Typically, in each conversation one issue is handled at a time. The coach listens to one describe the situation and begins to ask several open-ended questions to help guide the person into logical, critical, and adaptive thinking. After a period of time, the conversation naturally leads into the area of design. This is where the outcomes and tasks portion of the conversation transpires. Coaches always work to make sure they are not mentors giving knowledge and wisdom, but rather, they are helping the client work through the situation. Through this process, coaches must continually remember that the clients are the experts in the situations. After a course of action has been set, a coach will help the client set goals for commitment. This phase of the conversation is where the client will decide when everything will take place and what steps need to be taken to bring the issue or situation to its desired conclusion. After an established commitment, a coach will help the client identify areas of support. Areas of support can include seeing a mentor, consulting a friend, seeking another professional, or identifying other matters as the client navigates through the implementation of the issue at hand.

How to Find a Coach

There are three important guidelines to finding a coach. First, make sure the person you hire is non-biased. The best coach is someone who has no interconnectedness with the happenings of your life. Second, pick a coach that has adequate training and experience. The International Coaching Federation has an excellent tool, Credentialed Coach Finder, to assist in finding qualified coaches. Third, interview coaches before you decide on one. Listed below are a few questions you may want to ask before choosing a coach.

- What is your coaching experience (number of individuals coached, years of experience, types of coaching situations, etc.)?
- What is your coach-specific training (enrolled in an ICF-accredited training program, other coach-specific training, etc.)?
- What is your coaching specialty or areas in which you most often work?

PASTORAL COUNSELORS AND OTHER THERAPISTS

A clergyperson is also wise to be aware of persons they know and trust in the various counseling professions. This includes establishing a relationship, perhaps by requesting an introductory appointment, with the person to whom one will most likely turn when needed. Of course, knowledge of such persons is also useful for possible referrals a clergy might make. There are professionals who specialize in strengthening marriages or parent-child relationships. Likewise, there are those who specialize in the healing of depression or other mental health issues.

While each profession is to be respected and valued, it may be an accredited pastoral counselor who can effectively relate to a clergy's life and struggles. The American Association of Pastoral Counselors[29] has a tool on their website to aid the search for a pastoral counselor. If earlier chapters on burnout and compassion fatigue, stress, or some of the other challenging situations in ministry have stirred an inner recognition, quite probably a competent counselor or therapist should be added to one's resources for healing.

Almost always there is financial cost when engaging a counselor. Some agencies may have a sliding scale according to income, and there may be certain types of counseling provided in one's health insurance. Further, some denominations and judicatories may have funds to support a minister's need for counseling care. It never hurts to ask! While being wise about expenditure, it is much better to reach out for such help early rather than late.

In this chapter, we may have stirred your recognition of a number of relationships you support and that support you. And perhaps you also have heard gentle invitations to expand your "relational system."

FOR YOUR REFLECTION AND CONVERSATION

1. As you reflect on your family of origin and the family of which you are now a part, what strengths do you celebrate? Where is there room for growth? Is there any healing needed?
2. In what ways are you making sure you spend quality time nurturing your relationships with your marriage partner and children? How does this contribute to your self-care?

3. How does the discussion of "fictive kin" relate to you? In the past and present, who are some of the persons among your fictive kin, and how does or did that relationship enrich your life?
4. Who fills the roles of prophet, cheerleader, harasser, and guide in your life? Any gaps?
5. The chapter discusses friendships within one's congregation/agency and community as well as friendships with fellow clergy. What is your experience in each of these realms of friendship?
6. Do you have an *anam cara*, a spiritual friend or guide, a spiritual director, informally or formally? If so, how did this begin and how are you experiencing it now? If not, are you motivated to find one? If so, where will you search?
7. If you were to seek professional counseling, to whom would you turn?

Chapter Eight

Physical Self-Care

Human beings were never designed for the poorly nourished, sedentary, in-
door, sleep-deprived, socially isolated, frenzied pace of twenty-first century
life.

—Steve Ilardi, *The Depression Cure* [1]

As we turn to consider the care of our physical bodies, you may have an
initial feeling of resistance. You've heard before of the importance of exercising, eating right, and getting enough sleep. But knowing what one should
do and actually doing it are entirely different matters. When this topic came
up for one doctor of ministry student, she said emphatically, "I hate exercising! And you're not going to change that!" In this area, we already have
many habits and many reasons as to why we live life the way we do. And
changing even one of our habits is hard. Nevertheless, the importance of
physical self-care cannot be overstated.

In this chapter, we will first learn what the research says about how clergy
are doing in this area of self-care and explore some of the challenges we face.
We will then turn our attention to articulating a theology of physical self-care
and consider theological perspectives regarding our embodiment. With such
spiritual groundings, we will consider several aspects of such care. Exercise
and sleep have already been identified as important for stress management.
But we will go further in exploring these, as well as look at our physical need
for nutritious food.

HOW WELL ARE CLERGY DOING AT PHYSICAL SELF-CARE?

The Clergy Health Initiative at Duke Divinity School has been researching
that very question for many years with regard to United Methodist clergy in

North Carolina. Comparing the health of clergy to a demographically similar group in the general population in 2008, they found that clergy are experiencing higher rates of chronic diseases, such as diabetes, arthritis, high blood pressure, angina, and asthma. They also noted that many of these chronic illnesses are triggered or exacerbated by obesity and that nearly 40 percent of clergy surveyed were obese (body mass index of 30 or higher). This compared to an obesity rate of 29 percent in the general population.[2] Furthermore, diabetes, high blood pressure, and angina make one more vulnerable for heart disease, which is a prevailing cause of death.[3]

Recognizing that this research was done specifically on Methodist clergy in North Carolina, we can nevertheless assume that it also describes clergy in many other denominations and places. A couple of other studies support this assumption. A *Pulpit and Pew* 2001 research study showed "strikingly high rates of obesity in a nationwide survey of parish pastors."[4] And a 2002 study done by the Evangelical Lutheran Church in America found that 34 percent of its clergy were obese, compared with the national average of 22 percent.[5] Since obesity is a factor in the development of a number of illnesses, we can safely assume that clergy in general also experience higher levels of these chronic conditions.

When we turn to consider the mental health of clergy, we have comparable reason for concern. Research done by Duke's Clergy Health Initiative found that rates of depression for pastors were nearly double that for the general population in the United States. In surveys done in 2008 and 2010, between 10.5 and 11.1 percent of clergy reported symptoms indicating depression in the previous two weeks, whereas the general population's depression rate was at 5.5 percent.[6] The Evangelical Lutheran Church in America's "Ministerial Health and Wellness 2002" study found that 16 percent of male clergy experienced depression compared to the U.S. male rate of 6 percent, and 24 percent of female clergy experienced depression compared to the U.S. female rate of 12 percent.[7] Depression is a disease impacted by one's lifestyle and physical self-care.

As was discussed in chapter 4 on stress, both cardiovascular problems and depression are related to stress by mechanisms explained there. Research has also shown that obesity itself is associated with stress, through activated bodily processes. Furthermore, when stressed, we may engage in emotional eating or eat poorly by buying fast food rather than spend time cooking. We may feel too busy to exercise. Studies have also linked obesity to inadequate levels of sleep.[8]

The fact that so many clergy are experiencing such elevated rates of chronic diseases, obesity, and depression would suggest that they are not doing well in this area of physical self-care. And as the Clergy Health Initiative has discovered by listening to clergy speak to the issue, there are significant challenges that make it difficult to do better. Clergy tended to work more than fifty hours a week, were away from home around four evenings weekly, and had a widely varying schedule. Taking the time to exercise or cook a meal was difficult, and establishing a routine that incorporated physical self-care was challenging. Many considered such self-care as one more thing to do, but after they had completed ministry tasks. And of course, the work of ministry is never done. Clergy tend to put the needs of others and the congregation before their own needs, so even planned self-care time is easily set aside. Some regarded taking time for self-care as selfish, and thereby not to be held as a high priority. Such perspectives indicate that part of what is required for clergy to embrace the need to care for their bodies is attention to their beliefs and articulation of a theology of self-care that embraces care for one's physical body.

THEOLOGICAL PERSPECTIVES ON PHYSICAL SELF-CARE

There is much in the biblical text that affirms the goodness of the human body. In the story of creation, God is pictured as shaping the human body from the clay of the earth and breathing life into it. Human beings, male and female, are declared to be created in the very image of God, as image bearers. And God's pronouncement on life created on that sixth day was that it was "very good." The theological doctrine of creation affirms the goodness of the human body, its form shaped by the touch of God.

As the Psalmist reflects on the creation miracle of every human person, he is moved to praise: "For it was you who formed my inward parts; you knit me together in my mother's womb. I praise you, for I am fearfully and wonderfully made. Wonderful are your works; that I know very well" (Psalm 139:13–14). These words remind us that our bodies are wondrous. They are amazingly complex and beautifully coordinated to move us through life. Without intentional effort, our hearts beat and our breath moves in and out every minute of our lives. We have amazing abilities to see, to hear, to feel, and to think. Recognizing that God is the source of these wondrously made bodies reminds us that they are gift.

Several years ago, I (Ruth) spoke with a woman who was an artist. She had given one of her paintings to her daughter, happy to share the beauty she had created. But her daughter did not seem to value the gift, for year after year, it sat on the floor, leaning up against the wall, waiting to be framed and hung. This caused her artist mother much pain. If we give a gift to someone into which we have poured our creativity, and they don't take care of it, it is difficult to think that person appreciated our gift. Gratitude to God for these marvelous bodies involves caring for them, treasuring them, honoring them, and being good stewards of them.

The goodness of the human body is also shown in the life of Jesus. As Christians, we believe Jesus to be the incarnated presence of God. The divine took on human flesh; the sacred was embodied. As the Gospel of John says, "And the Word became flesh and lived among us . . . full of grace and truth" (John 1:14). There was nothing evil or so fatally flawed about the human body that it was unfit for the divine presence.

In his earthly ministry, Jesus was concerned for the bodies of others. Much of his time was spent healing sick bodies, touching leprous bodies, bringing sight and hearing back to bodies that were blind or deaf. The bodily well-being of others was of great concern. It was through his body, through hands that touched and a mouth that spoke, that God's healing power and presence were known. His body was the channel of God's love toward those who were hurting.

Even as Jesus sent out his disciples to use their bodies to heal the sick and preach the good news, those who still follow Jesus understand that we are the hands and feet of Christ. A dominant metaphor for the church is that of being the body of Christ. Our bodies together comprise the physical embodiment of Christ's spirit at work in our world. That is the message of this poem attributed to the Spanish Carmelite nun and mystic Teresa of Avila (1515–1582):

> Christ has no body now but yours.
> No hands, no feet on earth but yours.
> Yours are the eyes through which he looks compassion on this world.
> Yours are the feet with which he walks to do good.
> Yours are the hands through which he blesses all the world.
> Yours are the hands, yours are the feet, yours are the eyes, you are his body.
> Christ has no body now on earth but yours. [9]

The Apostle Paul writes in I Corinthians 6:19–20 these words: "Or do you not know that your body is a temple (or sanctuary) of the Holy Spirit within you, which you have from God, and that you are not your own? For you were bought with a price; therefore, glorify God with your body." Admittedly, Paul wrote these words in a passage where he was trying to convince the Corinthian Christians that what one does with one's body is important and that therefore sexual purity was important. Nevertheless, these verses contain a teaching that can be generalized beyond that. Our physical bodies are the dwelling place—the temple—of the Holy Spirit of God. It is through our physical bodies that God's presence is made known in the world and God's work is done. Through our experience of salvation, our bodies are not just our own but are to be used to glorify God. We are therefore to honor our bodies and treat them honorably. Inadequate care for them that leads to illness and disability will interfere greatly with our ability to serve God in ministry, as it is only through our bodies that this can occur.

There is more to how the human body is regarded in the Scriptures, however. In the holistic thought of the Hebrew Bible, the body is regarded as "the material, visible aspect of the individual self as person."[10] It is thereby essential to the unity of the person and not regarded as separate from it. That is, we are our bodies, rather than that we have a body. But while this perspective is predominant in the New Testament, one also finds some influences from the dualism of Greek thought. For example, Plato believed that the soul was superior to the body. In fact, the body was seen both as a prison for the soul and as a temporary feature of a person.

New Testament writers at times express this dualism of body and soul, including the thought that the body is a source of temptation and sin. In Romans 7, Paul speaks of the struggle he has with doing what he knows to be right. He finally cries out, "Who will rescue me from this body of death?" (Romans 7:24). And yet, it is not that the body is intrinsically evil and to be discarded. As Jewett writes, "The Christian looks forward not to the redemption *from* the body but redemption *of* the body (Rom. 8:23)."[11] Rather than the body being evil, we are to offer our bodies "as a living sacrifice, holy and acceptable to God" (Romans 12:1). That is, we are to use our bodies in willing service to God and others.

As can be seen from this exploration of biblical theology, the major doctrines related to creation, incarnation, the work of the church, and our future hope all uphold the goodness of the human body. Rather than viewing it as a prison from which the soul will escape, it is seen as an essential aspect of the person who is seeking to glorify God. This theological perspective underlines the importance of caring well for the bodies we are.

LEARNING TO HONOR OUR BODIES

Many of us, however, do not look positively upon our bodies. As I (Ruth) was driving home one evening, I chanced to hear a story on the radio that I have since reflected on. (I think it was a Moth story, although I have not been able to locate it.) The story line was about a woman's vacation experiences of enjoying a country club's hot tub, sharing it first with older men and then with women whose bodies were sleek and bronzed. She shared that she herself was five feet tall and overweight, having gained weight during a couple of pregnancies. These experiences prompted her to do some reflecting on her relationship with her body. On the one hand, she said she hated her body and had struggled with it much of her life, feeling it did not represent well the person she felt she was inside. But on the other hand, she realized that her body had served her well. Her body had worked hard to help create two beautiful babies. Although she had mistreated it during her younger years with drugs and alcohol, it had continued to function well. It had allowed her to take some wonderful trips where she had seen some amazing things. It had given her some great sexual experiences. She recounted the many ways her body had served and brought enjoyment to her. Realizing all that her body had faithfully done for her over the years, she ends the story with an expression of acceptance, embracing her body as who she is.

Probably many of us also experience a mixture of feelings toward our bodies, which may affect how we treat them. Our personal experiences of being teased about our bodies as children or our internalization of societal messages regarding how our bodies should look may have inculcated in us a sense of shame or dislike for our bodies. Even if we embrace cognitively the theological perspective that affirms the body's goodness, thus encouraging care for it, our lived experience of disliking our bodies or considering them unimportant may present obstacles. So part of caring for our bodies may be to befriend them, become more at home with them, listen to them, accept them, and regard them with compassion.

In her book *An Altar in the World*, Barbara Brown Taylor explores the practice of incarnation, or what she calls "the practice of wearing skin."[12] With typical forthrightness, she writes, "Whether you are sick or well, lovely or irregular, there comes a time when it is vitally important for your spiritual health to drop your clothes, look in the mirror, and say, 'Here I am. This is the body-like-no-other that my life has shaped. I live here. This is my soul's address.'"[13] She suggests that doing this may cause one to realize there is a lot for which to be thankful. "Bodies take real beatings. That they heal from most things is an underrated miracle. That they give birth is beyond reckoning."[14] She encourages us to wear our skin with gratitude, knowing that whatever we may think of our bodies, we can offer them to God and be useful in the world.

Similarly, in her book *Honoring the Body*, Stephanie Paulsell considers the practice of honoring the body to be a crucial part of Christian spirituality. She grounds this practice in the belief that all bodies are worthy of care and blessing. That includes one's own body, as well as those of others. She suggests that by recognizing that we *are* our bodies, not only inhabiting them, we may view them as having greater value.[15]

And yet our bodies are vulnerable and fragile, as God well knows and thus has compassion for us. "For [God] knows how we were made; [God] remembers that we are dust" (Psalm 103:13–14, adapted). Paulsell encourages us to embrace this task: "to learn to see our bodies and the bodies of others through the eyes of God. To learn to see the body as both fragile and deeply blessed. To remember the body's vulnerability and to rejoice in the body as a sign of God's gracious bounty."[16]

Not long ago, I (Ruth) experienced a time of severe lower back pain. Every small twist or turn or movement could cause me to have excruciating muscle spasms in my back. When driving, small bumps in the road or shifting my body while making a turn set off those spasms. It was debilitating, impacting everything I did and filling it with pain. I figured it must be a terrible disc problem that I would have to cope with the rest of my life. I went to the doctor, who diagnosed it as muscle strain, even though I could not remember having done anything to cause it. Finding it hard to believe, I nevertheless took the muscle relaxer and high powered anti-inflammatory medication she gave me. And much to my surprise, deep relief, and gratitude, it got better within a week or two. Remembering that experience makes me realize the fragility and vulnerability of my body and how severe injury or illness would dramatically impact my capacity to do ministry. It makes me intensely grateful for the health I now enjoy and for the wonder of being able to walk, sit, sleep, and drive without pain. Remembering this makes my life seem incredibly good and renews my commitment to care for my body so that it remains so.

Finally, the practice of honoring the body is also grounded in the conviction that we are able to enter into a deeper relationship with God through the needs of the body. With such a perspective in mind, it is to those needs that we now turn—specifically, the need for exercise, food, and sleep.

EXERCISING AND STAYING ACTIVE

Staying physically active and getting enough exercise requires considerable intentionality for most of us in contemporary American society. In past generations, work involved much more physical labor, and walking was often the means of transportation, such that exercise and physical activity were naturally incorporated into daily life. In many other countries of the world, this is still the case today. But in twenty-first-century America, our lives have become remarkably sedentary, as we work at jobs that mostly require sitting, transport ourselves by sitting in cars, and enjoy the entertainment of lounging in front of a television set or some other kind of screen.

We know, however, that regular aerobic exercise is one of the most important things we can do for stress management and self-care. Exercise helps us get rid of the extra adrenaline and cortisol that stress episodes dump into our system. As described in chapter 4, chronically high levels of these stress hormones circulating through our bodies can cause significant health problems. Exercise also helps all the systems of our body to function better and especially keeps our hearts and brains healthier. It decreases the risk of high blood pressure, diabetes, metabolic syndrome, heart disease, stroke, osteoporosis, and certain cancers. And it helps to boost mood, improve sleep, reduce stress, improve cognitive function, and control weight. [17]

Let's think about how much exercise we need to be healthy. The 2008 Physical Activity Guidelines for Americans, put out by the U.S. Department of Health and Human Services, advises healthy adults to get at least 150 minutes of moderate-intensity aerobic exercise, such as brisk walking, or 75 minutes of vigorous-intensity aerobic activity, such as jogging, each week. Other possible aerobic activities are swimming, cycling, racquetball, hiking, dancing, climbing stairs, and heavy yard work. In addition, it recommends that we do muscle-strengthening activities at least two days a week.[18] Stretching exercises are also important to help us gain more body awareness as to when we are feeling tense so that we can relax those areas, as well as having the health benefit of making us more flexible.

The Mind Body Medical Institute's *The Wellness Book* provides this guideline: "A brisk walk of 30–60 minutes 3–5 times a week is a level of exercise attainable by most adults and sufficient to produce the fitness standard that promotes health and decreases risk of disease."[19] But even less amounts of exercise have demonstrated positive health effects. In his book *The Depression Cure*, Steve Ilardi indicates that the best research shows that only ninety minutes of aerobic activity each week (a brisk half-hour walk three times a week) provides an antidepressant effect that is greater than that for the common antidepressant Zoloft.[20] In addition, those who are older, out of shape, or have a disability may have as much benefit from thirty minutes of slow walking as others do from vigorous activity.[21] What is important is that we begin where we are, start to physically exert ourselves, and then gradually increase exercise as we gain strength.

Recently, it has also been recognized that being too sedentary and sitting too much can cause cardiovascular and metabolic problems, even if one is regularly exercising. Research is showing distinct mechanisms in the physiology of inactivity that are different from that of exercising.[22] Thus, it is important that we be intentional in picking up our overall activity level and especially be attentive to not sitting as much. Even small efforts can be helpful. I (Ruth) will often choose to walk into other church offices and talk face to face rather than pick up the phone. This keeps me moving throughout the day. Someone else stands whenever she talks on the phone. Parking further from the building, taking the stairs instead of the elevator, taking breaks to stretch and walk around, and getting a standing desk to use for some of our work are also possibilities. Electronic activity trackers, such as Fitbits, are helping many to recognize their sedentariness and look for opportunities to get the recommended number of steps each day.

Many of us clergy are not getting sufficient aerobic exercise despite knowing that we should, so how can we get started and maintain this lifestyle change? Let's talk about some practical suggestions. It helps to choose an aerobic activity that one enjoys. I (Ruth) love walking outside in nature. Whenever possible, I choose to walk around the time of sunset, so I can watch the changing beauty of the sky. This so absorbs me with wonder that the physical effort I am exerting seems lessened, and often I am drawn toward thoughts of God.

Exercise becomes easier if we persist in it. I notice that my walking feels stiffer and takes more effort after a particularly busy time in which I have neglected it. But by the second day, the flow of walking returns, along with increased pleasure in moving, breathing hard, and exerting. Because of the interconnection of body and mind, I look forward to when I can take a break from work and go walking, knowing it is going to refresh and enliven my thinking.

It is helpful to make exercise interesting and absorbing. Some people may enjoy listening to music or a podcast. One woman discovered she loved listening to audiobooks but allowed herself to do so only while she was on her treadmill.[23] Others may exercise while watching a favorite TV show. Or perhaps an exercise video can make it more interesting.

It may also help to exercise with a friend, so that it becomes a social activity. A couple members of our church have been meeting very early every morning for years to walk together before work. This increases enjoyment and accountability, as well as nurtures friendships. My clergy brother enjoys a good game of basketball with other men several times a week and comes away invigorated. Others have found that hiring a personal trainer can get them started.

If exercise feels like a waste of time, you may need to make it purposeful. Consider activities that accomplish something, such as doing yard work. Some find purpose by having a reason and destination for their exercise. My father enjoyed walking to the store to get needed grocery items, and my son often bikes many miles to our family gatherings rather than drive.

It is important to create a schedule for when you are going to exercise, find times that work for you, write them on your calendar, and work hard to protect them. Whenever possible, create a routine, recognizing it may need to be flexible at times. Give yourself permission to take the time to do this. You will still have things that need to be done, but you deserve a little time off, and your body needs it. And more than likely, you will be able to think more creatively and clearly if you do. If needed, motivate yourself by making yourself accountable to someone.

Although we may be tempted to look upon exercise as a chore that must be done, Paulsell encourages us instead to view it as part of the spiritual practice of honoring our bodies and as a means "to open a space in which human beings can reach out toward the divine with their bodies."[24] Such are my evening walks, which in following the same path every day take on the semblance of walking a labyrinth. Following the same route opens up space to think, pray, or simply be in the moment, in my body, with mind relaxed. Furthermore, the exertion of stretching and moving enables us to know ourselves more fully as created by one who cherishes our bodies, so fearfully and wonderfully made.

EATING

Another way that we honor our bodies is by nourishing them with the right kinds and amounts of food. This is no small feat in our contemporary American society, which seemingly has an abundance of food, much of which has little nutritional value or is laced with chemicals. As I (Ruth) walk down the long row of chips and snacks in the grocery store, I wonder if we need to reconsider what the word "food" even means. Is it simply something we can eat or is it that which nourishes our body? Unfortunately, those can often be quite different in our society, in which agribusiness and food industries have changed the way food is produced, and often much less nutritious food is being marketed. Furthermore, with such an abundance of food, it is easy to eat more than we need, to shovel down food even when we are not hungry, and to do so almost unaware of what we are doing, as we continue to work at our computers or watch our videos. Changes in what and how we eat are related to the growing health problem of obesity in our country. Care for our bodies therefore entails attentiveness to these matters.

Because the U.S. government's (USDA) dietary recommendations are too often influenced by food industry lobbyists, we will use recommendations by the Harvard School of Public Health. These recommendations are based on the latest dietary research and are visualized as the Healthy Eating Plate and Healthy Eating Pyramid at The Nutrition Source on Harvard's website (https://www.hsph.harvard.edu/nutritionsource/healthy-eating-plate/).   Their healthy eating recommendations are as follows:

- At least half of your meal should consist of vegetables and fruits, with somewhat more vegetables (excluding potatoes). A variety of kinds and colors is best.
- A quarter of your meal should consist of whole grains—whole wheat, barley, quinoa, oats, and brown rice. Avoid refined grains, white flour, and white rice.
- A quarter of your meal should be made up of proteins. Fish, chicken, beans, and nuts are the best. Red meat should be limited, and processed meats (bacon, sausage) should be avoided.
- Use healthy plant oils and avoid partially hydrogenated oils.
- Drink water, tea, or coffee, and avoid sugary drinks. Limit milk and dairy products to one to two servings daily.
- Eat these high-quality foods in appropriately sized servings, rather than simply counting calories. Choose fresh foods rather than processed foods. And take a daily multivitamin, plus vitamin D.

Such healthy eating can make a definite difference in your body's health. Research shows that men whose diets most closely followed the Healthy

Eating Pyramid (which incorporates the above guidelines) were 20 percent less likely to develop a major chronic disease and 40 percent less likely to develop cardiovascular disease than those who had low scores in following this way of eating. Women who followed these guidelines decreased their risk for chronic disease by 11 percent and for cardiovascular disease by 30 percent over women who didn't eat healthily.[25]

One other dietary supplement that is important for brain health is omega-3 fatty acids. Made in leaves of plants, grasses, and algae, they are also found in animals or fish that feed on these. Grain-fed animals may produce meat in which they are lacking. Ilardi indicates that omega-3 fatty acids are important for the functioning of serotonin and other neurotransmitters and therefore valuable in the treatment and prevention of depression.[26] With clergy depression rates double that of the general public, it may be good to take fish oil capsules, a good source of omega-3 fatty acids. Furthermore, choosing organic food enables us to avoid harmful chemicals.

But it is not only what we eat that matters but also how we eat it. Mindfulness of what we are eating can make it a spiritual practice. This involves being present to the experience and enjoying the tastes and textures of what is being eaten. At a recent educational event that I (Ruth) attended, we were guided in eating a dark Hershey's kiss with mindfulness. It involved touching the wrapper, hearing its crinkles, smelling the rich chocolate, putting it in our mouths, and letting the flavor gradually melt into our taste buds. It took several minutes to eat one Hershey's kiss. The flavor was so rich and the experience so full that one Hershey's kiss was sufficient.

Such mindfulness not only enables us to fully enjoy the experience of eating, it helps us pay attention to our bodies so that we eat only what we need. Our appetite is designed to guide us in how much to eat, but it must be listened to and supplied with healthy food to be reliable. We may need to remind ourselves to slow down and be aware of our eating. Terry (Ruth's husband) does this by lighting a small table lamp or candle before each meal.

Honoring our bodies by eating nourishing food in this mindful way also helps us recognize the realities of our human embodiment and our need for God. Noticing our hunger and thirst reminds us of our bodily vulnerability and our dependence on the earth, the labor of others, and the sustenance of life by God.[27] When we sit down for a meal, we can do so with gratitude for all that has made possible this provision of food, by which we can care for our bodies and strengthen them for further service to God and others.

SLEEPING

Think of the last time you woke up from a full night of sleep, feeling rested and refreshed. Perhaps you even woke up before your alarm. How long ago was this full night of sleep? How often does this happen?

For many of us, this may be a rare occurrence, as sleep is one of the first things to get impacted by a stressed and busy life. When there's too much to do, it is easy to keep working late into the night but then still need to get up early in the morning. We may often feel that we don't have time for the recommended seven and a half to eight hours of sleep nightly. And so we plot to figure out the minimal amount we need to get by. Like Thomas Edison, who invented the light bulb, we may feel that sleep is a waste of time. Since his invention, we certainly tend to get much less. Ilardi indicates that in the early 1900s, Americans averaged nine hours of sleep nightly compared to the current average of 6.7 hours.[28] That nearly 30 percent reduction in sleep has left many of us sleep deprived, with significant consequences to our bodies and brains. We need to rediscover the wisdom of Thomas Dekkar, who said, "Sleep is that golden chain that ties health and our bodies together."[29] Research is indeed finding that adequate sleep is indispensable for both physical and mental health.

Just a few nights of sleep deprivation can cause memory and concentration problems, poor judgment, irritability, stress, and depressed mood. An extended period of disrupted sleep can trigger a depressive episode. Sleep deprivation studies have also found such harmful effects as increased inflammation, decreased immune function, impaired blood glucose monitoring, and increased blood pressure, conditions usually seen when people are experiencing high levels of stress. These can lead to increased risk for cardiovascular disease, stroke, diabetes, cancer, and infections. Insufficient sleep also is linked with weight gain through disrupting glucose processing, energy metabolism, and hormones that control appetite. It decreases leptin, which tells the brain that one is full, and increases ghrelin, which stimulates appetite.[30]

Although it may seem that nothing is happening while we sleep, major repair and rejuvenation work is going on. Restorative functions, such as tissue repair and removal of toxins, are occurring in the body. Sleep enables memory consolidation and brain processing, which enhances creative problem-solving and learning. Sleep is a time in which "essential housekeeping functions" are done, according to neuroscience professor Russell Foster. He considers it "arrogant" to think we do not need sufficient sleep. He writes, "It is not a luxury or an indulgence but a fundamental biological need, enhancing creativity, productivity, mood, and the ability to interact with others."[31]

Getting enough sleep is an area of self-care that I (Ruth) have come to realize is very important for me. Just one night of inadequate sleep reduces my capacity to concentrate and focus and makes me less motivated and more negative. Looking back over my life, the times I have struggled more with depression have coincided with times of sleep deprivation related to being awake at night with babies or having difficulty balancing demanding work with family care. Recognizing that sleep deficiency affects so negatively my capacity for joy and vitality in ministry, I consider it a spiritual discipline to put aside work and take time for sufficient sleep. The words of Psalm 127:2 are an encouragement: "It is in vain that you rise up early and go late to rest, eating the bread of anxious toil; for [God] gives sleep to [God's] beloved" (adapted).

So how can we improve the amount and quality of our sleep? Getting physical exercise is important because it improves sleep quality and leads to more restorative slow-wave sleep. Morning exposure to sunlight or bright light strengthens the body's internal clock, making it easier to fall asleep and stay asleep. When experiencing significant stress, we need to take steps to manage it. Anything that reduces stress will help us sleep better. Developing regular sleeping times and healthy bedtime routines can help. Reducing light an hour or two before sleeping, especially the blue light of many electronic devices, and then sleeping in as dark a room as possible also helps the body to sleep better.

AN INVITATION

We've taken a rather hard look at the consequences of not adequately caring for our bodies in this chapter. If you struggle in this area, we hope this has not been demoralizing but rather has been a wake-up call to action and an invitation to healthier living. Although there are many aspects to physical self-care, we have focused on the essential areas of exercise, eating, and sleep. Taking time for regular health monitoring, such as annual physicals, dental visits, and flu shots, is, of course, also essential, even while it is easy for many of us to neglect them. Relaxing through meditative practices and Sabbath as described in chapter 6 is also important for physical self-care.

FOR YOUR REFLECTION AND CONVERSATION

1. What thoughts do you have in response to the research indicating that clergy are having higher rates of physical and mental health difficulties than the general population? In your experience, why is it hard for clergy to attend to their physical self-care?
2. What theological perspectives provide you with spiritual motivation to care for your body?

3. How do you feel toward your body? What difference would it make if you were to befriend, listen to, accept, and regard your body with compassion?

4. How does your level of exercise and activity compare with the Physical Activity Guidelines for Americans? What makes it difficult for you to get sufficient amounts of exercise? Which of the suggestions might help you sustain healthy exercise levels?

5. How healthy is your eating, if assessed by the Harvard School of Public Health recommendations? What changes would you like to make in what and how you eat?

6. How often are you getting enough sleep? How do you feel when you do not get sufficient sleep? What might you do to better care for yourself in this area?

Chapter Nine

Self-Care through Inner Wisdom

Two-thirds of what we see is behind our eyes.

—Chinese Proverb

Some of the worst catastrophes in my (Dick's) ministry—attacks, church splits, pay cuts, being fired, and more—never happened. Oh, they happened in my head. But they never happened in fact. A worried and anxious imagination can pollute one's sense of reality and make effective leadership and ministry difficult. I could have used some of the inner wisdom that we will share with you in this chapter.

We are convinced there is a counterpart to that Chinese saying we quoted above. Something like two-thirds of what we hear comes from inside our heads. Our life experiences, our memories, our hurts, our fear, and our anxiety all rise up with clamor to be heard, particularly when we are coming into a hard patch of life or ministry.

We need inner wisdom, which is just as important to our well-being as the activities suggested in this book. In this way, we can move out of inner anxiety toward inner serenity and celebration of our strengths, gifts, and opportunities. In turn, this will open us to a clearer self-concept as well as an understanding of our role as clergy, its promise, and its limitations. Consider these steps to think realistically and recognize the good things in our lives.

RECONSIDERING OUR FAMILY OF ORIGIN AND ITS CONTINUING INFLUENCE

Out of his knowledge of systems and congregations, Rabbi Edwin Friedman wrote an important book, *Generation to Generation: Family Process in Church and Synagogue*. On the first page, he stated his thesis that all clergy

119

are "involved in three distinct families whose emotional forces interlock: the families within the congregation, our congregations [as families], and our own."[1] The influences from families in the congregation and the minister's family may include dead members as well as live ones and all that went on in those families. Change in any of those three families will have influence on the others. So an important part of inner wisdom is to reflect and explore, "What do I bring to ministry of help and hindrance from the family into which I was born and raised?"

Friedman used to ask students in his ministry seminars, "In what ways was your family a gift to you and your ministry?"[2] There is, of course, a counter question: "In what ways was your experience in your family a problem to your life and ministry?"

Often, the place to begin on family of origin work is to draw up a "genogram" of one's family over three or four generations.[3] Using symbols one can begin to explore. What are the recurring patterns from generation to generation—certain occupations, religious practices, abuse, addiction, strong bonds, cutoffs from each other? How does this help me understand some places in life and ministry where things don't go well?

And what about the family into which you were born? How many children, what gender, where were you in birth order? What was good and what was troubling? Was there physical, sexual, or emotional abuse? Was it sometimes chaotic with alcohol or other substance overuse? Were there arguments? Violence? Divorces? Deaths? Lisa Brookes has noted, "Family of origin work is getting unstuck emotionally and/or in your relationships in the present by healing the family or other wounds of the past."[4] Here are a few examples of discoveries from doing one's family of origin work.

Margaret Marcuson noticed that she was the firstborn female to a firstborn female, who was the daughter of a minister. Seeing this, she understood why she so often over functioned, and that meant someone else then under functioned. Her exploration of her family story went much deeper, with trips to relatives she had not seen in years, as well as visits to cemeteries to get in touch and know more of her sometimes tragic family story, its pain and its joys. She points out that family work is hard work, and further, no matter how much insight we have gained, this work never ends.[5]

Peter Scazzero studied a three-generation genogram. His grandparents, who were immigrants from Italy in an arranged marriage, had strict gender expectations with shades of abuse. He made some important discoveries to process on the way to being a better husband, father, and minister.

He realized, "I over functioned" to make Mama happy since her husband ignored her. "I over performed" because parental approval was often based on achievement, not unconditional love. "I had cultural, not biblical expectations for marriage and family. . . . I resolved conflict poorly," again more resembling his family of origin than the New Testament teachings he shared with others. And "I didn't let myself feel. . . . I did not know how to accept and process my own feelings."[6]

By coming to this awareness and learning from it, he was much more helpful to his family and to others. When people came to him struggling with their own family issues, he would reassure them, "All families are broken and fallen. There aren't any 'clean' genograms."[7]

As for my (Dick's) family of origin work, I was the baby, the second child and only son to a couple, with a strong father thirteen years older than my mother. My father died when I was ten, and my mother, older sister, and I struggled financially to survive. I now see how fragile we were, and so we didn't talk about our grief and tried not to argue too much. I loved and admired my father, his ministry, his missionary stories, and his kindness, and I trace the beginning of my call to ministry to wanting to continue his work at the time of his death.

I am so grateful to my mother and her aspiration for her children. She couldn't pay the grocery bill some months but constantly told my sister and me that we would be able to go to college. (We both have PhDs.) My mother was a gifted church pianist, and we often played (I on my baritone horn) together. That is a tender memory to this day. With instruments in hand, we were so kind and considerate of the other, but we somehow couldn't say out loud how much we missed Daddy. My sister and I also didn't know how to deal with our newly employed hardworking and fragile mother.

My mother joined forces with my father's successor, a single woman minister who had a large foster family. And so my family's gifts to my ministry include a deep respect and advocacy for capable women. But my father-shaped hole in my soul means that I may not be as effective with some men. I lost my dad early and so did not learn the hunting, fishing, horsemanship, mechanical gifts, and more that were associated with manhood where I grew up. As the baby in our original family and a middle child in our foster family, I lack some of the skill and enthusiasm needed for being a leader through complex situations and large projects.

Our family had another rather common practice. When any of us had a problem with another, we would tell someone other than the one about whom we were troubled. Years later I would learn the term "triangle" in family systems theory, but we had it down to an unconscious "art" long before.

I could say more about my family of origin and learn even more than I have—as I am sure Margaret and Peter could as well. The important thing is to start. The more family awareness becomes conscious, the better prepared we are for our marriages and ministries.

BECOMING AWARE OF CHURCH/AGENCY AS A SYSTEM
AND OUR PLACE IN IT

Systems thinking, according to Peter Steinke, is a way of conceptualizing reality. This view considers the interrelatedness of the parts in all their rich complexity. In a system, sets of forces interact with each other. When viewing groups of people as systems, it is understood that one person does not cause another to react. Rather all parts interact with each other and mutually influence each other.[8] Steinke notes, "Systems thinking deepens our understanding of life. We see it as a rich complexity of interdependent parts. . . . To think systemically is to look at the ongoing, vital interaction of the connected parts."[9]

In a congregation, denomination, or agency, there are many interrelated systems. There are economic, structural, relational systems, and more, each interacting with the others. And as we noted from Friedman, a congregation is also a system with three kinds of family groups interacting. This all too brief description of systems theory will point us to the wisdom found within it for clergy self-care.

One piece of this wisdom is knowledge and prudence in regard to the previously mentioned triangles. Edwin Friedman notes, "An emotional triangle is formed by any three persons or issues. . . . The basic law of emotional triangles is that when any two parts of a system become uncomfortable with each other, they will 'triangle in' or focus upon a third person or issue, as a way of stabilizing their own relationship with one another."[10]

It may be said that a person is "triangled" when caught in the middle of an unresolved issue. For example, two staff members or board members, having issues with each other, may turn to a third to hear their complaints and take their side. Or a member, uncomfortable with an issue a church is facing, such as whether to put the American flag in the sanctuary or whether to have a patriotic service on Veterans Day, may "triangle" the minister as the one who should be blamed for causing this "trouble."

How does a person deal with attempts to get "triangled in" to tensions between two other parties? The wisest course is to encourage the conflicting parties to deal directly with each other. One might ask such questions as, "Have you spoken to so-and-so? May I go with you [to talk with the other party]? May I tell so-and-so your concern?" Speed Leas notes that such responses convey an important message, "I'm no fun to complain to."[11]

Another aspect of systems understanding is that all communities have anxiety. And all churches/agencies have anxious persons within them. As Arthur Boers notes, it is part of the purpose of the church to welcome all who will come, including unhealthy and anxious people. A system's anxiety is an expression of what is happening among the anxious people within (and perhaps outside as well) the system. There are two types of anxiety: acute, which is situational and aroused by crises or irritations; and chronic, which is "perpetual, ongoing, and habitual."[12]

For those who share leadership (as clergy often do), usually the anxiety can be kept within manageable limits. This is done with prompt attention to threats and clear communication. Also, the opportunity for all to discuss and be involved in answering the threat is an important aspect.

The opening chapter of this book gave attention to the vast change and, in many places, drastic shrinkage in the numbers of people and resources for the Christian enterprise. There are agencies, seminaries, and churches that have had to close. Congregations have had to reduce the size of their staffs or move to having a part-time bi-vocational pastor. Acute anxiety is an appropriate response. Skillful and caring leadership to live through such crises and find a way is much needed.

Simultaneously there is chronic anxiety in persons and communities that may well be exacerbated by the acute crises. Chronically anxious persons may see the situation as much worse than it factually is. They may blame the leaders and threaten to withdraw gifts, attendance, and perhaps their membership itself.

So we have a family of families in a congregation and the bubbling up of both acute and chronic anxiety. Therefore, it is almost inevitable that some of the blame and pain for this will fall on the clergy. Richard Blackburn puts it this way, "The clergy collar is the screen upon which parishioners show home movies."[13]

This will be hard to take, particularly if one was drawn into ministry partly by the love and encouragement of one's faith community. In such situations, I used to quote a saying I thought I heard in a movie, "You never grow up until you have been disapproved of once." (The movie was *War and Peace*. The exact quote is "He was the first person in the world to disapprove of me. You're not really grown-up until that happens to you."[14]) Either way, it is possible that such a time can be a growing experience.

What is needed of the pastoral leader in anxious times, and what does the pastoral leader need in turn for one's own welfare? Edwin Friedman answers with the two words that have become famous—"nonanxious presence." He writes, "What is vital to changing any kind of 'family' is . . . the capacity of the family leader to define his or her own goals and values while trying to maintain a nonanxious presence within the system."[15]

If "nonanxious presence" seems beyond us, Arthur Paul Boers allows his and our efforts to at least be "less anxious" than the milieu around us. This means we offer a calmer perspective and give persons the freedom to accept or reject that offer. It may mean respectfully addressing harsh claims and opinions that have been directed at us.

It means reminding myself that I have the perspectives I do out of my family life pilgrimage, and so do those who may be harshly differing with me or criticizing me. My responsibility is to bring this calm perspective, not to persuade others or to succeed or to win in this anxious situation.

Closely related is the concept of the differentiated self. Steinke recalls this concept as offered by family systems pioneer Murray Bowen. Self-differentiation is

- defining yourself and staying in touch with others;
- being responsible for yourself and responsive to others;
- maintaining your integrity and well-being without intruding on that of others;
- allowing the enhancement of the other's integrity and well-being without feeling abandoned, inferior, or less of a self;
- having an "I" and entering a relationship with another "I" without losing yourself or diminishing the self in the other. [16]

Steinke concludes that self-differentiation means "being separate together" or "being connected selves."[17] It will be a lifelong process, and we will be tested as we seek to continue to grow in this vital perspective and way of life.

COGNITIVE THERAPEUTIC PERSPECTIVES

Having explored family systems theory as a guide to nurturing inner wisdom, we now turn to cognitive therapy as another psychological perspective that helps us gain self-understanding. First developed in the early 1960s by Aaron Beck, cognitive therapy is built upon the basic premise that the way in which we perceive or think about a situation is what determines our feelings and behaviors. We are often not aware of, and therefore do not question the validity of, these automatic thoughts, which emerge out of deeply held core beliefs about ourselves, others, and the world.[18] We assume that our interpretation is correct and, therefore, that the emotions and behaviors that emerge from them are in line with reality, not recognizing that there may be other ways of interpreting the situation.

A small example may help us understand the connection between automatic thoughts and feelings. Let's say that you meet an acquaintance in the hallway, but, instead of greeting you, he walks right by you. How you interpret his behavior, and what you tell yourself about it, will result in very different emotional responses. If you think he is purposefully ignoring you, you may feel hurt and sad. If you think he doesn't acknowledge you in public because he looks down on you, you may feel angry. You may feel worried, if you think he is angry with you. But if you think he is too busy and stressed to see you, you may feel concern for him.

Core beliefs about oneself and others are developed out of life experiences, especially those in early childhood. These strongly held beliefs then generate the thoughts that automatically provide us with interpretations. It is especially when we are under stress that negative core beliefs about oneself may easily be triggered and form the interpretive lens through which we look at a situation. There are many such possible negative core beliefs, including "I am inadequate," "I am different," "I am ineffective," "I am unworthy," and "I am unlovable." When activated, such core beliefs result in negative automatic thoughts and then painful emotions. [19]

We can gain greater self-understanding and perspective by noticing when we are experiencing distressing feelings and then paying attention to what thoughts or images are going through our minds or what we are telling ourselves. While we may not generally be aware of automatic thoughts, we can become conscious of them if we take the time to notice them.

Initially, we strongly believe these automatic thoughts, and so it is important to test them. Some of the questions we can ask ourselves are: What evidence is there that this automatic thought is or is not true? Is there another possible way to view the situation? What is the most realistic perspective? What would I say to a friend who was in this situation? By pausing to become aware of what is going through our minds and then reflecting on possible alternatives to our initial interpretation, we often become less certain of our negative interpretation. As a result, the intensity of our negative feelings also diminishes. As we become aware of our typical distressing automatic thought patterns, we can develop more realistic ways of addressing them.

Our interpretation of a situation may also be affected by what David Burns calls "cognitive distortions" or illogical ways of thinking. Some common cognitive distortions are:

- Magnifying/Minimizing—magnifying the bad and minimizing the good in a situation.
- Emotional reasoning—assuming one's feelings indicate the reality of a situation: "I feel like a failure, so I am a failure."
- Mind-reading—assuming one knows what a person is thinking without evidence.
- Discounting the positive—inability to receive compliments or affirm what one did well.
- All-or-nothing thinking—viewing things as all good or all bad, such that one thing going wrong makes the whole situation bad.
- Making "should" statements—criticizing oneself or others with what "should" be.

There are many other cognitive distortions including: overgeneralizing, jumping to conclusions, fortune-telling, labeling, and inappropriate blaming. Being aware of these cognitive distortions, and especially becoming aware of what cognitive distortions we tend to make, can help us in evaluating our automatic thoughts and negative self-talk.[20]

Furthermore, we also hold what Albert Ellis calls "irrational beliefs." Among these are believing that everyone should approve of what we do or that everyone should love us or that we need to be practically perfect in everything we do.[21] When stated as such, it isn't hard to see that they are irrational and unrealistic. And yet, as pastors, we may easily find ourselves wanting to please everyone and have everyone like us. Because this is unrealistic, we may end up feeling distressed when criticism and disapproval come our way.

Cognitive therapy suggests a cognitive restructuring approach that involves: (1) becoming aware of our automatic thoughts and how they are influencing our feelings and behaviors, (2) challenging the beliefs or thoughts that are hurtful and not realistic, and (3) replacing them with ones that are more in line with reality and more helpful.[22] One way to do this is to follow this adaptation of a four-step model suggested for stress management:

1. Stop—When you become aware of feeling stressed and upset or negative in your thinking, say, "Stop!" to yourself to break this pattern of responses.
2. Breathe—Breathe deeply and release tension, eliciting the relaxation response and diverting your attention away from the situation a bit.
3. Reflect—Consider the cause of your feelings of stress or distress and identify the unhelpful automatic thinking, cognitive distortions, and irrational beliefs. Ask yourself: What am I saying to myself? What is another way to look at this?
4. Choose—Choose how you are going to think and what you are going to do.[23]

Some time ago, a woman spoke to me (Ruth) about experiencing a great deal of stress and unhappiness at her job. She was increasingly being given work that others were supposed to do and then not given credit or rewarded for putting in this extra effort, even though it was making it hard to get her own work done. She repeatedly said to herself, "Nobody appreciates me here," and "Why should I do extra work, when someone else gets the bonus?" Feeling upset and irritated with coworkers, her relationships with them were tense. After she expressed these frustrations, we explored together what it would mean if she looked upon her job as serving God and helping others, rather than simply as earning money. She later reported back that work was going better. Each time she started feeling stressed because she felt she was being taken advantage of or given too much work, she would remind herself that she was serving God in her job. This kept her from feeling so stressed and enabled her to assist those needing her help.

MINDFULNESS

We now turn to consider the subject of mindfulness. Within the counseling world, mindfulness has become an increasingly favored approach for helping people live their lives more fully, as well as for addressing a number of mental health concerns, including stress and depression. But what is mindfulness?

Jon Kabat-Zinn, who developed mindfulness-based stress reduction, gives this frequently quoted definition: "Mindfulness means paying attention in a particular way: on purpose, in the present moment, and nonjudgmentally."[24] He indicates that by developing our capacity for relaxation, paying attention to what we normally don't notice, nurturing moment-to-moment awareness, and gaining insight, we can grow in wisdom.[25] Perhaps the definition provided by *Psychology Today* is also helpful to consider: "Mindfulness is a state of active, open attention on the present. When you're mindful, you observe your thoughts and feelings from a distance, without judging them as good or bad. Instead of letting your life pass you by, mindfulness means living in the moment and awakening to experience."[26]

At the heart of mindfulness are meditative practices. You have already been introduced to one popularized by Dr. Herbert Benson as "the relaxation response" and seen how it can become a spiritual practice by utilizing a meaningful religious word or phrase as its focal point. Sometimes it helps to begin by taking several deep diaphragmatic breaths to help turn our attention inward, breathing slowly in through our noses and out through our mouths. Then we can allow our breathing to fall into its own natural rhythm, as we focus on our breath or sacred word. As our minds get quiet and are no longer filled with thoughts, we may forget to use the focal word. But whenever our mind chatter starts up again, we can go back to silently repeating it to gain mental focus. Thoughts, feelings, and sensations that distract can simply be named and allowed to drift away like a cloud, while we turn back to focusing on our breath or focal word.[27] If we do choose a sacred word as our focal point, we will be engaging in a spiritual practice similar to that which Thomas Keating has named "centering prayer" and about which you can learn more on the Contemplative Outreach website.[28]

There are many meditative practices that develop our moment-by-moment awareness. One is simply to be in the present moment and notice what is in our awareness—what we are sensing, thinking, feeling, and experiencing. Another is to become aware of our breathing—to notice our breath as it goes in and out and what we experience as it does so. There is also the body scan meditation, which intentionally focuses awareness on each part of the body.[29] And yet another is to focus on our senses, taking in what is in our surroundings without judging anything as good or bad. We do this by mentally listing all that we smell, then hear, then touch, and finally see, ending this meditation by listing all that we are appreciating through our senses.[30]

When we regularly practice mindfulness, we may notice many beneficial effects. We may become more aware of how our minds work and notice the kinds of thoughts and feelings that naturally emerge. The mind has a natural bias to focus on the negative as a potential threat, as a part of being geared toward survival. This is particularly the case when we are stressed. We may notice that we spend much of our lives either ruminating about something that happened in the past or worrying about something that could happen in the future. This type of thinking can take up lots of space and emotional energy in our inner life and cause sad and anxious emotions. And yet the reality is that all we have in life is this moment, to be truly present to the people we are with and the experiences we are currently having.

Mindfulness practice not only helps us notice our thoughts and feelings; it teaches us to simply notice them and not immediately react to them. Furthermore, we can recognize them as just our thoughts and feelings and not necessarily the total reality of the situation. It enables us to realize we have choices as to where we will focus our attention and how we will respond. This doesn't involve numbing or denying our feelings. For example, if something happens that makes us very angry, instead of just spouting off, we can notice what is happening inside us, step away for a bit, help ourselves calm down, and from a wiser perspective decide what to do. We are thus better able to keep ourselves calm in stressful situations because we are attentive early to what we are experiencing in the present moment and we have some skills to direct our attention elsewhere in a way that helps us relax a bit (for example, by focusing on our breathing).

Those who practice mindfulness also begin to pay attention to the small joys of life, instead of rushing through the day oblivious to them. We may take time to notice the sunrise when we get up or the flowers on our way into work and spend a few minutes savoring the beauty. Or we may notice and enjoy the beloved face and endearing ways of a small child in the process of getting them ready for the day. These minutes of noticing, being in the present, enjoying, and savoring help us experience more gratitude, connectedness, and happiness.

Practicing mindfulness can help people to focus their attention and experience their minds as quieter and less distracted. This actually makes them feel much better and less anxious and depressed. Research shows that the more people's minds wander, the less they self-report being happy. This is because most often when our minds wander, we are engaging in rumination or anxious thinking. With a quieter, less distracted mind, we feel better.[31]

So you can see how mindfulness practices can help us take better care of ourselves in stressful situations. They help us notice early that we are starting to experience stress so that we can pay attention to the need for self-care. They give us some skills in how to calm ourselves down and relax through focusing our attention elsewhere so that the stress reaction is slowed or stopped. And with less emotional reactivity, more perspective, and a focused mind, we are able to see our options and make wiser choices on how to respond appropriately to the situation.

There is a significant amount of research indicating the many benefits of mindfulness meditation, including the reduction of negative emotions, the increase of positive ones, and the greater capacity for focus, attention, memory, and decision-making. Gray matter density increases in those parts of the brain related to memory, empathy, and emotional regulation. Compassion and altruism increase and relationships are enhanced.[32] Research into the use of mindfulness-based stress reduction with health-care professionals also demonstrates benefit, such as reduced stress and burnout, increased coping, improved empathy, increased self-acceptance, improved focus and clear thinking, and improved life satisfaction.[33] It thus has great potential for also being helpful for clergy.

These changes can occur because the brain has neuroplasticity. That is, it can continue to grow and change as neurons shift connections, even reconfiguring its structure. Research on meditation indicates that through tiny incremental alterations in neural structure, meditation can bring about significant brain changes. Neuroimaging scans have shown that contemplative practices, such as centering prayer by Catholic nuns and mindfulness meditation by Buddhist monks, have a calming effect by lowering the activity of the amygdala, which is the arousal center of the brain that warns us of danger.[34]

In considering this research from a spiritual perspective, Kirk Bingaman explains that the "higher neurological and spiritual functions (of meditation) help us begin to resculpt and regroove the neural pathways of our brains."[35] He argues that becoming a new creation in Christ and living more deeply the Christian life is much more related to spiritual practices than to steadfastly holding to a set of beliefs, although theological beliefs are important as well. But it is contemplative spiritual practices that can actually change us, so that we are less anxious and more filled with God's peace. He writes, "It will take a substantial period of time and the ongoing practice of mindful-awareness and meditation to exchange our anxious and fearful disposition for one that is geared more toward happiness, peace, and love."[36]

SELF-COMPASSION

Mindfulness involves more than attentiveness that focuses one's mind on the present. It also involves a healthy relationship with oneself that is accepting, patient, and compassionate. Often we are very hard on ourselves, particularly when we are under stress. But self-criticism increases the stress reaction, with more cortisol and adrenaline being released. In such situations, practicing self-compassion is another form of self-care.

Dr. Kristin Neff has been at the forefront of the science of self-compassion. She encourages us to consider what is involved in having compassion for someone. It requires that we notice that they are suffering and be moved by their pain, such that we want to help. Being compassionate involves being kind and understanding toward others when they make mistakes, rather than harshly judging them. She then asks us to imagine what it would mean to be as compassionate to ourselves, when we fail to live up to our standards or notice something about ourselves that we don't like. Instead of criticizing ourselves for our mistakes and inadequacies, it would involve talking to ourselves with kindness and understanding, just as we would a friend.

Neff thus indicates that self-compassion has three components. First of all, it involves self-kindness rather than self-judgment. Rather than ignoring our painful feelings or criticizing ourselves for our failures, we treat ourselves with kindness, gentleness, and understanding. This involves even comforting and soothing ourselves. Secondly, self-compassion involves recognizing that falling short, suffering, and experiencing things not going as we want them to are all part of our common humanity, rather than allowing ourselves to remain in the isolation of thinking we are the only ones who make mistakes or feel distressed. It involves realizing that life is not perfect, and neither are we, and this is the experience of all people. And thirdly, self-compassion involves mindfulness rather than overidentification with our negative feelings. This allows us to be with and acknowledge our painful feelings, rather than suppress or deny them, while also not merging ourselves with them so that they overwhelm us. [37]

Research shows that self-compassion is strongly linked to reductions in anxiety, stress, depression, rumination, perfectionism, and shame and to increases in life satisfaction, happiness, connectedness, self-confidence, optimism, curiosity, and gratitude. Those with self-compassion are more forgiving and caring of others and experience less burnout and compassion fatigue. [38]

We can nurture our self-compassion through intentional practices. When we are feeling badly, Neff encourages us to use "soothing touch." This simply involves giving ourselves a gentle hug, putting our hands over our heart, or in some other way soothing ourselves, as we would comfort a hurting child. As we do this, we can take several deep breaths, letting ourselves feel this soothing gesture.[39]

She encourages us also to take a "self-compassion break" when we're feeling stressed or emotionally distressed. After taking time to let ourselves bodily feel the discomfort, we can say to ourselves, "This is a moment of suffering" or "This is tough," acknowledging how hard it is. Then we can move on to saying, "Suffering is part of living" and bodily soothe ourselves, as above. Finally, we can say, "May I be kind (or accepting) of myself."[40] This is just a sampling of the many exercises and guided meditations that are available on the Self-Compassion website.[41]

The Scriptures frequently portray God's nature as compassionate. For example, we read in Psalm 103:13, "As a father has compassion for his children, so the Lord has compassion on those who fear [God]" (adapted). And in Isaiah 54:10 we read, "For the mountains may depart and the hills be removed, but my steadfast love shall not depart from you, and my covenant of peace shall not be removed, says the Lord, who has compassion on you." Jesus, in embodying the divine nature, demonstrated deep compassion for those who were hurting. Learning to be compassionate toward ourselves is therefore learning to view ourselves through the loving eyes of God. As we grow to trust in God's compassion for us, including the hurting parts within that are being healed by God's love and grace, and as we join God in this compassion toward ourselves, we are better able to be compassionate toward others.

GRATITUDE AND HABITS OF HAPPINESS

Before ending this chapter, we now turn to the field of positive psychology for insights that may further contribute to our self-care and the nurturing of a wise inner life. Rather than focusing on the negative emotions and mental illness, positive psychology studies the positive emotions and seeks to help people be happy and flourish. Happiness and joy in ministry not only indicate spiritual well-being and greatly facilitate effectiveness in ministry; they also are evidence of sufficient self-care, and so there is much we can learn.

Sonja Lyubomirsky has written a helpful book called *The How of Happiness*. She defines happiness as "the experience of joy, contentment, or positive wellbeing, combined with a sense that one's life is good, meaningful, and worthwhile."[42] She indicates that scientists of happiness have found that life circumstances only decide about 10 percent of happiness. Another 50 percent is determined by our genetic structure, as we each inherit a "happiness set point."[43] Some people are just born sunny and cheerful, and others are much less so. But 40 percent of happiness depends on our intentional activities to improve our level of happiness.

There are many evidence-based happiness-increasing strategies supported by scientific research. Some call these "habits of happiness." Among them are nurturing optimism, avoiding overthinking (self-focused negative rumination), avoiding social comparison, practicing acts of kindness, nurturing social relationships, learning to forgive, increasing flow experiences, savoring life's joys, developing strategies for coping, committing to one's goals, taking care of one's body, and practicing spirituality. But, according to Lyubomirsky, the "megastrategy for achieving happiness" is gratitude.[44] Therefore, we will now turn our attention to better understanding gratitude and how to nurture it within our lives.

Robert Emmons, who is the most prominent researcher and writer on gratitude, speaks of gratitude as "a felt sense of wonder, thankfulness, and appreciation for life."[45] He says that there are three aspects of gratitude. There is a perceptual aspect that notices all that is good in life. There is an intellectual aspect that recognizes that all the goodness that we enjoy comes from outside ourselves and that therefore we are beneficiaries of others— other people, God, or even pets. And finally, there is an emotional aspect to gratitude that appreciates and values both the gift and the intentions of the giver, such that we feel thankful and perhaps even love.

What is being described here is gratitude being elicited by the experience of grace. And grace and gratitude are at the very heart of the Christian faith. Our most basic experience of God is that of being a recipient of undeserved favor and love. And so the most fundamental and appropriate attitude toward God is one of gratitude, such that it grounds all that we do in serving God. Certainly in the Scriptures, we are told over and over again to "give thanks to the Lord, for [God] is good; for [God's] steadfast love endures forever" (Ps. 107:1, adapted). Paul agrees and writes, "Give thanks in all circumstances" (1 Thess. 5:18), and "Do not worry about anything, but in everything by prayer and supplication with thanksgiving let your requests be made known to God" (Phil. 4:6). Because our faith is based on grace, gratitude is an indispensable part of it. But what Lyubomirsky is claiming is that gratitude is also the key to experiencing joy, an intended part of the abundant life to which Christ has called us.

Research does indicate that gratitude boosts happiness in many ways. Gratitude focuses attention on the good and promotes savoring positive life experiences so that we experience maximum pleasure and enjoyment. It bolsters self-worth by focusing on what people have done for us and what we have accomplished, rather than focusing on our disappointments. When we are grateful for what we have, we are less materialistic and more likely to help others, all of which contribute to happiness. It helps us cope with stress by helping us to reinterpret negative life experiences positively and to find the blessings for which to be thankful.

Not long ago, I (Ruth) headed into a much-needed holiday break but without having sufficiently completed a writing project I had undertaken. As I found myself putting in long hours, day after day of this vacation, I recognized my potential to become grumpy. But I also realized that if I hadn't had this break to work on writing, I would not complete it on time, and therefore I could be grateful. Being grateful, rather than grumpy, was not only a far more pleasant experience, but it also enabled me to keep focused and productive.

Gratitude strengthens relationships with family and friends because we appreciate them and thus treat them better. It reduces comparison and envy, which undermine happiness, and it diminishes negative feelings, such as anger, bitterness, greed, jealousy, fear, and guilt. When we are grateful, it's much harder to feel these negative emotions. And finally, gratitude counteracts hedonic adaptation, that tendency to adapt to whatever has given us enjoyment until it no longer gives us pleasure and we start taking it for granted.[46] Emmons summarizes the research findings with these words: "Collectively, such studies present credible evidence that feeling grateful generates a ripple effect through every area of our lives, potentially satisfying some of our deepest yearnings—our desire for happiness, our pursuit of better relationships, and our ceaseless quest for inner peace, wholeness, and contentment."[47]

With such positive spiritual and emotional benefits, the cultivation of gratitude is a helpful aspect of self-care. However, we cannot just tell ourselves to be more grateful and expect our outlook to change instantaneously. Rather, what is required is our nurturing the disposition of gratefulness through a dedicated practice of noticing life's goodness and expressing our thankfulness. We can do this by keeping a gratitude journal in which we regularly take the time to write down the specific things for which we are grateful. Or we can write a letter of gratitude to someone who has been important in our lives and take the time to visit and read it to them. We can remember a difficult time in our lives and be thankful it is so much better now. We can learn prayers of gratitude. And we can savor what we experience through our senses.[48] Intentionally reflecting on life's goodness for which we are grateful and expressing that gratitude in whatever way is possible will, over time, deepen our spirituality, expand our contentment and joy, and increase our inner wisdom.

FOR YOUR REFLECTION AND CONVERSATION

1. What reflection and study have you done about the family into which you were born or adopted? What did you learn? What more would you

like to know? What connections do you see between your family heritage and your ministry?

2. As you reflect on your ministry, when did you use (or could you have used) nonanxious/less anxious presence? Self-differentiation?

3. What kinds of negative automatic thoughts do you tend to have, especially when stressed? Which thought distortions do you find yourself having? How might you challenge and make these more realistic and helpful?

4. To what extent do you tend to be self-critical? How might practicing self-compassion be helpful?

5. What are some ways you would like to begin nurturing a disposition of gratitude?

Chapter Ten

Self-Care through Laughter and Play

Laughter is the GPS system for the soul. Humor offers a revolutionary, yet simple, spiritual paradigm: If you can laugh at yourself, you can forgive yourself. And if you can forgive yourself, you can forgive others. Laughter heals. It grounds us in a place of hope.

—Susan Sparks[1]

I (Dick) once set out to write a book on humor as a tool of ministry. The thrust of it was to be that the many tasks of ministry—worship, pastoral care, administration, etc.—could be enhanced if the minister introduced gentle and relaxing humor into those situations.

However, it wasn't going well. I had to admit that most ministers (including me) weren't that funny or gifted with humor all or most of the time. Like many others, I enjoy a good laugh and sometimes help others laugh, but no one would think of me as a potential standup comedian. Though there are probably others, I only know one clergy who doubles as a standup comedian. That clergywoman is Susan Sparks of Madison Avenue Baptist Church in New York. Her delightful book that I quoted above, *Laugh Your Way to Grace: Reclaiming the Spiritual Power of Humor*,[2] has playful and profound gifts for laity and clergy alike.

Eventually, it hit me. The book I was attempting had a great topic but the wrong focus. Rather than making others laugh, my emphasis should be on the need for ministers themselves to laugh regularly and often. Humor, playfulness, enjoyment for its own sake—all this and more can be vital in one's resilience, both restoring and strengthening a minister's love and commitment to ministry. It is no accident that the word "recreation" divides into "re-creation," for that is what can happen when persons intentionally engage in play and humor frequently and faithfully. The book that emerged from my engagement with these ideas, *Laughter in a Time of Turmoil: Humor as Spiritual Practice*,[3] considers the connection between humor and flourishing.

Rae Jean Proeschold-Bell speaks of a study published by the American Psychological Association that shows there are five activities that when pursued regularly contribute to a positive outlook. The five are: engaging in spiritual activity, learning, social interactions, helping, and play. She notes that the first four of these are part of a clergy's day, and as to play, she "guesses clergy are no better at this than anyone else."[4]

We believe that ministers often do and can engage laughter and play for their own good. And so we offer suggestions for increasing these two aspects: fulfilling interests and activities; and humor and laughter.

THE SIGNIFICANCE OF VARIED INTERESTS AND ACTIVITIES

Much research points to the great importance of ministers pursuing their varied interests. They tell us that investment of oneself in deeply absorbing subjects and activities can support our vitality and joy. Here are three angles on this truth.

Restorative Niche

The Flourishing in Ministry Project out of Notre Dame University has noted the importance of clergy having a "restorative niche." "A restorative niche has two characteristics. First, it is something we can do well, something in which we can acquire and pursue a sense of mastery. Second, a restorative niche is something we do out of intrinsic motivation: simply for the joy we experience from the activity itself."[5]

While others might refer to these as hobbies, they do not believe the word "hobby" does justice to the essence of a restorative niche. These niches are areas in which there is deep interest, perhaps even passion, for activities where we aspire to excellence. While there is great variety in what might be one's restorative niche, it is urgently important that a person have at least one.

Of the ministers in their research project, only about one in four had such an activity, and most participated in it only about once every two weeks. However, those ministers who participated in theirs regularly—at least once a week—were among those they found at the very highest levels of flourishing. They note that "restorative niche" is a new concept in research literature but one so important that it needs more study. Early results point to its great significance.[6]

Flow

Closely related is Mihaly Csikszentmihályi's (pronounced "cheeks sent me high") discovery of the concept of "flow." "Flow" may happen in one's "restorative niche." Flow is a state of mind in which a person is fully and energetically engaged and completely absorbed in an activity of one's choosing.

The creator of this theory began to investigate the experience of artists, most particularly painters. He wanted to know what was happening when artists became so involved in their work that they would lose any sense of time and disregard their need for food, water, and even sleep.

His work aroused great interest and the discovery that "flow" may be more widespread than he earlier thought. Indeed, it may be an important part of the activities we choose for our self-care. While there are many varying lists of the factors involved in flow, at least some of the following are present:

1. *Clear goals.* These goals may challenge a person's skill set but be perceived as attainable.
2. *Concentration and focusing.* There will be great energy and effort that delves deeply into the chosen challenging task.
3. *A loss of self-consciousness.* One becomes deeply immersed and lost in the activity.
4. *Distorted or altered sense of time.* A person may lose all track of time or interest in time as usually experienced.
5. *Direct and immediate feedback.* One can recognize success and failure and can correct mistakes.
6. *Balance between ability level and challenge.* The tasks selected are neither too easy nor too difficult but challenging enough to hold one's concentration.
7. *A sense of personal control of the activity.*
8. *An intrinsically rewarding activity*—that is, it feels effortless to engage in this experience.
9. *A sense of absorption and focus* in that awareness is narrowed down to the activity itself.[7]

Not all of these qualities are needed for one to experience flow, but certainly some of them will be present. Martin Seligman asks, "When does time stop for you? When do you find yourself doing exactly what you want to be doing and never wanting it to end?"[8] However you answer that may be where you experience flow. Seligman also notices that there is no mention of positive emotion in that list of flow characteristics. "In fact, it is the absence of emotion, of any kind of consciousness that is at the heart of flow. Consciousness and emotion are there to correct your trajectory; when what you are doing is seamlessly perfect, you don't need them."[9]

What are some experiences of flow? Here are examples from clergy friends. Ron Erickson experiences it in woodworking and woodcarving. He is fascinated by it, loves to take advanced courses, and can sink himself into it days at a time, creating unique and exquisite pieces of art.

Terry Rosell, our seminary colleague, experiences flow in pottery making. He returned to it some thirty years after loving it in college and spends hours of delight in the activity itself and in what he can make for others. Recently he made a complete set of chalices and trays for serving communion at the church where he is a member.

I (Dick) experience at least some aspects of flow in three activities. One is music—playing my baritone/euphonium in bands. While I like to practice by myself and at band rehearsal, flow sometimes happens during performances when it all comes together, we get it right, and I am ecstatic about being part of such beauty (at least to my tin ears!).

Another is writing. Throughout my parish and then teaching ministries, I have greatly enjoyed drawing together what I have learned from experience, reading, and reflection. In this I hope to make a modest contribution and carry on a conversation with the larger community. I enjoy the process and am sometimes pleased with the product. Recently, I took courses in creative writing at a community college and was delighted in beginning efforts at creating poetry and fiction.

Yet another is gardening and yard work. This is a partnership with my wife, Mary Ann—she designs, plans, and purchases. I make it a reality: digging, planting, weeding, watering, fertilizing, trimming—and enjoying all the beauty that emerges. I may be the rare person who actually enjoys mowing my yard. It allows time to ruminate about a sermon or this chapter. It's one of the few things in my life where I can see clearly that it's done . . . at least for a few days.

Multiple Mindedness

Cynthia Lindner, professor at the University of Chicago Divinity School, did research on a related but somewhat different aspect of enriching activities. She wanted to investigate what makes pastors effective. She interviewed a dozen ministers seen as effective by colleagues and congregations. With each, she did an hour-long interview with open-ended questions inviting them to describe their vocational lives. These interviews were recorded, transcribed, and analyzed for common themes.

Out of the variety of narratives she heard, she discovered that they held in common an "awareness of their own complexities—their multiple and sometimes competing interests, perspectives, and engagements—and the energy and creativity these engendered." Among these effective ministers, she found those who "edited magazines . . . were journalists and bloggers . . . served in city and state government . . . performed in comedy clubs . . . [were] jazz-musicians."

She emerged from this study deeply impressed by what she called "ministerial multiple-mindedness or ministerial multiplicity." These ministers, she noted, found their identity not singular but rather an integration out of the many relationships and communities in which they engaged. Lindner concluded,

> When clergy cultivate multiple selves rather than constraining themselves for the sake of conventional expectations of ministry, they report sustained resilience and generativity in their work. I found that pastors whose sense of worth and agency is not reliant on a single circumscribed role experience less compassion fatigue and are significantly less likely to avoid confrontation, capitulate or explode.[10]

To the best of our knowledge, Linder did not include bi-vocational ministers in her study. However, it occurs to us that when ministers engage in at least two income-producing activities, there are some opportunities to claim and practice the multiple mindedness of which she speaks.

LAUGHTER WITHOUT JOKES?

We now move on to consider laughter and humor. There is a growing awareness that there is a gift of healing and relief in laughter itself quite apart from jokes or other humorous stimuli. Dr. Lee Berk noted, "If we took what we know about the medical benefits of laughter and bottled it up, it would require FDA approval."[11] The Jewish mime Samuel Avital has noted that laughter affects and exercises every cell in the body: "When you laugh, the whole system vibrates, a dancing diaphragm, dancing cells. All the cells are happy, and when you are happy you will have a longer life. If you don't furnish your cells with this vibration of dancing . . . you are robbing them of life. So laughter is a transformer."[12]

Madan Kataria, an Indian physician, has discovered, developed, and promoted what he calls "laughter yoga." It started some years ago, when he met with a small group of friends each morning for a brief time of jokes and laughing together in his home city of Mumbai. Eventually, they realized they didn't need the jokes. They would simply gather and laugh.

And so this "merry medicine man" has pioneered and advocated a new technique of group laughter based on yoga. This has grown to thousands of laughter clubs in at least seventy-five countries. One can experience his enthusiastic leadership and laughter process by watching and participating in his TED Talk. [13] It will be most enjoyable to watch it with friends who also like to laugh.

I (Dick) have attended a laughter yoga group in my city, led by a person who had been trained in the Kataria laughter yoga method. A small group of eight or nine of us gathered at a holistic health center. Our leader guided us in playful laughter sounds. Then she invited us to stand, walk randomly around our meeting area, look each other in the eye, and laugh. Every few minutes, she would consider another unlikely event about which we were to laugh, for example, "Imagine you just learned your bank account is overdrawn. . . . You had a fender bender coming here and your car is a mess" and other such statements.

As does Dr. Kataria, she told us that contrived laughter has the same or almost the same benefit as spontaneous laughter, so feel free to "fake it till you make it." Some distinguish the difference as "voluntary laughter" and "involuntary laughter." For nearly an hour, we strolled moving from person to person, looking each other in the eyes, and laughing at her outlandish imagined reasons for our laughter. Then she invited us to sit comfortably relaxed and reflect for a few moments. With a cheerful little hug from our leader and a small monetary contribution, we were on our way.

I was glad to have this experience and enjoyed being there. However, my interests led me another way. I decided to pursue my laughter with the many other opportunities to use humor and jokes. Certainly, Dr. Kataria has touched on something vital—we need all the laughter possible. We are wise to reach out to the doorways that may lead us further into this healing gift.

VARIETIES OF HUMOR

It is fascinating to think of the endless types, styles, and forms of humor. Many years ago, Evan Esar tried to list and classify all the types of humor there are as a contribution to the "budding science of humor." He listed and described at least fifty kinds of jokes and other humor. To give you a small idea of what he found, he speaks of wisecracks, epigrams, riddles, conundrums, jokes, anecdotes, and tricks. He explores techniques of humor including the chain, the pendulum, blunting, reversibles, Spoonerisms, fuddle talk, and much more. [14] There are nearly endless kinds of humor and numerous places of humor that one can attend to each day.

However, there is humor that enriches and builds up, and there is humor that attacks and destroys. In our search for humor as self-care, how does one evaluate, sort out, and decide? We personally have found the classifications offered by Peter Berger to be a helpful starting place. He offers this in his book *Redeeming Laughter: The Comic Dimension of Human Experience*. [15]

Berger notes that humor as the capacity to perceive something as funny is universal. Every human culture has humor in some form. True, what persons find humorous varies greatly from age to age and culture to culture, but the presence of humor is constant. In one section of his book, he writes of comic forms of expression in our culture. Basically he sees four types with different impact and different uses. The common theme he sees in all these varieties of humor is the perception of incongruence.

Benign Humor—the Comic as Diversion

This type of humor simply evokes "pleasure, relaxation and good will. It enhances rather than disrupts the flow of everyday life."[16] This is children's humor: laughter at one's self, which is at one's own quirks and foibles; mellow amusement that helps one deal with the minor irritations of the day. This type of humor can be enjoyed by oneself or with others. It does not have to be deliberately produced; it can just happen.

Some ways we share our benign humor may be through "knock knock" jokes, puns and other plays on words, humorous quotations, and limericks. The amusing animal antics on YouTube provide other examples. For those who still read a newspaper, this kind of humor may be found on the comics page in Family Tree, Marmaduke, Garfield, and Dennis the Menace, among others.

Berger took a chapter from the history of American humor for his example—Will Rogers with his seemingly random comments about the world, government, Congress, commenting, "All I know is what I read in the papers." A couple of his quips—"Always drink upstream from the herd." "I don't make jokes. I just watch the government and report the facts." The spirit of his humor was in his quote, "I never met a man I didn't like." Describing his humor, he once said, "I don't think I ever hurt any man's feelings by my little gags. I know I never willfully did it. When I have to do that to make a living, I will quit."[17]

This is humor that provides a few moments of vacation from life's worries by providing a harmless diversion. There is a kind of magic here, an enchantment that can be valued indeed.

Tragicomedy—the Comic as Consolation

A newspaper ad—
Lost—Dog, faded brown, three legs, one ear missing,
blind left eye, broken tail, recently neutered.
Answers to name "Lucky." Sorry, no rewards.

Tragicomedy is "that which provides laughter through tears. It is mellow, forgiving. . . . Above all it consoles. . . . The tragic is not banished, not absorbed. It is, as it were, momentarily suspended."[18] Some African American comedians excel in tragicomedy.

Rodney Dangerfield, with his classic line "I don't get no respect," was a tragicomedian, as was Charlie Chaplin. As Chaplin went through his struggles with machines and with people who ignored or abused him, he bore those injuries in ways that drew a smile or a chuckle. He once said, "Playful pain—that's what humor is. The minute a thing is over-tragic, it is funny."[19] He also commented, "My pain may be reason for somebody's laughter, but my laughter should never be the reason for somebody's pain."

Berger's example was Yiddish writer Sholem Aleichem and his reflections on the people with whom he lived in a Ukrainian Shtetl, a small Jewish village, in the late nineteenth and early twentieth century. These people lived under terrible conditions: deep poverty, denied mobility, often subject to vicious attacks by soldiers or police. Amazingly, in that setting, his writing overflows with comic characters and situations. He felt that his mission was to give voice to what he termed "an orphan people" as well as to create laughter in a wretched world. One of his most famous stories was about Tevye the milkman. His stories formed the basis for the musical *Fiddler on the Roof.*

There are others who testify to the helpfulness of this kind of laughter. Viktor Frankl, Holocaust survivor and creator of logotherapy (therapy through finding meaning and purpose in life), reflected on those dark days in the death camps: "Humor was another of the soul's weapons in the fight for self-preservation. It is well known that humor, more than anything else in the human makeup, can afford an aloofness and an ability to rise above any situation, even if only for a few seconds."[20]

It is good to also be sensitive to other people's use of tragicomedy. I (Dick) remember calling on a delightful elderly woman, long confined to a wheelchair. She greeted me, "Why hello, pastor. I'd love to get up and make you a cup of tea." I salute such playful courage.

We also remember sitting with families after a death to offer care and to plan a funeral. As they remembered and shared memories, there often was laughter along with the tears. As caregivers, we are not to impose our tragicomedy on another's pain, but when they express it, we will recognize the courage of their laughter and join in.

Wit—Comedy as an Intellectual Game

Another type of humor, wit, uses intellect to make a point or offer an insight. While the previous two types of humor are gentle and sensitive to others' feelings, the person engaging in wit ignores the emotional impact on others in favor of making a brilliant point or offering a clever insight.

As Berger observes, "Wit . . . has no interest beyond itself, is dispassionate, detached from any practical agenda. . . . Wit always employs paradox and irony. . . . The most effective wit employs spare means to achieve a rich result. Wit is sharp, pithy, pointed."[21]

There are two main ways to practice wit. One is the joke, a very short story that ends with a punch line that offers some sort of insight. The other is the epigram, a compact statement that makes a pronouncement on some subject in an entertaining way.

H. L. Mencken was one of the masters of epigrams. Here are a few of his:

- "Conscience is the inner voice that warns us that someone may be looking."
- "Puritanism—the haunting fear that someone may be happy."
- "A man may be a fool and not know it, but not if he is married."[22]

How did those strike you? With each of these, I laughed—and then started objecting. Wit can be great fun, but not if you are the butt of the joke or the subject of the epigram.

This may be the disadvantage of wit. The laughter it engenders may relax our own critical thinking so that we may start believing something that is not true. For there are two dangers in wit—it can hurt, and it can lie. At the same time, when stung by an epigram, perhaps it will sharpen our thinking.

That may stir much thinking and reflecting and thus disrupt our spontaneous humorous repartee. Still, as we look for humor to enjoy as self-care, some thought and reflection on its building aspects and its detrimental aspects should be part of our choices.

Satire and Irony—the Comic as Weapon

Satire, in Berger's thought, is "the deliberate use of the comic for purposes of attack."[23] The attack may be directed at institutions, governmental or religions. Or it may be directed against individuals, professions, or theories. He notes, "Benevolent satire is an oxymoron."[24]

There are at least two levels of power where satire may be engaged. For one, persons may engage it against persons of near equal power. This is often done in political contests, for example, between competing candidates for the same office. Satirists do this to destroy, question, or cut down to size the potential threat of the competitor. Weaknesses may be attacked, or strengths may be made to look like weaknesses.

Or, sometimes, satire is one of the last resort methods of the underling, the defeated, and the mistreated. Persons may not have "the law" or money or police or military power on their side. Their only weapon is their humor, including satire of the persons who oppress them. They still have free thoughts, ideas, and humor. And so they exercise this to keep alive the fire of resistance.

Satire can take many forms—political speeches, newspaper editorials, comedy shows, or protest pamphlets. Novels can be the medium of extended and developed satire. George Orwell's *Animal Farm* and Tom Wolfe's *Bonfire of the Vanities* are two such examples. Late night talk shows and programs such as *Saturday Night Live* engage a variety of the types of humor we have mentioned, but they come down strongly on wit and satire.

Satire may sometimes seem to be the only recourse when oppressed or speaking on behalf of the oppressed. When doing so, it is wise to remember two cautions. One, like wit, satire can distort, even lie. Two, the satirical attitude may become an addictive habit that sours one's spirit so much that other forms of discourse are hard to imagine.

We should also point out that there is a kindred approach—irony. With irony, one also points out the failures and problems—with or without humor. However, it is offered in a more forgiving mood with awareness of the weakness and frailty of the human person—including one's self.

HUMOR AND PLAY AS A SPIRITUAL PRACTICE?

Susan Sparks offers a fascinating take on the spiritual dimension of humor. She begins with the Celtic concept of "thin places." These are places where the boundary between human and the holy is so thin one can almost break through. She quotes theologian Marcus Borg, "Thin places are places where the veil momentarily lifts, and we behold God."[25]

Thin places have many forms. Some are geographical; others may be in music, poetry, literature, or art. Some may find their "thin place" in the presence of a devout and holy person.

She continues, "Another thin place we don't often think of is laughter. It clears our hearts of insecurity, neediness, and stale expressions. It opens our hearts anew for the words or songs or silence we were meant to receive. With laughter, our hearts are laid bare before God."[26]

Robert McAfee Brown offers a kindred perspective. He notes that in Isaiah 11:2, the prophet mentions six gifts of the spirit. However since seven is a sacred number from scriptural times on, he proposes another gift of the spirit—the saving grace of humor.

He doesn't mean any old humor. He refers to a sense of humor that "has to do with *seeing things in proper proportion*, which means (among other things) having an appropriately modest view of ourselves." Therefore, he elaborates, this involves "an ability to laugh *at ourselves*. It involves a willingness to be cut down to size and emerge liberated rather than devastated by the experience" (italics his).[27]

Peter Berger, who has contributed much to this chapter, concludes by speaking of comic laughter as "transcendence in a lower key," a present experience and sign of God's great surprises to come, which is therefore, as his title implies, "redeeming laughter."[28]

We approach this question of humor's function by reflecting on spiritual practices as described in chapter 6. There we noted that spiritual practices are shared activities that address fundamental human needs to form a way of life. Further, each of these practices creates openings in our life where God's grace, mercy, and presence may be made known.

We contend that the practice of humor is a valid spiritual practice, certainly to be exercised in concert with the other spiritual practices we mentioned. Engaging in the spiritual practice of humor and play/playfulness can yield many fruits:

- hope and hopefulness when contending with depression and despair;
- perspective on problems and topics that may seem daunting;
- rebalancing of one's priorities;
- breathing space in conflict and criticism;
- quite often, a softening of the sides and opinions in a conflict;
- a nudge toward forgiveness of others and of myself;
- once in a while, a "thin place";
- a deeper, perhaps chastened, self-understanding;
- a rekindling of joy, including joy in serving the calling to which I am called;
- and thus resilience in our life and work.

HOW DO I MAKE HUMOR/PLAY A GREATER PART OF MY SELF-CARE?

The most basic step is to be aware of your need for more humor/play/creativity in your life (if you do) and to decide to give fitting attention to meeting this need. With this recognition, you may recognize where you want a solitary activity and where you want social experiences.

Then it is important to make your need known and to stake out the time and resources to make it happen and give it priority. Dick's friend Lee found great release in his weekly (Tuesday evening) competitive table tennis club. Though he was responsive to the crises of persons in his congregation and community, he observed that, once people knew his love and renewal by this evening, these crises rarely happened Tuesday evenings!

It may be necessary to find ways to shake loose and recover or discover your playful self. Annette Goodheart has written of numerous ways to relax one's way into a more playful, humorous life. Here are just a few of her many, many, suggestions: Tell someone about your embarrassing moments. Laugh with a baby or play with small children. When your own children are grown, find some other children to play with and enjoy. Do something out of character. Tell someone what you laughed about. Have a family reunion with or without your family.

Do a winking meditation while staring into someone's eyes in deep meditation. Say, "Seriously." Throw a unique party, perhaps a slumber party for adults or something else that touches happy memories. Risk looking foolish. Consider a pillow fight. Play "gigglebelly"—a group of people lie on the floor, each with one's head on another's stomach. Laughter will almost certainly happen spontaneously. Add the words "tee-hee" to just about any statement. Form a "serious anonymous" group.[29]

My (Dick's) personal practices include keeping a file of jokes, articles, fun e-mails, and such. I also have a shelf of books on humor and joke books where I can spend a relaxing hour. One of my favorite books pokes fun at my ethnic group—*Scandinavian Humor and Other Myths*.[30] I like to spend time with playful friends. And sometimes, I dare to write about humor.

We hope that this chapter has stirred some memories and recognitions, touched some longings, and stimulated your creativity to claim valuable humor-play gifts for the stewardship of self-care. William Barclay once wrote, "Jesus promised his disciples three things—that they would be completely fearless, absurdly happy, and in constant trouble."[31] In this chapter, we have worked on the "absurdly happy" aspect—the spirit of joy, laughter, play. May such a life be yours. And may it renew and enrich your ministry.

FOR YOUR REFLECTION AND CONVERSATION

1. As you reflect on this chapter, what are you doing well with play and humor? What changes—additions and subtractions—would you like to make in your life?

2. Do you or anyone you know suffer from geliophobia? Have you or anyone you know benefitted from gelotology? (Geliophobia is the fear of laughter. Gelotology is the study of laughter and its effect on the body, including treatments using laughter. Sorry, we couldn't resist putting these words in. They amused us.)

3. Have you ever experienced "thin places" as mentioned in this chapter? Have you ever experienced "thin places" in play and humor? Tell another about it.

4. When in your life was it easiest to find things to laugh about and to play? What discoveries do you make from this reflection?

5. When has humor—your own or someone else's—been helpful or possibly even redemptive in your Christian life and ministry?

6. Where are you—from denying to being skeptical to being convinced—about the suggestion that humor is a spiritual practice? What—if any—difference does this point of view make?

Chapter Eleven

Financial Self-Care

Lord, you keep our minister humble, and we'll keep her/him poor.

—Prayer for a Pastor

While you may have chuckled at this well-known church adage, we all agree that it really isn't funny. For many of us, it hits rather too close to home. We know firsthand about negotiating a ministry salary and then living within its confines. We understand that following the call of our hearts to serve the kingdom means we will never be rich by the world's standards. We're generally okay with that choice until it's time to purchase a home, put our children through college, enter retirement, or obtain expensive medical treatment. In those situations, our vocational callings may seem at odds with the realities of our economic system, and we may experience a "tug-of-war between our money interests and the calling of our soul."[1] That struggle, if left unattended, can cause deep division within ourselves that robs us of inner peace, sows discontent in our vocation, and sometimes even produces guilt or shame for prioritizing material needs. While the struggle is real, with some care and attention, it can be greatly lessened, if not overcome.

MONEY: THE ELEPHANT IN THE ROOM

"The Bible is relentlessly material in its focus and concern. It refuses to let its passion be siphoned off into things spiritual. . . . Everywhere the Bible is preoccupied with bodily existence."[2] Our sacred texts will not let us off the hook when it comes to matters of finance and economics; both the Hebrew Bible and the New Testament point us to a Creator God who is profoundly concerned with our proper use of and relation to money and possessions. Thus, financial knowledge informed by living faith is an essential part of

149

both discipleship and witness, especially for those who lead others. Integration is a top priority of financial self-care: bringing our faith to bear on our finances so that our finances can reflect our faith.

No one wants to talk about money, but we must. Financial matters consistently top the surveys listing areas that ministers feel least equipped for managing and leading.[3] Similarly, financial reasons are cited as one of the reasons that ministers leave the ministry.[4] Most recently, a *Washington Post* article about clergy suicide cited financial issues among other significant stressors.[5] Ministers—whether they be launching nonprofit community ministries, chaplaining at local hospitals, leading worship gatherings, baptizing new members, equipping employees and volunteers, spearheading capital campaigns, or advocating for racial and economic justice—are at the same time struggling to pay their bills and worrying about their future. Ministry kids are either doing without the private lessons, traveling sports teams, techno gadgets, cars, concert tickets, and other experiences their peers enjoy, or parents are financing them on credit cards. Ministry households with debt of any kind are likely unable to pay for children to attend college without borrowing more and becoming even further indebted.

A constellation of issues has created an increasingly complicated economic landscape for ministers. Because seminaries and denominational entities can no longer afford to offer full scholarships as in the days of strong denominational identity and big endowments and because persons rarely leave life and lifestyle behind to attend theological school, emerging ministers are often encumbered by significant debt loads. Educational debt levels are at an all-time high, and the *Wall Street Journal* reported this surpassed consumer debt for the first time in 2010.[6] Fewer churches offer full-time, fully funded staff positions; increasingly, churches seek ministers who will serve part-time, rendering bi-vocational service necessary.[7] Not only do clergy frequently graduate from seminary wracked with educational debt, but they are also faced with limited income prospects for discharging the debt. While clergy and other religious workers report generally high job satisfaction and high meaning derived from their work, salaries are lower than for other professions.[8] On top of personal financial concerns, some ministry leaders may experience pressure from their organizations to increase pledged giving, clean up financial messes, or work money miracles. They serve not only as spiritual guides but also as primary fundraisers. Unfortunately, preparation for such a role is often lacking in ministry training.

Ministers dealing with personal financial strain are caught in a predicament few others understand. As congregational leaders, they are expected to teach biblical stewardship and model healthy money management for their members; they are sought for solid advice and godly counsel. Nonprofit sector clergy direct and launch community services, and helping agencies often striving relentlessly to procure not only initial investments of financial resources but also consistent, ongoing funding. Likewise, pastors are lead fundraisers within their congregations; their giving and generosity encourage others to be generous and faithful. Chaplains and pastoral counselors spend their days bringing nonanxious presence to those in crisis and high-stress situations, but when they experience financial stress or crisis, there is often nowhere to turn for help. It is nearly impossible to admit making money mistakes or to disclose the burden of huge medical bills (especially if the organization pays for "good" insurance!) to one's leadership team, personnel committee, or HR department. As a result, ministers suffer in quiet isolation.

ANGIE'S STORY: PART ONE

Because I (Angie) have walked this road myself, I have a heart and passion for others in ministry who face economic challenges. I also understand the guilt and shame associated with these difficulties. Writing out my own story remains uncomfortable.

Once upon a time, financial worries kept me up at night. More than twenty years ago, I married an associate pastor and brought debt into my ministry marriage. Just two years out of undergrad, I carried a moderate student loan balance, but I also had some consumer debt. Fortunately, my husband was debt-free. His ministry salary was modest but dependable. My search for a permanent position in our community's public schools, however, yielded only temporary contracts (and therefore only semi-regular pay) in the first couple years. Finances were a source of stress as we began our life and family together.

Over time he moved into senior ministry roles, and our financial situation improved on his income side. As we added children to our family and relocated, though, I left my career in secondary education to care for young ones, only supplementing the family income with part-time employment as a private tutor, retail clerk, and even nursing home dishwasher. We managed but barely. We could not afford to save, and emergencies forced us to use credit cards even when we knew it was unwise. Our budget was certainly tight, but we stayed afloat until my husband developed a heart condition that landed him in intensive care twice and later required surgery. Astronomical hospital and doctor bills soon followed. Without savings our only options were payment plans to discharge the medical bills at a slow but manageable rate over time.

Fast-forward several years. Those medical balances were decreasing, and student debt, after numerous hardship deferments, had diminished slightly by income-based repayment. I worked steadily part-time as a church youth/children's ministry director, and we were again holding our own. Working in that part-time position, I discerned a call to full-time vocational ministry.

Both my husband and my faith community encouraged me to attend seminary.

We had one major concern: finances. Taking into account current financial status and prior economic hardships, we believed that faithful stewardship forbade us from borrowing money at that time. With that in mind, we began to search for a theological school that was either ultra-affordable or offering a full scholarship. Thankfully, I received a full-tuition scholarship for an experimental master of divinity program, and I graduated without adding to my undergraduate debt, which had grown from $25,000 to $38,000 with accruing interest.

My first official ordained call was to copastor a small, family-sized church with my husband. Because it was a single full-time position with a salary unable to meet all our needs, we chose to work bi-vocationally as I previously mentioned in chapter 2. Our choice enabled us to earn enough to provide for our family and to attain financial stability. Securing other ministry positions to supplement our church income proved challenging, but we were determined to work in other ministries rather than simply seek any type of work. Thus, the search lasted many months. Eventually, he landed in chaplaincy, and I accepted a grant-funded position in the seminary where I had matriculated. The transition to a bi-vocational work style was stressful on many levels. Scheduling is certainly tricky, and the lengthy job search disrupted any financial stability we had previously achieved. Now five years into the shared ministry journey, we are finally experiencing freedom from the stress and strain of economic challenges. We are grateful for the opportunities to serve a church we love and to earn wages outside its meager budget.

I know my story is not unusual. I've heard similar stories from the seminarians with whom I work and the clergy with whom I socialize. Perhaps bits and pieces of it resonated with your own story. I am particularly interested in this topic not only because I have lived these realities but also because my seminary work, directing the Money and Ministry Program, is part of the national Economic Challenges Facing Future Ministers initiative, a research and educational initiative funded by the Lilly Endowment and engaged by sixty-seven theological schools. Additionally, "Faith, Finances, and Flourishing" is the working title and emphasis of my own doctoral research. Much of the practical wisdom shared in this chapter arose out of that 2017 research project with several working clergy.

FAITH, FINANCES, AND FLOURISHING

While this chapter cannot resolve the broad and deep economic challenges and the accompanying stress that ministers may experience, our team is committed to equipping ministers for facing these realities with courage and competence. We offer some suggestions in the sections that follow to support and encourage faith leaders in congregations and other organizations and to open the door for authentic conversations about money and our ministries. We are convinced that ministers who prioritize money management and financial preparation as both spiritual and practical discipline will be better prepared to lead congregations in faithful Christian stewardship and to experience personal financial well-being. Our prayer is for ministers to live faithfully into their calls without the burden of financial stress.

Personal Strategies for Financial Wellness

While the subject of money may be taboo in social circles and faith communities, its presence is constant. Money impacts nearly every aspect of our individual lives. About it our faith speaks abundance, and the world screams scarcity. Amid these competing voices and a culture given to excess and constant striving after wealth, we may feel trapped by money's hold over our lives. Then when we gather into groups and organizations, we bring those feelings along with our combined experiences, learning, mistakes, attitudes, beliefs, and values to the whole system. Those of us who aspire to lead in matters of faith and witness face the daunting task of making sense of the complicated variety of dispositions toward financial resources as we seek the good of our organizations. No wonder we are stressed and worried about money matters!

Lynne Twist in her book, *The Soul of Money*, asserts, "Each of us experiences a lifelong tug-of-war between our money interests and the calling of our souls."[9] But what if it doesn't have to be that way? What if we could bring the highest ideals and dreams of our Christian vocation to bear on our money? And vice versa, what if we could bring all our resources and possessions into line with the world-changing aspirations of our call to ministry? What if our financial lives were fully integrated into our rich and meaningful lives of Christian service? What we're talking about is wholeness, and it is essential if we seek financial wellness. With some intentional reflection and critical thinking, we can transform our attitudes, assumptions, and practices, thus freeing ourselves from money's grip so that our resources can flow freely through our lives in ways that nurture us and impact the world around us.

Understanding Our Own Money Stories

Self-awareness plays an important role in all aspects of our lives, and our finances are no exception. Each and every one of us brings a lifetime of lessons learned about money to our individual lives, as well as to the organizational systems of which we are a part. Understanding these lessons and the ways in which they influence and impact our money management is a critical piece of integrating our lives toward wholeness. Whether you realize it or not, you have a money story—an autobiography of sorts. Bits and pieces of your story are told through your attitudes toward money, your habits with money, and the feelings that money evokes.

Consider your childhood for a few moments. What are your first memories about money? How was money discussed (or avoided) in your family? What did you learn about money at church? All those memories have shaped your money story. You may have learned to be secretive about money. If your family was poor, you may have resented schoolmates who were wealthy. You may have heard at church (albeit incorrectly!) that money was the root of evil. Perhaps you never had a job as a teenager and therefore never learned to manage; conversely, you may have been required to work for your own pocket money. I (Angie) heard a conference leader share that as a child her mother delegated the checkbook balancing to her;[10] every time her mother wrote a check or made a deposit, she attended to the subtraction or addition in the checkbook registry. Whatever your story is, the road to wholeness includes a rest stop for understanding your story and reflecting on all the ways in which it influences your views and your habits.

Margaret Marcuson, in her book entitled *Money and Your Ministry*, suggests six tips for exploring your family's money story.[11]

1. Write one page that expresses what you learned from your family of origin about money. Read it to see how that learning is expressed in your ministry.
2. Ask your parents, if they are living, what they learned from their parents about money. Stay curious rather than judgmental, and talk in person if possible.
3. Observe how your siblings and close relatives deal with money. Is it different from or similar to the way you deal with it?
4. Assess your extended family connections. Do you know who are the most and least financially successful person(s)? To whom are you most connected? What are the family attitudes toward the most and least?
5. Notice the attitude toward gift-giving in your family. Is it balanced, or do some give more than others? Are gifts freely given or with strings attached? What is your family's attitude toward charitable giving?
6. Consider the strengths you received from your family in this area. Even if your values and approach differ, try to generate at least one idea.

Marcuson insists that when we begin to understand our money stories, we are increasingly able to gain new perspective on this area of our lives. As our awareness grows, so does our ability to make different choices in our personal lives and to experience less anxiety during potentially stressful financial seasons in our organizations.

Clarifying Our Values

We've all heard it said that "if you really want to know a person's priorities, look at their checkbook." Certainly, we could add debit card receipts, smartphone banking apps, and online banking statements to be more contemporary, but the sentiment remains the same. How we allocate our resources defines, in large part, who we are and what we become. We spend, save, invest, and give based on our values. Once in a financial coaching session, a seminary student confessed to me (Angie) somewhat jokingly that she evidently valued fast food because drive-thru restaurants constituted the majority of her debit card transactions. Now we might snicker, but at the same time her confession may hit dangerously close to home. Most of us can relate on some level.

The journey toward wholeness necessitates at least a short stop to clarify our values. If we don't want to trek through life known only for our love of fast food, then we must consider what it is that we really and truly value. Stop reading, reflect for a few moments, and take the time to make some notes. What is important to you? How would others describe you? What do you hope your legacy will be? To what ideals do you aspire? The answers to these questions are your values, and only you can respond. Perhaps you listed family, compassion, generosity, financial stability, social justice, gender equality, advocacy, spirituality, evangelism, or simplicity. Whatever they are, these priorities are uniquely yours.

What would happen if you really prioritized those ideals? In *The Soul of Money*, Lynne Twist writes, "What you appreciate appreciates."[12] She is convinced that if we direct our energy and attention to our values, we can be empowered to relate differently to and with our money. If we focus on what's lacking, we become obsessed with what we don't have or seemingly can't obtain. We forfeit peace of mind and happiness. If, however, we direct our attention and our energy toward our capacity to attain the ideals to which we aspire, we actually grow, and our capacity increases. It is a matter of attitude and perspective. Our view of the world and our role in it can be perceived as limited or limitless depending on our focus. If we appreciate and tend to the cultivation of our values, we can "become expressions of those qualities in whatever we do in our interactions with money."[13]

Articulating a Personal Theology of Money

Praying for the opening of the U.S. Senate on April 18, 1947, Chaplain Peter Marshall spoke the following words: "Give to us clear vision that we may know where to stand and what to stand for—because unless we stand for something, we shall fall for anything."[14] In my (Angie's) seminary experience, every student was required to write *credo* papers in theology class; these "I believe . . . " assignments gave us opportunities to articulate our beliefs on the various doctrines of Christianity. I wrote about God, revelation, Christology, Pneumatology, Soteriology, Eschatology, and Ecclesiology, but no one ever asked what I believed about money and possessions. Though the Hebrew Scriptures and the New Testament speak at length about our relationship with and our use of resources, neither seminary nor ordination required me to develop a theological perspective on this topic. Since that time, as I've served congregations and also a theological institution, I've become convinced that this is indeed important work for clergy to undertake.

Theological reflection is the next stop on our journey toward financial wholeness. Margaret Marcuson deems it such foundational work that her book opens with a chapter devoted to knowing what you believe about money. Undeniably, a healthy theology of money is critical for clergy who have accepted God's call to God's work as their life's work. In order for us to fulfill our calling, we must understand scriptural teaching and be able to articulate it not only for ourselves but also for those whom we lead.

So what do you believe? It's complicated to be sure. The entirety of Scripture is overwhelming and not entirely consistent. Thankfully, there are biblical scholars who've done incredible work of culling, distilling, and organizing. Walter Brueggemann's *Money and Possessions* for the Interpretation Series is an excellent resource that covers both Hebrew Bible and New Testament section by section and highlights the ways in which both testaments point us toward similar themes. Also, Luke-Acts scholar Luke Timothy Johnson has written excellently in *Sharing Possessions: What Faith Demands.*[15] With regard to financial ministry in particular, Henri Nouwen's *The Spirituality of Fundraising*[16] and Kerry Alys Robinson's *Imagining Abundance*[17] are excellent, concise resources.

Start somewhere. Study prayerfully. Take your time. What you believe now will no doubt evolve over time, but this reflection will pay dividends both in your personal financial management and in your financial leadership. The work of articulating your money theology will be well worth the investment.

Practical Strategies for Financial Wellness

Living fully into wholeness surely bids us beyond reflection. Besides transformed thinking, there are some regular practices that can lead us further along the path to financial wellness. By taking action to bring our resources in line with our deepest values and our vocational dreams, our relationship with money can become a place of transformation for our individual lives and even for our organizations. Financial discipline and planning, in this sense, holds the potential to emerge as spiritual practice.

Knowing Where Our Money Goes

Before you can take action toward financial wellness, you must know where your money goes. Now, it sounds simple enough, and it is. But our contemporary tendency toward technological, eco-friendly, "paperless" living enables us to earn, save, spend, and give without much effort on our part. It's quite easy to lose track of direct deposit payroll, debit card swipes, smartphone payments, and automated billing. As a result, we may or may not have any sense of bank balances, fluctuating seasonal expenses, wasteful expenditures, or even interest earnings. Tracking the money that flows to and through our lives offers us a window with which to view our current financial status, our strengths and weaknesses, and our potential for transformation.

Tools for tracking your money are widely available whether you prefer old-school pencil and paper, computer, or handheld device. If you'd like to see charts or graphs of earning and spending trends, go with software, smart device applications, or web-based programs. Some are free, while others are available for purchase. If you don't mind data entry and still use paper checks, programs like Quicken or QuickBooks might be for you. Among techno-savvy adults, You Need A Budget (YNAB) is a wildly popular app for tracking and budgeting, especially on a smartphone. Web-based programs like mint.com are capable of linking your bank accounts, credit cards, and other creditors in one virtual location and generating charts for easy visual tracking. Likewise, some banks and credit unions offer similar apps and web-based programs for persons who have accounts at their institutions. Whatever your preference, you can find a tool that can help you get a sense of where your money goes.

Aligning Financial Commitments with Our Values

Once you have a sense of how resources flow through your life, you are in a position to make decisions about managing those resources. Unfortunately, we sometimes discover through tracking that our own finances fail to align with our deepest vocational commitments and our highest aspirations for our lives and our world. This disconnect between our financial reality and our values is likely one of the reasons that those of us who've dedicated our lives to service and spiritual matters get so frustrated with money matters. To overcome that dissonance, we must figure out a way to align our money and values. This is an important step on the journey toward wholeness.

Reallocating our resources to bring them in line with our deepest soul commitments may be necessary. Tracking your money shows you where it comes from and where it goes, but you alone can change the flow. *The Soul of Money* reminds us, "It takes courage to direct the flow, but with each choice, we invest in the world as we envision it."[18] What would it take for this finances-values alignment to take place? What are you willing to sacrifice? What are you willing to engage? Whether you have a little or a lot, you can take steps toward integrating your values and your money habits. Analyze your situation and start where you are; the sum of your choices over time can add up to the wholeness you seek. If your financial situation is bleak and seems impossible, seek out a professional in your community that can accompany you on this journey.

Practicing Healthy Habits

John Wesley's wisdom on financial practices was sound in his day,[19] and it remains solid in our age. First, gain all you can. Work hard, and earn as much as possible. Implicit in his teaching, of course, are Christian ethics; resources must be gained through honest means without harming others. Second, save all you can. Basic financial literacy applies here: in order to save, earnings must exceed expenses. This principle requires us to live well within our means. It is not a call to hoard our resources but instead to plan for the unexpected and to prepare for the future. Third, give all you can. Giving is an integral part of our Christian witness. When we give with deliberation and discipline, we declare our contentment in God's provision and demonstrate our trust in God's sufficiency. All are important choices that call us to carefully assess and distinguish between our needs and wants both present and future, as well as to make thoughtful decisions regarding our contribution to our community and our world.

Of course, none of this is possible without a plan. Goal setting is crucial for those of us who seek increasing financial wellness. After reflecting on your own money story, clarifying values, articulating theology, tracking resources, and considering values-money alignment, you are positioned to set some goals that will enable you to integrate your finances with your faith and vocation. Each goal should be linked to your passions, commitments, and dreams, not simply some random financial achievements that you don't particularly care about. As you set goals, be sure to include specific action steps required to achieve them. What exactly will you do? Goals should also be measurable and time-driven. How will you know a goal is met? What is the timeline for attaining it? Finally, if at all possible, enlist a partner(s) in holding you accountable. Work together with your spouse if you're married, or convene a confidential clergy group to discuss money matters together.

ANGIE'S STORY: PART TWO

Throughout all the years of my family's financial struggle, one factor remained constant as we sought both to manage our money well and to live our faith publicly: our commitment to giving. In fact, we became tithers in the earliest years of our marriage when our checkbook rarely indicated surplus; we had enough but just barely. I'll admit that I was reluctant at first because I could not see how giving a significant percentage of money away every month would benefit our economic situation, even though I trusted in God's ability to provide and believed God's promise of faithfulness. But on paper the numbers did not make any sense at all. How could we give when we were ourselves barely scraping by?

Little did I realize then that disciplined, regular giving involved so much more than numbers written in a ledger or bank statement. I confess that in those early days I sometimes thought about all that our tithe could buy at the market or the mall, the new cars we couldn't afford, and the college savings we couldn't amass. Despite all the ways in which we could have utilized those resources, we continued to give through the local church—week after week, month after month, year after year. With the arrival of each new calendar year, we renewed our commitment and continued evaluating and re-evaluating our income and our ability to give in increasing amounts.

Time marched on as it is in the habit of doing, and at some point I realized that I had ceased to dream about other uses for our tithe but instead began to look for additional opportunities to give beyond our commitment. I discovered the joy and satisfaction that comes from being generous. The habit of disciplined generosity over time produced a heart that delighted in giving, and I became a changed person. My entire outlook on financial commitments to our local church and to other ministries was transformed, not by the ability to make exceedingly large donations but simply through the faithful habit of dedicated giving. I know that I won't ever be a wealthy philanthropist, but I can experience in my own life the very same joy that comes from giving out of my own resources whether they be abundant or meager.

GENEROSITY AND WELL-BEING

In their book *The Paradox of Generosity*, Christian Smith and Hilary Davidson identify and describe the transformation that I (Angie) experienced as my own generosity blossomed. According to their extensive research, in offering ourselves for the well-being of others, "we enhance our own standing, and in letting go of some of what we own, we better secure our own lives."[20] Our own flourishing is facilitated when we give ourselves away. Likewise, the reverse is also true; our own sense of well-being is diminished when we hold too tightly to our resources. Certainly, a wide range of religious teaching reinforces and supports this notion.[21]

- "One man gives freely, yet gains even more; another withholds unduly, but ends up impoverished."—Hebrew Proverb
- "Giving brings happiness at every stage of its expression."—Buddha
- "They who give have all things; they who withhold have nothing."—Hindu Proverb
- "Whoever tries to keep his life will lose it, and whoever loses his life will preserve it."—Jesus of Nazareth

Now Smith and Davidson have established it as a quantifiable sociological fact. Their 2010 survey, which included interviews and observation studies, yielded fascinating results about Americans' dispositions toward generosity. Several themes emerged from the data they collected. A strong association exists between generosity and happiness, health, and purpose; more generous persons enjoyed higher levels of happiness, health, and purpose. Just as generous practices influence personal well-being positively, ungenerous practices affect well-being negatively. These associations evidence the paradoxical nature of generosity: by giving we receive and by grasping we lose. Science confirms what wise teachers have been trying to teach us all along. And yet more Americans remain ungenerous rather than living truly generous lives and experiencing the greater well-being that could be theirs.

The notion of generosity and its impact on personal well-being is critically important for those of us who lead people and organizations in matters of faith and service. Just by reading this book, you have demonstrated your own interest in well-being. Undoubtedly, you would like to see others experience it as well. Some of the best news from their research includes the notion that generosity can be cultivated and that generosity is not limited by income or financial status. By engaging in regular, repeated giving over time, we (and those whom we lead) can grow increasingly generous. Smith and Davidson remark, "If one really *wants* to [become a generous person], simply start *behaving* like a generous person."[22] May we experience not only financial wholeness but also the health, happiness, and purpose of living generous lives.

FOR YOUR REFLECTION AND CONVERSATION

1. As you reflect on this chapter, what financial self-care are you doing well? Where do you sense the need to change?

2. What are some themes that emerged from your personal money story? How do you see those themes at work in your personal finances and your financial ministry?
3. What is rising to the surface as you consider a theology of money? What embedded theology from the past is no longer helpful? What new ideas are you embracing?
4. Do your values and vocational dreams currently line up with your finances? Why or why not? What will you do to bring them into alignment?
5. How do Wesley's *gain*, *save*, and *give* manifest in your life? Which area(s) do you need to nurture? What will you do to begin intentionally cultivating that area?
6. Before reading the chapter, how would you have described your state of financial well-being? How would you describe it now? What commitments will you make to financial self-care?

Chapter Twelve

Intellectual Self-Care

When I pray, I talk to God. When I study, God talks to me.
—Twentieth-Century Torah Scholar[1]

This quote was a wonderful eye, heart, and mind opener for me (Dick). I had long felt a harmony with the divine One when I studied, whether for my own interest or to have important things to share in my ministries of proclamation, caregiving, and teaching.

While some separate devotional from scholarly study of scripture (considering all the literary, historical, contextual questions of a Bible passage), I did not. Openness to all these questions and the knowledge gained by asking those was a mystical, revelatory experience. Indeed, Dwight L. Moody once wrote, "When I pray, I talk to God but when I read the Bible God is talking to me."[2]

Bible study, yes, but also there is a similar wonder exploring other subjects. Whatever we study, it is about God's world, God's people, and God's infinite creativity. Such learning may enrich one's life and ministry.

If this does not resonate with you, perhaps you have not found the kind of study-learning that fits you or the reason for exploring it. This chapter may open doors of discovery and growth that makes such study and learning more revelatory and enjoyable for you. Read on.

THREE BOXES, THREE ORGIES

As we explore, one of our guides will be Richard Bolles (an Episcopal clergy, incidentally). Bolles was mostly known for his frequently updated book, *What Color is Your Parachute?*[3] and for the life/career planning workshops he led and trained others to do.

163

He also wrote another book with the title *The Three Boxes of Life and How to Get out of Them*.[4] In this book he offered a broader view of life/work planning than his *Parachute* book. As I (Dick again) mentioned in chapter 3, one of my life-changing experiences was a two-week training course with Bolles as he helped us experience the wise guidance provided in both these books.

In *Three Boxes*, he considered three aspects of our lives—work, leisure, and learning. He spoke of three boxes as the way we ordinarily experience them. He noted that, when we are young, most of our time and energy is given to the box called learning. In our adult years, most of our time and energy is devoted to the box called work. And when we are old and retired, most of our time and energy is in the box called leisure. In each era of life, there may be small attention to the other two activities, but all too often we live in a box of education, then a box of work, and then a box of leisure.

At times Bolles changed the image from "boxes" to "orgies" and would comment something like this, "For most people, when they are young, there is an orgy of education. When adults, there is an orgy of work. And when they are old there is an orgy of leisure. Life should be more than three orgies!"

Rather, he advocated lifelong learning, lifelong work, and lifelong leisure. True, in each chapter of our life, one of these—learning, work, or leisure—will have the larger focus. But there should be adequate attention given to each of these through life, Bolles believed, and so do I. In this chapter, we will explore the educational component.

If lifelong learning does not excite you, and if, perhaps, earlier education may not have been all that pleasant for you, consider other possibilities. Still guided by the broad wisdom of Bolles, we will help you ask: why do I want to learn, and therefore what do I want to learn; how do I best and most enjoyably learn; and how do I find the time and resources to be able to do this? I will recast this to speak specifically to us pastors, priests, counselors, and chaplains.

WHY AND WHAT DO I WANT TO LEARN?

Before you go on, stop and ask yourself a basic question. Take a piece of paper or a blank page on your computer, and at the top of it, put this question: "What and why do I want to learn?" Let your mind wander over what beliefs or skills or playful interests might be enticing to explore. Close this book and reflect for a while. Think about what might be interesting or fun or enriching in your life. What knowledge would contribute to your present work? Give this the time you need.

When you have taken that step, consider these responses we have heard from other clergy and from ourselves. Read over this list and see if it resonates with you or suggests still other possibilities for your "Why and What" list:

1. *I want to learn (or improve) some skills and practices I seemed to miss in seminary but need in my ministry.*

   In the light of ministry experience, I am more ready to re-explore important aspects of my seminary education that are significant in my present responsibility.

2. *I am overwhelmed with the tasks and responsibilities ahead in the next few weeks/months/years. I would like to be more prepared and find resources for this need.*

   An away time of study and exploring supporting material may contribute to my effectiveness as I anticipate the busy and high demands of my ministry in the present and near future.

3. *I would like to learn how to manage my time more effectively.*

   There is never enough time to do what I want to do. I would like to learn how to prioritize, organize, and use my time more efficiently. (This book has some brief suggestions in chapter 13, but your interest may go beyond our basic guidance.)

4. *I would like to be better at dealing with the conflicts that come up in my life and work and to be able to present my ideas and needs more effectively.*

   Conflict transformation and assertiveness are needed practices that may change the course of a congregation or a life. These are identifiable skills and strategies with methods that can be learned.

5. *I want to discover ways to deal with my isolation and loneliness.*

   There will be new people to meet in any group learning experience where people are together because of a shared interest. There are also courses to help improve one's people skills.

6. *I would like to learn a new "restorative niche," hobby, craft, or activity for my relaxation and enjoyment.*

   In search of a new hobby, art, or skill, it may be fun to take courses to explore this possible interest. I may discover that "this is not for me" or "I have found something I enjoy and want to learn more."

7. *I need to renew my spirit and/or mind.*

   Perhaps days in a retreat center, with or without a spiritual guide, or time alone (with or without a stack of books or disks) or with a close friend away from the present situation is what I need at the present.

8. *I want to re-explore the foundations of my faith, heritage, Bible study methods, and content.*

9. *I feel called to reconsider my stance on pressing theological and/or ethical issues, open to either reconfirming and deepening my stance or changing it.*

Clergy are sometimes stunned to realize that they don't believe the same things they used to as regards theology or ethics. Societal views on topics such as economics, patriotism, and sexuality change and need response from religious leaders. Occasionally, these changed or questioned positions overwhelm and cause one to leave ministry. Before leaving, it might be wiser to study and learn about the range of options and the reasoning behind each position. Perhaps change and growth rather than withdrawal is a possibility.

10. *I need perspective on the vast ferment of change within the Christian church and to explore thoughtful and relevant responses to it.*

As we noted in the first chapter, there are strong winds of change in the Christian movement, both in one's own country and globally. It may mean that ministry will be more difficult; it certainly means that some of the ways clergy do their work must change. Perspective for clergy and laity is much needed.

11. *I may want to change the form of ministry I do, perhaps to chaplaincy, counseling, teaching, or organizational leadership. And so I may need to gain the knowledge and credentials so that I can enter that kindred ministry occupation. Or I may wish to grow and consolidate my wisdom-skills in the ministry I am doing.*

When another form of ministry seems appealing, it is essential to learn important information from those within that type of ministry. Talk to people who are doing that specialty. One might ask such questions as these: How did you get into counseling or chaplaincy or . . . ? What do you like about it? What do you dislike about it? Who else might be able to tell me about their joys and struggles in that occupation? Clarity and information about necessary requirements, steps, and credentialing requirements may happen.

If one wishes to be more focused, grounded, and skilled in the ministry one is doing, a doctor of ministry program may best meet that need. Various seminaries often have specific focuses and specialties to offer. One might find a place to grow, research, and become more knowledgeable and skillful in the ministry one loves.

12. *I want to learn how to engage computers, the Internet, and social media for ministry and not be overtaken or overwhelmed by it.*

As we will discuss shortly, Internet media can be an invaluable window on the world of learning. Various media sites can enhance ministry, pastoral care, worship, and more. Or it can hinder these things.

It is also imperative that clergy be aware of the hazards of addictions to either computer games or online pornography. If caught in the snares of either hazard, it is important to seek help. Learning and counseling resources can help.

What do you think? Does this list suggest other reasons you want to learn? Feel free to change or modify these to fit your interest more closely. Or add new ones. It is important to know—what at this point of my life has the highest priority for my learning and growth?

HOW DO I PREFER TO LEARN?

As you begin to identify what you would like to learn, the next question is: how do you prefer to learn? Do you like to learn with others or by yourself? Would you like to learn at your own pace or at the pace set by a curriculum or instructor or group?

Do you want to be taught with methods created for adults or those created for children? The "fifty-cent" words for this question are andragogy (adult teaching) and pedagogy (child teaching). "Pedagogy" is probably how most of us experienced elementary, secondary, and perhaps later education. There was an outside authority who set the standards and created the curriculum. Then there was a person who knew all this and was entrusted to teach those who didn't know. This was learning for the joy of learning and for future reward. It has been an effective method for many, but not all, young and old learners. (Of course, "pedagogy" is rapidly changing these days as well.)

On the other hand, andragogy—adult learning as identified by educator Malcolm Knowles—suggests education starting from where adults are and addressing what adults want to learn in the way that adults prefer to learn. Adults bring more life experience and a reservoir of past knowledge. They are more interested in learning as regards one's present life situation, needs, and issues.

Therefore, Knowles suggested, adults should be involved in the planning and evaluation of their learning. Experience, rather than lecture, is the basis for learning activities. Mistakes are experience-producing opportunities for learning. The greatest interest will be in topics of direct importance to one's personal life or work challenges. Adult learning, therefore, will be more problem-centered and problem solving than content-centered.[5]

Both these educational methods have their gifts for the learner. At the same time, there may be a door to richer lifelong learning if aware of this distinction as one asks both what and how do I want to learn.

There is yet another question about the "how" of learning—do I want to learn primarily with my "left brain" or my "right brain" or both? (Since this distinction was first identified, there has been much nuanced study of the brain. These terms are still useful as metaphors for interests and styles of learning, and we will use them that way.) The left side of one's brain is rational, analytical, objective, and sequential. Subjects using mostly left brain emphasize logical thinking, analysis, and accuracy.

On the other hand, the right side of one's brain is intuitive, holistic, subjective, synthesizing. Right brain subjects emphasize aesthetics, feeling, and creativity. Right brain–sensitive courses open doors to love of music, to artistic experience, to imagination, and to poetry, myth, and story.

Though most of us probably want to be "whole brained" using both left and right portions of our brain, much education emphasizes left brain. Some may feel right brain starved. So as you choose your own lifelong learning plan, this may be another important clue for how you want to learn.[6]

There is still another angle on learning—the combination of human, media, and print components. If you want to learn something, how important is the human interaction with fellow learners or with the teacher/guide/mentor?

As a seminary professor, from time to time I (Dick) was asked to do a directed or independent study with a student. I learned there was a wide variety of ways that experience can be optimal. With some, after an initial meeting of setting goals, objectives, and resources, the student would love to dig in on his or her own and only occasionally need another meeting in fulfilling the course responsibility. With others, a weekly check-in was important. Perhaps this was for clarification or correction but also out of the need for human contact. If you wanted to learn something from a mentor, what would be your preferred pattern of meeting with the person and doing the learning on your own?

Another aspect of this question is how do you relate to media-based education? Is it pleasant and enjoyable for you to learn from a media-based course of study where there is little or no direct human interaction? If so, there are vast opportunities. If not, after trying it, there are many other options.

Learning Needs

One more topic to explore—do you have any learning needs that call forth creativity to negotiate a good learning experience for you? For example, like many older adults, I (still Dick) have experienced deterioration of sight and hearing. With excellent hearing aids, two sets of glasses, bright lights on my music stand, and constant reminders to my directors to speak loud enough for such as me, I still enjoy learning and performing in community concert bands. These issues are not confined to the old. We have known young students who did not know what others were seeing and who improved dramatically after an eye examination and glasses with corrective lenses.

In addition to physical limitations that you may need to consider, there are other less-evident ones that are best addressed early, rather than after you are into your learning journey. The following five paragraphs on this topic were provided, at our request, by learning specialist Virginia Fortner, PhD,[7] and are included here with her permission.

Are you a one-right-answer Convergent Thinker that expects the type of teacher who gives you that style of study outline and tells you the "best answer" and steps to reach it? Or are you a Divergent Thinker who is comfortable with all the possible answers to a given question and a teacher who allows the process of learning to bring you to your own best answer? Productive education today encourages an "open-ended" approach that allows for many possible answers shared without judgment, mindful listening, and thoughtful choosing of criteria for deciding answers. Ministers and religious educators do best knowing their thinking style and including the opposite style's expectations in study group activities. If didactic "one right answer" lectures or sermons aren't balanced with consideration of others' ideas, the divergent, random thinkers' creativity is lost. If thinking becomes too random and does not organize and become productive, convergent thinkers will tune out.

A friend of mine, a seminary graduate, tells me she is dyslexic and how much more time she had to devote to make any sense out of reading assignments in order to be an effective student. Reading makes up a lot of adult learning time. Figuring out "what the words say" (decoding) is the vital first step that may be helped by reading aloud, tutoring, or making useful pronunciation/spelling/vocabulary lists. "What the words mean" (comprehending) is understanding meaning—catching enough of an author's word-picture to "make a movie" in your own head. Comprehension is also required to gain from lectures and follow group discussions. Lindamood-Bell.com[8] is the best intensive reading remediation suggested to me (Virginia). Some very bright learners need to read out loud to themselves for material to stick in their minds. Others may outline in various ways while many highlight important points to remember. Some actually write the phrases or summaries to digest what they read. If you have a diagnosed learning disability or struggle with reading or test-taking, you may wish to search online seminaries and other learning sites that provide supportive services.

Educators recognize the necessity for recognition of emotional needs in relation to learning. Online searches can point the way to seminaries and other learning resources that support extra time in test-taking, outlets for anxiety, and psychological guidance for fear of failure or other factors that might stand in the way of success.

It is a good idea to know your best learning channel and accommodate it as you can while making ways to shore up your less-developed channels. If you prefer seeing things written—about 70 percent of learners are visual—

ask for handouts or PowerPoints and take notes. If listening is your preference (20 percent), you may even close your eyes and jot down an occasional
note to remember a lecture. Many prefer a combination of visual and audito-
ry channels. A few need to see, hear, and draw/gesture/move to solidify a
new concept. Choose where you sit—up front to give visual attention or hear
clearly, in back if your movements divert others' attention from instruction.
People who know American Sign Language often use it unconsciously as
they listen to speakers.

In addition, mobility and transportation issues need to be addressed for
enjoyable participation. Since the American Disabilities Act, handicapped
accessibility has become the rule, and county or local transportation facilities
are increasingly available.

WHERE DO I WANT TO LEARN?

When one has asked the why, what, and how questions of learning strategy,
the question of where becomes simpler. A good place to begin might be to
find and visit with a "resource broker," that is, someone who probably won't
be the one to teach you but who knows who or what might be helpful to
you—for example, a resource librarian at a public, seminary, or university
library or the continuing education director at a university or seminary. There
may also be persons with helpful suggestions among your colleagues and
friends.

If you wish to learn by yourself, a librarian may point you to excellent
print or media resources, or a seminary professor in your field of interest
might provide a syllabus and bibliography from a course close to your interest. Or you may be able to find a person near you who shares your interest
but is farther along in the topic or skill that draws you.

Various kinds of media also make much learning available. For example,
I (Dick) had received the catalogs for "Great Courses," which provide summaries, outline, and video or audio lectures by leading scholars on a wide
variety of topics. Though these courses generally cost less than $200, I
hadn't purchased one. And then, to my delight, I discovered that the local
public library was carrying a number of them. I have enjoyed them, and they
cost me nothing!

Friends have pointed out the vast range of free online university classes
taught by leading professors at excellent universities. There are many listings
of these. One might go to "Open Culture"[9] and look around for a course that
responds to your interest for a start.

If the preference is for learning with others, then colleges, seminaries,
retreat centers, mental health associations, nearby churches, and more offer
onetime or limited-time courses that draw together a knowledgeable leader

and persons who share an interest or passion. Again, the resource brokers may have valuable suggestions if you talk with them about what is your interest and what you would like to learn.

Travel may be the learning experience that appeals to you. There are group tours for pleasure or learning or both. Of course there is individual travel as well. As our colleague Dr. David May says, "Travel is the greatest antidote to prejudice."[10] Travel to and life within, however brief, a much different culture helps us experience persons of beauty, dignity, and creativity. In short, one perceives a whole different world. Some international travel may also open one's eyes to poverty, hardship, refugees, and hunger.

WHAT IF I DON'T KNOW WHAT TO LEARN?

Perhaps this brief exploration of so many learning possibilities has left you confused rather than enthused. You may have perplexity over where to go next. For starters two inquiries, side by side, may lend some clues. For one, conversations with trusted friends and colleagues as well as lay leaders in your ministry might be helpful. A question to ask them might be, "Where is my ministry going well and where is change and possible improvement needed? From all I have learned so far, what more do I need to study to grow deeper in ministry?"

At the same time, listen to yourself. Ask: what fascinates me, what enriches me, what brings me joy? What arouses my curiosity? What do I enjoy?

The responses from trusted friends and one's own questions about delight and fascination may converge at least in part. If this does not happen, choose from both sets of insights—others and your own inner delight.

If it still feels unclear or if you are considering a change in the focus and place of ministry, it may be wise to go to one of the regional centers of the Ministry Development Council. These centers offer a variety of types of counsel, discernment, and encouragement for clergy and their spouses. One of their specific opportunities is the Vocational Consultation Program. Their website describes this service: "The reasons for clergy seeking involvement in the Vocational Consultation program are multiple and varied. They may be giving consideration to the search for a new call or they may wish to maximize their gifts in their current placement but need guidance. Strengths and weaknesses will be explored, and the client will be assisted in developing an action plan for both personal and professional development."[11]

A GROWTH EXPERIENCE WORTH EXPLORING

As we think of lifelong learning and growth, there is one more possibility that should be mentioned. That is the "clergy renewal leave" or "sabbatical."

What is it? It is an extended period of time for a minister to rest, seek spiritual renewal, learn, possibly travel, and gain perspective and increased vigor for ministry.

"Clergy renewal leave" or pastoral sabbatical comes after an extended time of service and has as its purpose the gaining of perspective, new wisdom or skills, and fresh energy for that ministry. Some churches and agencies grant a three-month leave after six years (or four years) of service, for example. Some renewal leaves may be shorter, a month or so. For whatever period of time, one is relieved of everyday responsibilities and is free to engage in specifically chosen and planned opportunities for growth.

How does this come about? Ideally a church or agency has a policy in place when a minister is called. Or, perhaps, if this is a new idea to those involved, it is discussed and negotiated as part of the terms of accepting the call. Some denominations are helpful by stating the importance of clergy renewal, recommending a sabbatical policy, perhaps even providing wording for this policy. If this has not happened, a minister and supportive lay leaders can initiate discussion, years in advance of the first such renewal time provided. At any rate, it is wise for clergy and employing community to plan two to three years ahead.

If one is granted, say three months, how should a sabbatical be spent? The one clear answer is that it should not be a carbon copy of anyone else's. This is a time to discern, to dream, to brainstorm, with spouse, with friends, with church leaders. A. Richard Bullock and Richard J. Bruesehoff, in their guide to sabbatical planning, advise to think in three blocks:

- resting, including sleeping more, exercise, visiting friends, etc.;
- renewal, focused study on selected topics of importance to self and community; and
- rebirth, including plans for returning to the community in a different place both for clergy and community.

Another clergy described these three steps as letting go, living in God's presence, and reorientation. Still another used the terms decompression, transition, and reentry.[12]

Though I took part in many enriching educational experiences while serving in parish ministry, I (Dick) had only one true sabbatical. It happened when I was sixty-two and after nearly forty years of service.

I felt the need not only for rest but for a new perspective. Finally my purpose came clear: I wanted to engage in mutual learning and perspective with pastors and seminarians in developing countries. Friends—missionaries Gam and Alice Shae—helped outline the trip and made contacts and arrangements so that I could experience this.

I spent a month in Indonesia and a month in Myanmar (Burma) meeting people, worshipping with them, leading pastors' retreats, meeting students, and speaking to their classes. In those brief times, I experienced much gracious hospitality and made unforgettable friends. I also had a weekend in Singapore where I visited at some length with a professor who teaches pastoral care in an Asian setting, and I worshipped-spoke at a Chinese church. My sabbatical closed out with two weeks in Thailand, much of it debriefing with the Shaes and visiting students I had taught.

I returned rested, refreshed, and enthused to sustain and revive my congregation's commitment to local and world mission. Several members commented that if they had known how much more energetic and effective I became, they would have sent me much sooner!

When others hear this story, the response is often "That sounds like a very busy sabbatical. I would want a lot more 'down time.'" That's as it should be. Each sabbatical should fit the interests, lifestyle, and needs of the person taking the sabbatical and the community she or he serves.

Melissa Bane Sevier, who out of her own experience has written a lovely "spiritual companion" for those taking sabbaticals, offers cautions as to when a minister's renewal leave should not happen. She points out that if one is deeply burned out or there are serious marriage or family conflicts or a major decision-making time for the church or a church conflict, this renewal leave should be postponed to a more fitting time.

Further, such leave is not for the purpose of deciding whether to stay or leave one's present ministerial responsibility. While certainty is impossible, one should plan to stay at least a couple more years after this renewal time. [13] On the other hand, I am aware that one church granted their pastor, Greg Hunt, renewal time so that he could explore "whether God or fatigue was nudging me to change forms of ministry." After that time of rest, study, and prayer, he resigned and entered a new form of ministry. [14]

Of course, such planning needs to include spouse and family—how they will be impacted and whether they should be part of some of the travel or other experiences. Also, provisions for the community so that leadership is present and growth for congregation or agency is also possible is an important topic. The two books just mentioned provide much wisdom and guidance on this topic. Our purpose is to stimulate interest and possibility thinking about such times as one avenue of intellectual and spiritual self-care.

WHAT ABOUT FINANCES? HOW CAN I AFFORD IT?

This chapter has listed many motivations for lifelong learning as well as ways and places to do so. If this seems impossible financially, give it some thought. A good question might be: what is possible for me right now, and how can I take steps for more extensive learning experiences in the future?

One might start with learning opportunities with no financial cost. These include the online resources we mentioned as well as libraries and resource brokers. Further, there might be someone who might have things to teach you who will guide you free of charge.

I (Dick) was once approached by a pastor who had a long reading list required for his doctor of ministry studies. He asked me to meet with him once a month to discuss a book on that list. He could not pay me but would provide the book if I didn't have it and would buy me lunch while we visited. I was glad to do it. He met an educational requirement. I found it stimulating, and we became better friends, all at very little cost to him.

Further, allowance for continuing education needs to be an item of conversation when any minister and employing community are negotiating their contract. Depending on resources, the allowance may be small. But it should be explained, utilized, and interpreted before, at the beginning, and during one's ministry tenure.

If ministry renewal leave or sabbatical seems far beyond even imagining, one might learn how to write an excellent plan and proposal and submit it to the Lilly Endowment Clergy Renewal Programs.[15] They consider requests for grants up to $50,000, which can include up to $15,000 for congregational expenses associated with the clergy renewal program.

Or explore one of the programs of the Louisville Institute Pastoral Study Project, which provides grants of up to $15,000 for pastoral leaders "to pursue a pressing question related to Christian life, faith, and ministry."[16]

While a minority of those who apply will receive such grants, it's worth trying. If that doesn't work out, there are many other options to pursue. Many seminaries will be hospitable to a minister who would like to come, use the library, visit with faculty, enter into chapel, and other aspects of seminary life. Some seminaries have semester-long or yearlong pastor-in-residence offerings.

To be sure, persons in bi-vocational ministries will have many complications in arranging study leave beyond the finances. Creativity and flexibility will be needed.

In this chapter, you have been invited to consider in what way enriching ministry for the long haul needs a lifelong learning component. Then you were offered a number of questions and strategies to find that which will be enriching and life giving for you.

While preparing this chapter, we came across an essay passionately advocating for lifelong learning, written by Laura Rodgers Evans. We enjoy her enthusiasm and share her conclusion as the final words of this chapter.

Blood, sweat, tears, hunger, fights, bruises, and laughter all come in the midst of learning. How will you cope and keep striving to *be?* . . . Keep your whole self involved in life-giving learning: how are we pursuing self-awareness, self-care, and self-extension? Are you experiencing valuable side effects, like self-confidence and treasured friends? Are you ready to learn? Let's go.[17]

FOR YOUR REFLECTION AND CONVERSATION

1. What was your best learning experience ever? What made it so for you? What was your worst learning experience ever? What made it so?
2. In the light of the things discussed in this chapter, how would you describe yourself as a learner?
3. What invitations, hungers, longings, if any, did this chapter stir for you?
4. What barriers exist to make your responding to those invitations difficult?
5. What are the steps you will take to overcome those barriers?
6. What is needed to change learning-education from one more responsibility to self-care for you?

Chapter Thirteen

Basic Steps to Self-Care

Matt Bloom, principal investigator for the Flourishing in Ministry Project at the University of Notre Dame, "finds that the widespread language of self-care in clergy roles ignores the larger environment in which ministry takes place. 'What is left out is that there are ecosystems of wellbeing.'" [1]

How will we clergy in our various ministries be able to live in "ecosystems of wellbeing"? Two basic things must be true: (1) one's employing community (whether church, agency, or institution) must believe in the importance of self-care and thus provide space, time, and resources for the minister's renewal and growth; (2) the minister will need to claim and exercise this provision for self-care that renews one for ministry. And at times, perhaps quite often, one will need to advocate for such self-care provisions.

We hope that this stirs a light of recognition in some readers—aha, this is what we are doing to keep me alert, alive, and growing. Quite probably, others will realize how far their situation is from what is needed. How do minister and community ever get to such a place? We offer a few basic steps in that direction.

STEP ONE: INCREASE YOUR SKILLS IN ADVOCATING FOR A BALANCED LIFE WITH NEEDED SELF-CARE

We can ask and negotiate for the self-care time we need. How does one do that effectively? Part of it may be to negotiate a realistic job description and self-care protocol (more on this shortly). To do this, there are valuable clues from the advocates of assertiveness training.

Alberti and Emmons define assertiveness in this way: "Assertive behavior promotes equality in human relationships, enabling us to act in our own best interests, to stand up for ourselves without undue anxiety, to express honest feelings comfortably, to exercise personal rights without denying the rights of others."[2] They note three barriers to expressing oneself and one's needs effectively: (a) a person doesn't believe they have the right to be assertive; (b) the person may be anxious and fearful about speaking about one's needs; and (c) one may lack skills for effective self-expression.[3] Their book provides guidance to overcome these barriers.

Assertive behavior honors the self while at the same time honoring the other, caring for both sets of needs. This is true whether the "other" is an individual or an organization.

Therefore, assertiveness is distinctive from:

* aggressiveness—where one may use force, out shouting, out arguing the other, sarcasm, or bullying.
* passiveness—accepting others' decision, keeping quiet, pretending some demand is okay with you when it really isn't.
* passive-aggressiveness—appearing to accept the other's demands, but instead responding with procrastination, forgetting, dawdling, pouting, or giving the other the silent treatment.[4]

Assertiveness, by contrast, is genuine concern for the rights of all, self and the various others in one's life. It is also learning how to communicate this clearly. It is a love of neighbor and of self, neither selfish nor denying the God-given rights and needs of oneself.

For most of us, this attitude and these skills are not inborn; they need to be learned. Though there is more that we can say about these skills, all one's training in communication and caregiving will be useful. Good books (including the two we are referencing here) or workshops can provide growth in this vital skill. Suffice it to say, assertiveness uses "I" language. It is honest and direct, with words as well as nonverbal communication, and is socially responsible.

There is one specific method that may be of particular help as a step toward a working agreement with one's employer about self-care time and schedule. Sharon and Gordon Bower speak of a technique they call the DESC Script. As the initials imply, it has four steps.

Describe the situation as you see it. Do so in behavioral terms. What is the situation, and how is it impacting you and your employer's best interests?

Express your feelings about this situation. "I" messages and descriptions of your emotions about the current situation will be useful.

Specify what it is that you want. This is the step many people miss, but it is vitally important. As you speak about what you need for your self-care, be specific, clear, and reasonable. A basic, concrete statement of what you are asking is essential for this transaction to succeed.

Consequences. Describe the consequences of fulfilling or not fulfilling your request. Communicate about benefits both for your employer and for you if the request is granted. Of course, you don't know the exact outcome, but you can speak realistically and hopefully about what constructive change will in all likelihood happen with the granting of your request.[5]

The request of the third step, the "Specify" step, may be quite simple, such as recognizing that you will take a given amount of time for an interest or supporting your child's activity. It may be more complex, such as needing to be relieved of certain responsibilities. Or it may be a major request, such as asking for more help, time for an educational experience, or a sabbatical.

Whatever the request, it should be carefully prepared and tried out first on a trusted confidant—perhaps spouse or fellow clergy for feedback on how to make it better. Once these steps have been taken, it may also be good to share it with a trusted leader, perhaps the chairperson of the board that is making the decision before presenting it to the whole group.

Doing the DESC process does not guarantee that your request will be granted. Perhaps it will occasion discussion or further study. It may be denied. The nature of the denial and reasons for it may well have information helpful for making your next DESC proposal. If this step has stirred in you awareness and courage to speak of your needs as well as those of the other, you have done well.

Of course, there are also times not to be assertive. One should not be assertive when caring for an individual or organization that is in deep crisis, grief, or pain. Such are the times to suspend one's assertive claims and to support persons and community through the crisis. Probably one should not be assertive about one's self-care at times when many other members of the organization are giving beyond themselves to achieve something important. And quite probably one should not be assertive on these matters if it follows too closely a previous request, discussion, and decision making. At the same time, it is important to remember that temporarily yielding on self-care claims does not mean abandoning them.

STEP TWO: BECOME MORE EFFECTIVE IN TIME MANAGEMENT

Our experience is that self-care activities energize and equip us to do our work more effectively and efficiently. At the same time, it is always good to pause and explore some important questions: What part of my work takes more time than it should? What are my time wasters? When and why do I procrastinate? How can I do the work I am called to do with greater effectiveness and possibly lighter time investment? Where do I start in addressing these issues?

Self-Cohesion

Robert Randall in his book *The Time of Your Life: Self/Time Management for Pastors* suggests a different approach than most others use in exploring the use of time. He begins his book, "The essence of time management is self-management. . . . It is the state of a pastor's self that determines the pastor's responsiveness to time management issues in ministry."[6]

While most books on time management go from "outside in," he approaches this subject from the "inside out." This approach chooses to help us clergy enhance our inner life so that we can become better stewards of time in our ministry. "When we become more cohesive and understanding of ourselves, we can respond more empathically to the time-related needs of parishioners and to our own time needs."[7]

Reflecting on Jesus' counsel, "Be wise as serpents and innocent as doves" (Matthew 10:16), he suggests self-cohesion has two aspects in regard to self and other:

- Being *wise* with oneself—using one's head when self-cohesion is threatened.
- Being *affirming* with oneself—keeping your heart straight. These in turn should lead to—
- Being *wise* with others—realistic about others, recognizing their needs, problems, issues.
- Being *affirming* with others—including those who don't keep their promises or don't follow through, seeing possibilities, and more.[8]

Of course, Randall acknowledges, self-cohesion exists on a continuum between "firm" and "weak." There will be fluctuations, as crises, criticisms, successes, and failures come and go. Self-cohesion can be threatened by disease, loss, criticism, or rejection.

Still, with firm self-cohesion, persons have a positive self-image and the ability to regulate the tensions experienced. They are comfortable in their own skin, and their thoughts are balanced and realistic. They are able to live in the present and in the seasons of their life. When one operates from a reasonable amount of such inner strength, there will be wise and considered time management in the various aspects of ministry. Randall counsels to know yourself and claim your strengths. From this you may have corresponding effectiveness in managing your time.

Role Clarity

In their book, *Switch Off: The Clergy Guide to Preserving Energy and Passion for Ministry*, Heather Bradley and Miriam Bamberger Grogan apply their expertise in the corporate world to guide more effective functioning in ministry. When one says yes to some activity, one is also saying no to others. Therefore, they counsel to find and use one's "off switch." There are three questions in regard to this off switch: "Where am I taking on stuff that isn't mine? How much is enough? What do I need to say yes to? Say no to?"[9]

In exploring these questions, they point out three types of roles. There are outer roles that provide the structure and process of the system—job titles, job descriptions, and specific tasks. These answer the question, "Who does what?" There are inner roles that have to do with the emotional functioning of the system. For example, what values does the system need? Inner roles may include "devil's advocate, cheerleader, initiator, or peacemaker." These respond to the question, "How do we work together?" Then there are ghost roles—powerful influences that come from a variety of sources. They speak of people ghosts, circumstantial ghosts (such as a church anniversary), and cultural ghosts, which are societal influences that exist within and without the church. The question here is "What forces exist but cannot be observed?"[10]

This awareness leads to a number of illuminating explorations. Where are the poorly filled roles that I seem to be taking on? Where is there role creep where I am assuming more responsibility than I should? Where is there role confusion or role overlap? What ghost roles fall on me? Where am I experiencing role nausea? From what roles can I legitimately be released?

There authors conclude there are four tools needed to be able effectively to engage one's "off switch." These are: role analysis, reality check, boundary analysis, and control analysis. They provide charts and searching questions to move through each of these tools. This compact book provides provocative questions and exercises to guide us clergy through this vital process, too briefly described here. Claim your fitting roles and shed or delegate roles that are not fitting for you. Consequently, you will use time more effectively.[11]

Attention to Details

There is great wisdom for time management in those concepts of self-cohesion and role clarity. At the same time, there are many opportunities close at hand to save a bit of time that can be used for other things. Let's consider just a few such ways:

1. Recognize your time wasters, and reduce the use of them. Social media, online shopping, video games on work time, procrastination, hours spent on hymn selection, wild goose chases on irrelevant subjects—these and more can eat up hours of valuable work time.

2. Ask yourself: when are your highest-energy and most creative times? What tasks should be addressed in those times? Two ministers who are good friends answer this question in exactly opposite ways. One knows that the early hours of the day are the height of his creative energy. He better attack that sermon, article, or other difficult task then. The other finds his creative juices late at night in a quiet house after everyone else has gone to bed.

3. Find ways to focus and organize which work responsibilities to meet each workday. For some, not all, this means list making. I (Dick) am one of those. A checklist of the large and small tasks—calls, letters, contacts, appointments, projects, beginnings, investigations—is helpful to me. To come to the end of the day with all or most of the items crossed out is quite satisfying and instructive as to how to approach the next day and week.

4. Recognize and claim the value of small steps. Break down a major task by noting steps that will take one in the direction of accomplishing it. For example, Fred Craddock has described a series of steps one can do throughout the week to engage a Bible text and mine it for truths to be expressed in the sermon that will come from it. [12] Identifying the small steps can be helpful for a variety of tasks, including major studies and comprehensive plans.

5. Double up. Use the time when put on "hold" for any praying, thinking, or tasking near at hand. When waiting to see a hospital patient, one can meditate on scripture for next Sunday's sermon quietly in the chapel or get some exercise by walking around the hospital grounds.

6. Add your own wisdom to these basic suggestions.

STEP THREE: USE SELF-CARE CREATIVITY IN ENGAGING MEDIA

The vast growth of media and technological resources for enriching ministry is one of those "good news, bad news" dilemmas. The good news is all the gifts media brings. A minister can access much help for sermon preparation through the Internet. It can enhance worship and education, bringing beautiful images, great scholars, interviews, and photography from around the world into our meeting places. E-mails and texting are quick and easy means of communication. Constant contact can be used to send information to large numbers of people, such as prayer requests or newsletters. Churches and agencies can offer websites to present themselves to all interested, including their witness to the world. Worship services can be streamed as well as archived so that worship becomes more accessible to those incapacitated or at a distance.

Through social media a minister has greater freedom of movement while being available and in touch with a vast variety of people and their needs. Further, much of a community can be alerted to news of importance to all. Facebook and other social media sites can build a community of care. One minister reaches out to a hundred mothers of preschoolers in this way. The Internet can help one keep current on news of the world. In all this, as Bruce Epperly notes, social media can be vehicles of spiritual transformation. [13]

The bad news is that, at times, social media is preferred to meeting persons in live, face-to-face settings. Sometimes, quick communication such as a brief e-mail does not communicate clearly. The bad news also is that without boundaries a minister can be available to congregants or clients 24/7. And more bad news—engaging and managing media can be extremely time consuming and, let's face it, time wasting. Media addiction, including but not limited to video gaming and online pornography, is widespread.

So how can ministers practice self-care in this area of ministry? An important place to start is to see media as our tool, not our master. Too little attention has been paid to this important insight. When we realize its truth and take thoughtful charge of this aspect of our life, several options may occur. In these days of information overload, be wise and selective regarding what news sources you view and how to evaluate the truth of what is reported.

Further, recruit volunteers who are more comfortable and adept in this world than you may be. Discover how to partner with such gifted folks to combine their creativity and ingenuity with your sense of the important gospel truths and community enrichment you would like to convey. Also learn to take a "media Sabbath." These are times when you will be turned off to outside messages and stimuli for all but the most serious crises. Family meals and other special times warrant our full attention. If you'd like to learn more about taking a break from your devices, there are even apps to help you. [14]

Finally, be aware how lasting (and sometimes widespread) are the things you say online. It is especially important not to deal with conflict on the Internet. And so, in Epperly's counsel, "pray before sending." [15]

APPLICATION: JOB DESCRIPTION

A practical and needed place to combine these skills is in the minister's job description. I (Nate) often meet with church search committees to help them define what gifts they need in their next minister and what services the minister should provide. Too frequently, I am appalled with the shallow responses they give and their failure to recognize a minister's need for rest and renewal.

Clearly, a job description is needed not only for the minister but to clarify and educate the religious community. This might start with the purpose and goals of the congregation and what they need from their minister to help them accomplish these. There should be discussion of ministerial tasks and priorities as well as realistic understanding of time investment needed for each task. Clarity as to whom the minister reports is always important but especially so in times of conflict or when doing a performance evaluation. Along with the congregation's expectations about availability, office hours, and more, there should be in place a way to discuss and develop the pastor's capacity for leading the community into shared ministry. This can be an opportunity to use the self-care skills mentioned in this chapter to both educate and negotiate a working partnership. Teach about the time needed to prepare and perform the tasks assigned. Be sensitive to roles, including ghost roles and role creep. Clearly and assertively state the responsibilities of the laity and the legitimate needs of the minister so that all may live in an "ecosystem of well-being."

I (Nate) also urge churches to see these job descriptions as fluid documents that can evolve as the congregation grows in its understanding of what their minister does and what its responsibilities as a faith community are.

STEP FOUR: WRITE AND FOLLOW A SELF-CARE COVENANT

Another vital step is to move beyond considering possibilities and toward making first commitments. We suggest that you write a self-care covenant. In chapter 6, we suggested creating and following a "rule of life," which Marjorie Thompson described. If you did that, here are some other areas to consider to add to that. This covenant should select a step to be taken in each of at least four areas of self-care: physical, relational, intellectual, and spiritual. Each of these steps should be beyond what you are currently doing, challenging but not impossible. Writing this may make you aware that you have overemphasized some parts of your self-care and neglected others. This is an opportunity to begin to change that.

As with the rule of life, this covenant needs to be shared with another, someone you ask to be your accountability partner. This could be a clergy colleague; perhaps you could both write self-care covenants and be each other's accountability partner. Or it could be another caring professional, a member of your family, or a friend who knows you well. You and this selected person should discuss and choose how frequent check-ins should happen. Then schedule the first check-in. It may be wise to share this with a supportive person from your employing community.

Select a time period for your covenant, perhaps somewhere from three to six months. Then it is time to reconsider—what was impossible, and what was too easy? What growth steps should be included in your next self-care covenant?

We believe these are vital steps to engaging your employing community as well as becoming and continuing to be the minister you are called to be, with greater joy and effectiveness in how you spend your days.

FOR YOUR REFLECTION AND CONVERSATION

1. What are your strengths and what are your challenges in speaking clearly and assertively about what you need? What, if any, are gender differences and challenges in assertively stating one's needs? How does this impact you?
2. What has been your experience with people, cultural, and circumstantial ghost roles?
3. What are your wisest practices in time management in your ministry? What are your biggest time-wasting temptations? How do you deal with them?
4. How has your ministry changed, grown, or been enhanced through your use of various media? Where is this distracting for you? What are your wisest strategies?
5. How do you feel about writing a self-care covenant for the next few months? Are you willing to try it? If so, who will you ask to be your accountability partner?
6. Which of these—or your own—suggestions hold promise for negotiating and making the space you need for self-care time and activities?

Chapter Fourteen

A Theology of Self-Care

> By and large a good rule for finding [true vocation] is this. The kind of work
> God usually calls you to is the kind of work (a) that you need most to do and
> (b) that the world most needs to have done. . . . The place God calls you to is
> the place where your deep gladness and the world's deep hunger meet.
>
> —Fredrick Buechner

Earlier, we suggested that some of our ministerial malaise may be due to
"theological amnesia." In this chapter, we call you (as well as ourselves) to
theological remembrance and renewal, particularly in regard to self-care.
Buechner's well-loved description of vocation reminds us that all God's
people are called. Further, there are clues to discern this vocation, this calling. This is true for the persons we serve, and it is true for us ministers.

THE GRACE AND HOPE OF OUR CALLING

We start this theology with awareness of the grace that invites us into this
particular calling. We are not in our ministries because we are holier, more
spiritual, more learned, or wiser than others. If we listen carefully to those
with whom we minister, we can find those who have much to teach us in
each of these regards. Rather, we resonate with Paul's words in Ephesians
3:8, "Although I am the very least of all the saints, this grace was given to me
to bring to the Gentiles the news of the boundless riches of Christ." A place
to begin is gratitude for the privilege of being called into this life of service.

Within this gracious call, there will be times when we feel overwhelmed.
The One who calls us into this high and holy privilege knows that occasionally the challenges of ministry may feel impossible and like more than we
can carry. But the promise is we do not carry it alone. Again, it is Paul who

witnesses to God's provision in such times: "We are afflicted in every way, but not crushed; perplexed but not driven to despair; persecuted but not forsaken; struck down but not destroyed; always carrying in the body the death of Jesus, so that the life of Jesus may also be visible in our bodies" (II Cor. 4:8–10).

Our theology of self-care guides us in this time of—as we said at the beginning of this book—a five-hundred-year rummage sale and a perfect storm. When we look at church and ministry in contrast to what it was, we are tempted to despair. Though despair literally means "without hope," we are called to hope, difficult as it sometimes is. Charles R. Pinches has well said, "We underestimate what is required in hope because we underestimate God or overestimate ourselves."[1]

Indeed, there are times in the hazards of our calling when we urgently need to claim the Christian hope of which Paul speaks, embody it, and communicate it with those we serve. As Gabriel Marcel has well stated, "Hope is for the soul what breathing is for the living organism. Where hope is lacking, the soul dries up and withers."[2] Hope is not our own doing. It is the gift of God who calls us to discipleship and service.

PROMISES AND COMMITMENTS IN OUR CALLING

As we reflect on the gracious call of God into our unique vocation, it is good to recall and renew the promises we made at the outset of our ministries. For many of us, this was expressed in a code of ethics that we gladly accepted on the day of our ordination or commissioning.

However, in the heavy demands and wear and tear since then, this may have grown fainter—in our minds and perhaps even in our practice. And so part of our theology of self-care guides us to seek forgiveness for any lapses or failure and to recommit to the promises we made.

We are called to consider the inner wisdom of the code(s) of ethics for our professions and to recommit to them. It might be fruitful to consider when you were helpful to a person or community by following some parts of your code of ethics and when you or another minister were not helpful by not following the guidance of one's code.

Do your religious families, professions, or denominations have a code of ethics for clergy? If not, you might want to explore my (Dick's and other members of the writing team] denomination's code and its accompanying learning guide referenced in a link in this endnote.[3] If you serve a nondenominational organization or if your denomination does not have such a guideline, you might want to consider the one created by the National Association of Evangelicals referenced in a link on this endnote.[4] The National Council of Churches of Christ does not have a code of ethics for clergy, apparently leaving that to the various member denominations, but they do offer a twenty-first-century social creed referenced in a link on this endnote.[5] Some of the professional societies for ministry specializations also have codes of ethics. As fellows in the American Association of Pastoral Counselors, each year in order to renew our affiliation, we (Ruth and Dick) have to state we have read this code in the past year and are in conformity to it. It is accessible through a link on this endnote.[6]

Each of these contains wise moral guidance born of experience. There is certainly inner wisdom in reading, reflecting, and perhaps discussing with another, with such questions as these: Where does this express the heart of my calling? Where do I disagree with a certain provision and why? Where must I separate myself from this code? In what ways do I hope to go beyond this code of ethics? Such explorations may contain renewal in aspects of our lives that have not been addressed elsewhere in this book.

DIVINE SUSTENANCE ALONE AND IN THE COMPANY OF OTHERS

Disciplined self-care is one of the ways we are sustained, and hope is renewed in times of stress and danger. This is much needed for we ministers share the humanity, finitude, and limitations of the rest of God's people. Only God never slumbers nor sleeps. The rest of us need our sleep and more. We get hungry and tired, fearful and hurt. Intentional rest from our labors, such as Jesus provided for the disciples, is essential for continuing renewed ministry. This was an important discovery for me (Angie). Truly one cannot fill glasses from an empty pitcher. In order to adequately provide care for those with whom I've been entrusted, I must first care for myself.

Sometimes this care can be found in solitude with God. As the Psalmist recalls, "But I have calmed and quieted my soul, like a weaned child with its mother" (Psalm 131:2). This is truly a gift, one in which some of us claim and find renewal even more than others. As we earlier noted, there are spiritual practices of renewal that fit each of us in our varied personality types.

At the same time, solitude should not be confused with being isolated from others in our struggles. More often than we like to admit, we may be in deeper distress than need be, for we declare like Elijah, "I alone am left" (I Kings 19:14). In God's revelation to Elijah, he was instructed whom to anoint as kings and whom to anoint as his successor. Further, he was reminded that there were seven thousand who had not bowed their knee to the false god Baal (I Kings 19:15–18). Alone, Elijah? Open your eyes and see all who share your faith and to whom you can turn for support and strength.

Alone? By your own choice? Open your eyes and find the person or persons who can console, strengthen, and support you.

God's call to struggling ministers therefore includes the guidance to abandon a "Lone Ranger" mentality. The invitation is to community—to fellowship. In the New Testament, the Greek word is "koinonia," which refers not only to one's communion with God but to the presence of God that is mediated in a group of believers.

This "group" may be one other person—a friend, a mentor, a coach, a counselor, a spiritual guide. Or it may be an intentional small group. Perhaps it is family. Or it may be the rich friendships that are sometimes the by-product of working together on something—a class, a mission project, or the program and mission of a church.

THE MANY SURPRISES AND GIFTS IN SELF-CARE

One of the gracious surprises in these communities of self-care is that they often cross the lines of conservative and liberal Christians and of denominations that may not have had much conversation with each other. Throughout working on this book, we have been enriched and informed by thoughtful writers from across this theological spectrum, and we hope what we have prepared will likewise be helpful to Christians who may have different views and priorities. Indeed, Rabbi Friedman saw an ecumenism crossing Christian-Jewish lines when clergy related to each other on the life processes of their congregations.[7]

What is potentially helpful spiritual self-care is as wide as the suggestions in chapters 6 to 13 and probably even wider. As a former teaching colleague, Maynard Hatch, professor of religious education, used to say, "You cannot not teach religious education." (Read it again. The double negative is intentional.) The implication is that, as we live out our lives in front of our children, youth, and others, we are communicating what we believe in everything we do whether we are aware of that or not.

Likewise, we cannot do any kind of self-care that is enriching to us and not be doing spiritual self-care. Whatever is pleasing and empowering to you is spiritual self-care. As I (Dick) mentioned earlier, I experience this often as I play at a practice or performance of a concert band. I am so relaxed and joyful that it often puts any tensions I was feeling back in perspective. Any self-care activity that does that for you, even once in a while, is spiritual self-care. When I (Dick again) was a younger pastor, an hour or two of pickup basketball would drain the tensions from my body and send me back renewed.

Of course, that does not remove the importance of explicit practices of spiritual self-care, as those are discovered and practiced. Foundationally, we believe in God who loves the world and who communicates with us, God's children. God reveals presence, guidance, care, and strength both wordlessly and with words. We are called to commune with God in the glories of creation, in the practices of one's Christian community, in group disciplines, and in solitary prayer and meditation.

Though some of us feel very scattered as we enter into these sacred opportunities, the desire to enter into communion with God, find strength, and serve God is important. And however difficult we find it, we leave with more strength and peace than if we had never tried.

This self-care is a journey, not a destination; a process, not the end of the process. We and our commitments are always a work in progress. With this in mind, we forgive ourselves when we fail and trust in God's forgiveness, but we get up and start again on the road of being growing ministers.

By God's grace, we are led into ministry. And by God's grace, we are offered many healing self-care practices to strengthen us when the demands of ministry seem about to overwhelm us. I (Nate) realize I am useless to everyone if I am burnt out, miserable, and depressed. Putting more of an emphasis on self-care has made me a better listener, less stressed, and more sensitive in counseling situations.

But these gifts of self-care are not offered to just us clergy. And our self-care is never an end in itself; always it is a means to serve and strengthen the communities of faith and the world beyond.

ECCLESIOLOGY OF SELF-CARE

This theology of self-care thus leads to an ecclesiology of self-care. For what we have been advocating for clergy is sorely needed by most of the population! We have earlier mentioned how many of the illnesses today are "lifestyle" illnesses and those caused or worsened by stress. Years ago, Roy Oswald stated this vividly, "I see intentional self-care as a vehicle for change, not only in our hurting congregations, but in a battered world."[8]

At the very least, we are called to witness and invite the churches, agencies, and communities we serve into these health-enhancing, life-enriching self-care practices. The "how" as to the ways this is done will vary in our numerous places and styles of ministry. It may begin simply by living a holistic healthy life, strengthened by self-care practices—doing this in one's faith community. As Oswald also commented, "Each of us makes a powerful theological statement the moment we enter a room."[9]

Each person in a system influences the system. The system in turn influences the individual. Change in one—say in the direction of greater health and vigor—may well have impact on others in the system.

Or our ecclesiology of holistic self-care may also lead us in specific directions, programs, and practices. Perhaps we will initiate a parish nurse program to bring education, attention, and support to people in their health issues. We might be led to regular services of prayers for the sick. Possibly discussions on the topics mentioned in this book and sessions led by holistic health professionals in your community will be a helpful process. I (Ruth) frequently find that I need to encourage those who come for pastoral counseling to focus on some dimension of self-care that is lacking. Whether exercise, nurturing friendships, or developing spiritual practices, attentiveness to self-care can be crucial for their healing and greater well-being.

Rev. Dr. Michael Minor is a parable of where this can lead. When he came to tiny one-hundred-member Oak Hill Missionary Baptist Church in Hernando, Mississippi, he discovered a population with huge health problems and frequent deaths from obesity-caused illnesses. And so he took drastic steps—he banned fried chicken from church potlucks and set up a walking track around the church perimeter! The church now has a machine that provides readings on blood pressure and body-mass index, donated by the American Heart Association. In the kitchen, there is a plaque, "No Fry Zone."

People responded to Rev. Minor's gospel of healthy living, and persons in his church are now going out as teams of "health ambassadors" to other churches. These efforts have grown into a national outreach program in his denomination, the National Baptist Convention. He has also obtained grants to train people to encourage enrollment for health care insurance. [10]

BACK TO THE FUTURE

We have spoken of the overwhelming and disturbing changes in the world, church, and ministry. We went on to describe the dimensions of pain that ministers were experiencing in an occupation often overstressed and subject to compassion fatigue. Then we explored a wide variety of ways that ministers can be renewed through specific self-care practices.

Are the practices we offered an adequate response to the severity of this historical crisis that church and ministry now face? We believe the answer is yes. At least self-care is one part, a vital component of surviving and thriving in such times.

About 2,500 years ago in another of those "five-hundred-year garage sales," the prophet speaking in Isaiah 40 addressed a discouraged, defeated people, exiled from their homeland, hearing rumors and hoping against hope to be allowed to return to their homeland.

At first he challenged, "Why do you say O Jacob . . . 'My way is hidden from the LORD, and my right disregarded by my God'?"

Isaiah then called them back to a faith that had grown faint within them: "Have you not known? Have you not heard? The Lord is the everlasting God, the Creator of the ends of the earth." And though you may have grown faint and weak, God has not. "[The Lord] does not faint or grow weary; [God's] understanding is unsearchable."

Our God is present with us in all this, Isaiah counsels. God "gives power to the faint, and strengthens the powerless." True, there are those who are not experiencing this presence and power right now—"Even youths will faint and be weary, and the young will fall exhausted."

However, it is time to trust again and to experience the sustaining power of our Creator: "But those who wait for the Lord shall renew their strength, they shall mount up with wings like eagles, they shall run and not be weary, they shall walk and not faint" (Isaiah 40:27–31 adapted).

Our prayer is that these promises will be kept again. We hope that ministers who are feeling the crush of a changing world and shrinking church will be strengthened by renewing self-care practices. We pray there will arise a mighty body of religious leaders—resilient, creative, energetic, courageous—ready to participate in God's new story for church and world.

When that happens, to God be the glory. Amen.

FOR YOUR REFLECTION AND CONVERSATION

1. How did you respond to this book's first chapter and its descriptions of the crisis in ministry? As you think about yourself and your friends in ministry, did it seem overdrawn and exaggerated, or did it ring true?

2. What self-care practices are most enriching for you? What other practices are you planning to begin?

3. Do you have a theology of self-care? If so, in what ways is it similar, in what ways different from the one offered in this chapter? If not, how does this theology/credo strike you? What would you want to add, change, delete?

4. As you reflect on your ministry setting, what is most needed for the resilience/renewal/revival of clergy, laity, and church today and tomorrow?

Notes

1. MINISTERING DURING A RUMMAGE SALE
AFTER A PERFECT STORM

1. *The Green Pastures*, by Marc Connelly, music by Hal Johnson, produced by Laurence Rivers Inc., Mansfield Theater, New York, February 26, 1930–August 29, 1931.

2. As quoted in Charles L. Rassieur, *Stress Management for Ministers* (Louisville: Westminster Press, 1982), 13.

3. As noted in Peter Carey, *Santos Woodcarving Popsicles* (blog), March 15, 2009, accessed December 27, 2017, http://santospopsicles.blogspot.com/2009/03/every-500-years-church-has-rummage-sale.html.

4. Jeffrey D. Jones, *Facing Decline, Finding Hope: New Possibilities for Faithful Churches* (Lanham, MD: Rowman & Littlefield, 2015), 29–30.

5. Dan Edwards, "The Great Emergence by Phyllis Tickle," *Bishop Dan's Blog*, March 15, 2009, accessed July 13, 2017, http://bishopdansblog.blogspot.com/2009/03/great-emergence-by-phyllis-tickle.html.

6. Phyllis Tickle, *Emergence Christianity: What It Is, Where It's Going, and Why It Matters* (Ada, MI: Baker Books, 2012), 25.

7. Jones, *Facing Decline*, 29–30.

8. Jones, *Facing Decline*, 30.

9. Robert Putnam and David Campbell, *American Grace: How Religion Divides and Unites Us* (New York: Simon and Schuster, 2010).

10. Putnam and Campbell, *American Grace*, 91–133.

11. As cited in Linda A. Mercadante, *Belief without Borders: Inside the Minds of the Spiritual but Not Religious* (New York: Oxford University Press, 2014), 2.

12. As noted in Jack Wellman, "Why We Are Losing So Many Churches in the United States?" *Christian Crier* (blog), October 26, 2013, accessed January 5, 2017, http://www.patheos.com/blogs/christiancrier/2013/10/26/why-we-are-losing-so-many-churches-in-the-united-states/.

13. Wellman, "Why We Are Losing?"

14. Terry Rosell, "Why People Don't Trust Preachers and What to Do About It," class lecture and PowerPoint provided to the authors, July 3, 2017.

15. As quoted within Emily McFarlan Miller, "Survey Reveals Public's Skepticism about Pastors," *Christian Century* 14, no. 5 (March 1, 2017): 13.

16. Rosell, "Why People Don't Trust Preachers."

17. "Study Finds Clergy Sexual Misconduct Widespread," *Christian Century* 126, no. 21 (October 20, 2009): 14.

18. Patricia M. Y. Chang, "Factors Shaping Clergy Careers: A Wakeup Call for Protestant Denominations and Pastors," *Pulpit and Pew*, Duke Divinity School, 2005, 5–6.

19. K. Meek, M. McMinn, C. Brower et al., "Maintaining Personal Resilience: Lessons Learned from Evangelical Protestant Clergy," *Journal of Theology and Psychology* 313, no. 4 (2009): 339–347.

20. Greg Crow, "Region, Role, and Size as Risk Factors in Clergy Attrition," Association of Nazarene Sociologists and Researchers conference, March 26, 2010, Crowne Plaza Hotel, Lenexa, KS.

21. Barbara G. Wheeler, Sharon L. Miller, and Daniel O. Aleshire, "How Are We Doing? The Effectiveness of Theological Schools as Measured by the Vocations and Views of Graduates," *Auburn Studies* (New York: Auburn Theological Seminary, December 2007), 5.

22. Lovett H. Weems Jr. and Ann A. Michel, *The Crisis of the Younger Clergy* (Nashville: Abingdon, 2008), 1–10.

23. PAALT (Pastoral Attrition Action Learning Team), *Report on Our Survey*, 5th ed. (Valley Forge, PA: American Baptist Ministers Council, June 9, 2015).

24. As reported in Jack Wellman, "Average Pastor Salaries in United States Churches," *Christian Crier* (blog), December 15, 2013, accessed January 5, 2017, http://www.patheos.com/blogs/christiancrier/2013/12/15/average-pastor-salaries-in-united-states-churches/.

25. Anthony Ruger, Sharon Miller, and Kim Early, "Taming the Tempest: A Team Approach to Reducing and Managing Student Debt," *Auburn Studies* (New York: Auburn Theological Seminary, October 2014), 14.

26. "Top 2 Causes for Pastors Leaving Ministry and More Statistics," Standing Stone: Strengthening Shepherds (website), accessed February 28, 2017, https://www.standingstoneministry.org/top-2-causes-for-pastors-leaving-ministry-and-more-statistics/.

27. H. B. London Jr. and Neil B. Wiseman, *Pastors at Greater Risk* (Ventura, CA: Gospel Light, 2003), 13.

28. G. Jeffrey MacDonald, "Move to Part-Time Clergy Sparks Innovation in Congregations," *Faith & Leadership*, March 21, 2017, accessed December 26, 2017, https://www.faithandleadership.com/move-part-time-clergy-sparks-innovation-congregations?utm_source=albanweekly&utm_medium=content&utm_campaign=faithleadership.

29. PAALT, *Report on Our Survey*.

30. PAALT, *Report on Our Survey*.

31. Richard Krejcir, "Statistics on Pastors: 2016 Update," Francis A. Schaeffer Institute of Church Leadership Development, accessed February 15, 2017, http://files.stablerack.com/webfiles/71795/pastorsstatWP2016.pdf.

32. Joe Roos and Cheri Herrboldt, "Forced Termination: A Guide to Healing for Pastors and Congregations," *The Mennonite*, November 2017, 16.

33. Michael Weise, "Murmurs from the Outside: What Former Pastors Are Saying to the Church," *Comparative Report of Six Studies on Pastoral Attrition*, 2004, submitted to the Pastors Institute and symposium participants in response to the October 4 and 5 symposium, Louisville Institute for Pastoral Study.

2. SELF-CARE IN A VARIETY OF MINISTRIES

1. Jo Ann Deasy, "How 2016 Graduates Are Faring," Association of Theological Schools, Commission on Accrediting, November 2016.

2. Thomas Skovholt and Michelle Trotter-Mathison, *The Resilient Practitioner*, 3rd ed. (London: Routledge, 2016), 41.

3. As quoted in Lovett H. Weems Jr. and Ann A. Michel, *The Crisis of Younger Clergy* (Nashville: Abingdon, 2008), 55.

4. Bruce G. Epperly and Katherine Gould Epperly, *Four Seasons of Ministry: Gathering a Harvest of Righteousness* (Bethesda, MD: Alban, 2008), 117.

5. Epperly and Epperly, *Four Seasons*, 120.

6. Epperly and Epperly, *Four Seasons*, 124.

7. Epperly and Epperly, *Four Seasons*, 5.

8. https://www.faithandleadership.com/move-part-time-clergy-sparks-innovation-congregations?utm_source=albanweekly&utm_medium=content&utm_campaign=faithleadership.

9. L. G. Jordan, A. M. Townsend, and E. W. D. Issac, *The Baptist Standard Church Directory and Busy Pastor's Guide* (Nashville: Sunday School Publishing Board, 1993).

10. Terrell Carter, personal conversation with Dick Olson, April 19, 2017.

11. Young Sun Jin, "A Study of Pastoral Burnout Among Korean-American Pastors" (DMin Thesis, Liberty Theological Seminary, 2009), 26–53, http://digitalcommons.liberty.edu/cgi/viewcontent.cgi?article=1165&context=doctoral.

12. Jin, "Study of Pastoral Burnout Among Korean-American Pastors," 54.

13. Jin, "Study of Pastoral Burnout Among Korean-American Pastors," 57.

14. Samuel Park, personal conversation with Dick Olson, May 11, 2017.

15. As reported in David Masci, "The Divide Over Ordaining Women," The Pew Research Center, September 9, 2014, accessed July 28, 2017, http://www.pewresearch.org/fact-tank/2014/09/09/the-divide-over-ordaining-women/#comments.

16. Marsha Wiggins Frame and Constance L. Sheham, "Care for the Care Giver: Clues for the Pastoral Care of Clergywomen," *Pastoral Psychology* 52, no. 5 (May 2004): 369–380.

17. Adelle M. Banks, "Pastor-Mothers Balance Pulpit and Parenting," *Christian Century*, May 31, 2011, 15.

18. "Daughters Provide as Much Elderly Parent Care as They Can, Sons Do as Little as Possible," *American Sociological Association News*, accessed on July 28, 2017, http://www.newswise.com/articles/daughters-provide-as-much-elderly-parent-care-as-they-can-sons-do-as-little-as-possible.

19. David J. Kundtz and Bernard S. Schlager, *Ministry Among God's Queer Folk* (Cleveland: The Pilgrim Press, 2007), 1.

20. Bethany Meier, interview with Angela Jackson, November 8, 2017.

21. Dionne Boyice, interview with Angela Jackson, November 9, 2017.

22. Sean Weston, interview with Angela Jackson, November 9, 2017.

23. https://clgs.org/about-clgs/.

24. http://www.welcomingresources.org.

25. http://www.awab.org.

26. Jose Martinez, personal correspondence with Dick Olson, December 23, 2017.

27. https://www.ptsd.va.gov/professional/co-occurring/moral_injury_at_war.asp.

28. Ronald A. Heifetz and Marty Linsky, *Leadership on the Line* (Boston: Harvard Business Review Press, 2002), 53.

3. BURNOUT AND COMPASSION FATIGUE

1. As quoted in Tyler Lee Kruger, *Keys to Resilient Practice in Contemporary Chaplaincy* (DMin Dissertation, Lancaster Theological Seminary, 2010), 10.

2. Roy Oswald, *Clergy Self-Care: Finding a Balance for Effective Ministry* (Herndon, VA: Alban, 1991, 1998).

3. Christina Maslach and Michael P. Leiter, *The Truth About Burnout: How Organizations Cause Personal Stress and What to Do About It* (San Francisco: Jossey-Bass, 1997), 9–16.

4. Merriam Webster Dictionary online, accessed November 3, 2017, https://www.merriam-webster.com/dictionary/burnout.

5. Wikipedia, "Herbert Freudenberger," accessed November 3, 2017, https://en.wikipedia.org/wiki/Herbert_Freudenberger.

6. Maslach and Leiter, *The Truth About Burnout*, 17.

7. Robert J. Wicks, *The Resilient Clinician* (New York: Oxford University Press, 2008), 9.

8. The American Institute of Stress, accessed November 3, 2017, http://www.stress.org/military/for-practitionersleaders/compassion-fatigue.

9. Chris Marchand, *An Investigation of the Influence of Compassion Fatigue due to Secondary Traumatic Stress on the Canadian Youth Worker* (DMin Dissertation, Providence Seminary, 2007), 17.

10. Wicks, *Resilient Clinician*, 29.

11. Wicks, *Resilient Clinician*, 29.

12. Denise Hill, Mark Jeske, and Maureen Kelly, "Compassion Fatigue," PowerPoint provided to the authors, October 6, 2017.

13. Maslach and Leiter, *The Truth About Burnout*, 17–18.

14. Dennis Portnoy, "Burnout and Compassion Fatigue: Watch for the Signs," *Health Progress*, July–August 2011, 48.

15. Thomas M. Skovholt and Michelle Trotter-Mathison, *The Resilient Practitioner: Burnout and Compassion Fatigue Prevention and Self-Care Strategies for the Helping Professional*, 3rd ed. (London: Routledge, 2016), 107–109.

16. J. Gill, "Burnout: A Growing Threat in the Ministry," *Human Development* 1, no. 2 (Summer 1980), 22.

17. Maslach and Leiter, *The Truth About Burnout*, 17–18.

18. Judith A. Schwanz, *Blessed Connections: Relationships that Sustain Vital Ministry* (Herndon, VA: Alban, 2008).

19. G. Lloyd Rediger, *Coping with Clergy Burnout* (Valley Forge, PA: Judson Press, 1982).

20. Wayne Muller, *Sabbath: Finding Rest, Renewal and Delight in Our Busy Lives* (New York: Bantam Books, 1999), 3, quoted in Kirk Byron Jones, *Rest in the Storm: Self-Care Strategies for Clergy and Other Caregivers* (Valley Forge: Judson Press, 2001), 9–12.

21. Jones, *Rest in the Storm*, 23–48.

22. Fred Lehr, *Clergy Burnout: Recovering from the 70-Hour Work Week and Other Self-Defeating Practices* (Minneapolis: Fortress, 2006), 11.

23. Richard N. Bolles, *The Three Boxes of Life and How to Get Out of Them* (Berkeley: Ten Speed Press, 1978); *What Color Is Your Parachute?* (Berkeley: Ten Speed Press, 2003).

24. Oswald, *Clergy Self-Care*, 79.

25. Compassion Fatigue Awareness Project, accessed November 10, 2017, http://www.compassionfatigue.org/pages/selftest.html.

26. Consulting Psychologists Press, accessed November 10, 2017, https://www.cpp.com.

27. Ayala Malakh Pines, Elliot Aronson, and Ditsa Kafry, *Burnout: From Tedium to Personal Growth* (New York: Free Press, 1981), 4–5.

4. STRESS

1. Paul Bowden, ed., *Telling It Like It Is: A Book of Quotations* (Seattle: CreateSpace, 2011), 234.

2. Hans Selye, *The Stress of Life*, revised ed. (New York: McGraw-Hill, 1978), 1.

3. Herbert Benson and Eileen Stuart, *The Wellness Book: The Comprehensive Guide to Maintaining Health and Treating Stress-Related Illness* (New York: Birch Lane Press, 1992), 180.

4. Tracy B. Herbert and Sheldon Cohen, "Stress and Illness," *Encyclopedia of Human Behavior*, volume 4 (Cambridge, MA: Academic Press, 1994), 325, accessed August 12, 2017, http://kungfu.psy.cmu.edu/~scohen/encyclo94.pdf.

5. Tracy B. Herbert and Sheldon Cohen, "Understanding the Stress Response," Harvard Health Publishing, 1994, accessed December 31, 2107, https://www.health.harvard.edu/staying-healthy/understanding-the-stress-response; Sheldon Cohen, Denise Janick-Deverts, and Gregory E. Miller, "Psychological Stress and Disease," *JAMA* (*Journal of the American Medical Association*) 298, no. 14 (October 10, 2007), accessed December 31, 2017, http://sites.northwestern.edu/foundationsofhealth/files/2013/03/07-JAMA-Psychological-stress-disease.pdf.

6. Herbert and Cohen, "Understanding the Stress Response," 328.

7. Richard N. Fogoros, "An Overview of Atherosclerosis," *Verywell*, updated August 7, 2017, accessed December 31, 2107, https://www.verywell.com/what-is-atherosclerosis-1745 908.

8. American Psychological Association, "Stress Weakens the Immune System," February 23, 2006, accessed December 31, 2017, http://www.apa.org/ research/action/immune.aspx; Herbert and Cohen, "Understanding the Stress Response," 238–329.

9. Paul Gilbert, *Overcoming Depression* (New York: Oxford University Press, 2001), 17.

10. Stephen S. Ilardi, "The Diagnosis and Treatment of Depression: A Lifestyle-Based Approach," continuing education workshop sponsored by Saint Luke's Health System, March 11, 2015.

11. Stephen S. Ilardi, *The Depression Cure* (Cambridge, MA: Da Capo Press, 2009), 35–36.

12. Ilardi, *Depression Cure*, 20.

13. Gilbert, *Overcoming Depression*, 19–21.

14. Ilardi, *Depression Cure*, 37.

15. Gilbert, *Overcoming Depression*, 50–60.

16. Herbert and Cohen, "Understanding the Stress Response," 326.

17. Kelly McGonigal, *The Upside of Stress* (New York: Avery, 2016), xii.

18. McGonigal, *Upside of Stress*, 4.

19. McGonigal, *Upside of Stress*, 11.

20. McGonigal, *Upside of Stress*, 16.

21. McGonigal, *Upside of Stress*, 33.

22. Scott Kelly, interview with Rachel Martin, on NPR's *Morning Edition*, October 17, 2017.

23. McGonigal, *Upside of Stress*, xxi.

24. Yu X., Fumoto M., Nakatani Y., Sekiyama T., Kikuchi H., Seki Y., Sato-Suzuki I., and Arita H., "Activation of the Anterior Prefrontal Cortex and Serotonergic System Is Associated with Improvements in Mood and EEG Changes Induced by Zen Meditation Practice in Novices," *International Journal of Psychophysiology* 80, no. 2 (May 2011), 103–111, abstract accessed December 31, 2017, https://www.ncbi.nlm.nih.gov/pubmed/21333699.

25. Sonja Lyubomirsky, *The How of Happiness* (New York: Penguin Books, 2007), 112–124.

26. Center for Spirituality and Healing, University of Minnesota, "How Does Nature Impact Our Wellbeing?" accessed June 17, 2016, https://www.takingcharge.csh.umn.edu/enhance-your-wellbeing/environment/nature-and-us/how-does-nature-impact-our-wellbeing.

27. Richard Louv, *The Nature Principle*, cited by Lecia Bushak, "Benefits of Ecotherapy: Being in Nature Fights Depression, Improves Mental Health and Well-Being," *Medical Daily*, October 26, 2013, accessed June 2, 2016, http://www.medicaldaily.com/benefits-ecotherapy-being-nature-fights-depression-improves-mental-health-and-well-being-261075.

5. A STARTING PLACE

1. As reported in Steven Petrow, "Resilience Isn't Just Being Tough; It's a Skill You Can Develop. Here's How I Did It," *Washington Post*, August 30, 2017, accessed December 28, 2017, https://www.washingtonpost.com/lifestyle/wellness/resilience-isnt-just-being-tough-its-a-skill-you-can-develop-heres-how-i-did-it/2017/08/29/9d077a1e-881f-11e7-a50f-e0d4e6ec070a_story.html?utm_term=.748f54225475.

2. Thomas M. Skovholt and Michelle Trotter-Mathison, *The Resilient Practitioner: Burnout and Compassion Fatigue Prevention and Self-Care Strategies for the Helping Professional*, 3rd ed. (London: Routledge, 2016), 125, italics theirs.

3. Martin E. P. Seligman, *Flourish: A Visionary New Understanding of Happiness and Well-Being* (New York: Free Press, 2011), 16–22.

4. Pauline Boss, *Loss, Trauma, and Resilience: Therapeutic Work with Ambiguous Loss* (New York: W.W. Norton Company, 2006), 48.

5. Al Siebert, *The Resiliency Advantage* (San Francisco: Berrett-Koehler Publishers, 2005), 5.

6. Sheryl Sandberg and Adam Grant, *Option B: Facing Adversity, Building Resilience, and Finding Joy* (New York: Alfred A. Knopf, 2017), 111.

7. Al Siebert, "The Resiliency Quiz," The Al Siebert Resiliency Center (website), accessed January 11, 2018, http://resiliencyquiz.com/index.shtml.

8. Emmy Werner, "Resilience and Recovery: Findings from the Kauai Longitudinal Study," *Focal Point: Research, Policy, and Practice in Children's Mental Health* 19, no. 1 (Summer 2005): 11–14.

9. Werner, "Resilience and Recovery," 11–14.

10. Werner, "Resilience and Recovery," 11–14.

11. As quoted in Diane Coutu, "How Resilience Works," *Harvard Business Review*, May 2002.

12. http://strengthscopeus.com.

13. Sandberg and Grant, *Option B*, 10.

14. Nan Henderson, "What Is Resiliency, and Why Is It So Important?" *Resilience in Action* (blog), November 2, 2012, accessed December 26, 2017, https://www.resiliency.com/blog/.

15. Joan Borysenko, *It's Not the End of the World: Developing Resilience in Times of Change* (Carlsbad, CA: Hay House, 2009), 32–33.

16. Siebert, *Resiliency Advantage*, 54.

17. Siebert, *Resiliency Advantage*, 93.

18. Martin Seligman, "Building Resilience," *Jay Dixit* (blog and website), accessed August 3, 2017, http://jaydixit.com/psychology/failure-and-resilience/martin-seligman-on-building-resilience/.

19. Borysenko, *Not the End of the World*, 25.

20. Robert J. Wicks, *The Resilient Clinician* (New York: Oxford University Press, 2008), 16.

21. Aaron Ungersma, *The Search for Meaning: A New Approach in Psychotherapy and Practical Psychology* (Sydney: Allen and Unwin, 1961), 28–30. See also Viktor Frankl, *Man's Search for Meaning* (New York: Washington Square, 1959).

22. Sandberg, *Option B*, 29.

23. Sandberg, *Option B*, 134–139.

24. Gregory Hamel, "Problems That Past Lottery Winners Have Faced," Pocket Sense (website), accessed December 26, 2107, https://pocketsense.com/problems-past-lottery-winners-faced-8708.html.

25. Coutu, "How Resilience Works."

26. Skovholt and Trotter-Mathison, *Resilient Practitioner*, 131.

27. Wicks, *Resilient Clinician*, 46.

28. Boss, *Loss, Trauma, and Resilience*, 57.

29. Skovholt and Trotter-Mathison, *Resilient Practitioner*, 127.

30. Skovholt and Trotter-Mathison, *Resilient Practitioner*, 128.

6. SPIRITUAL SELF-CARE

1. Henri Nouwen, *Sabbatical Journey* (New York: Crossroad Publishing Company, 1998), 97.

2. Barbara Brown Taylor, *An Altar in the World: A Geography of Faith* (New York: HarperOne, 2009), 176.

3. https://www.16personalities.com/free-personality-test   or   http://www.humanmetrics.com/cgi-.

4. Bruce G. Epperly and Katherine Gould Epperly, *Tending to the Holy: The Practice of the Presence of God in Ministry* (Herndon, VA: Alban, 2009), 8–9. For another perspective, see Cheer P. Michael and Marice C. Norrisey, *Prayer and Temperament: Different Prayer Forms for Different Personality Types* (Charlottesville, VA: The Open Door, 1991).

5. Epperly and Epperly, *Tending*, 11.

6. Jason Micheli, *Cancer Is Funny: Keeping Faith in Stage-Serious Chemo* (Minneapolis: Fortress Press, 2016), 165.

7. Micheli, *Cancer*, 37.

8. Micheli, *Cancer*, 181.

9. Micheli, *Cancer*, 191.

10. Micheli, *Cancer*, 193.

11. Micheli, *Cancer*, xii.

12. Micheli, *Cancer*, xxi; Dick Olson told this story in similar and same language in a book review for the *Journal of Religion and Disability* 21, no. 3 (2017).

13. Wesley Granberg-Michaelson, "An Anchor in the Storm," *Sojourners* 46, no. 4 (April 2017): 15.

14. Granberg-Michaelson, "Anchor," 15.

15. As quoted in Granberg-Michaelson, "Anchor," 16.

16. Granberg-Michaelson, "Anchor," 16.

17. Granberg-Michaelson, "Anchor," 17.

18. Granberg-Michaelson, "Anchor," 17.

19. Joy M. Freeman and Tabatha Johnson, eds., *Still a Mother: Journeys through Perinatal Bereavement* (Valley Forge, PA: Judson Press, 2016), 2.

20. Johnson and Freeman, *Still*, 2–3.

21. Johnson and Freeman, *Still*, 39.

22. Johnson and Freeman, *Still*, 45.

23. Johnson and Freeman, *Still*, 69–70.

24. Johnson and Freeman, *Still*, 70.

25. Johnson and Freeman, *Still*, 76.

26. Johnson and Freeman, *Still*, 78.

27. Peter Scazerro, *Emotionally Healthy Spirituality* (Grand Rapids, MI: Zondervan, 2006), 13.

28. Scazerro, *Emotionally*, 14.

29. Scazerro, *Emotionally*, 17.

30. Scazerro, *Emotionally*, 17.

31. Scazerro, *Emotionally*, 157–158.

32. Scazerro, *Emotionally*, 45.

33. *Faith and Leadership*, "Laura Everett: Riding My Bicycle Is a Spiritual Discipline," August 8, 2017, accessed January 17, 2018, https://www.faithandleadership.com/laura-everett-riding-my-bicycle-spiritual-discipline.

34. *Faith and Leadership*, "Laura Everett."

35. *Faith and Leadership*, "Laura Everett."

36. *Faith and Leadership*, "Laura Everett."

37. Laura Everett, *Holy Spokes: The Search for Urban Spirituality on Two Wheels* (Grand Rapids, MI: Wm. B. Eerdmans, 2017).

38. Wayne Muller, *Sabbath: Finding Rest, Renewal and Delight in Our Busy Lives* (New York: Bantam Books, 1999), 7.

39. Muller, *Sabbath*, 37.

40. Muller, *Sabbath*, 20.

41. Arden Mahlberg, "Getting Our Bearings: Sabbath Reorients Clergy to God and to the World," *Sustaining Pastoral Excellence*, accessed March 15, 2017, https://www.faithandleadership.com/programs/spe/articles/200707/bearings.html.

42. Mahlberg, "Getting Our Bearings."

43. Muller, *Sabbath*, 162.

44. Muller, *Sabbath*, 165.

45. Muller, *Sabbath*, 55.

46. Muller, *Sabbath*, 183.

47. Herbert Benson and Eileen Stuart, *The Wellness Book: The Comprehensive Guide to Maintaining Health and Treating Stress-Related Illness* (New York: Birch Lane Press, 1992), 45–46.

48. Herbert Benson and Marg Stark, *Timeless Healing: The Power and Biology of Belief* (New York: Scribner, 1996).

49. Marjorie Thompson, *Soul Feast: An Invitation to the Christian Spiritual Life* (Louisville: Westminster John Knox, 1995), 146.

50. Thompson, *Soul Feast*, 150.

51. Dorothy C. Bass, ed., *Practicing Our Faith*, 2nd ed. (San Francisco: Jossey-Bass, 1997), xi.

52. Bass, *Practicing*, 5, italics theirs.

53. Dorothy C. Bass and Don C. Richter, eds., *Way to Live: Christian Practices for Teens* (Nashville: Upper Room Books, 2002).

54. Dorothy C. Bass and Susan R. Briel, eds., *On Our Way: Christian Practices for Living a Whole Life* (Nashville: Upper Room Books, 2010).

55. Richard Foster, *Celebration of Discipline* (New York: HarperCollins, 1978).

56. Nancy Roth, *Spiritual Exercises: Joining Body and Spirit in Prayer* (New York: Seabury, 2005).

57. Wendy Wright, *The Rising: Living the Mysteries of Lent, Easter, and Pentecost* (Nashville: Upper Room, 1994); *The Vigil: Keeping Watch in the Seasons of Christ's Coming* (Nashville: Upper Room, 1998); *The Time Between: Cycles and Rhythms in Ordinary Times* (Nashville: Upper Room, 1998).

58. Barbara Brown Taylor, *Leaving Church: A Memoir of Faith* (New York: HarperOne, 2012).

59. Taylor, *Altar in the World*, xv.

60. Taylor, *Altar in the World*, xv.

61. Taylor, *Altar in the World*, 82–83, italics ours.

7. RELATIONAL SELF-CARE

1. As quoted in Judith A. Schwanz, *Blessed Connections: Relationships That Sustain Vital Ministry* (Herndon, VA: Alban, 2008), forward.

2. Gary Chapman, *The 5 Love Languages: The Secret to Love that Lasts* (Chicago: Northfield Publishing, 2015.

3. Helyn Strickland, "We Are Family: The Significance of Fictive Kinship Among Twenty Year Invested Employees in a Minimum Security Psychiatric Hospital" (DMin Dissertation, Central Baptist Theological Seminary, 2017), 87.

4. Strickland, "We Are Family," 75.

5. Strickland, "We Are Family," 19.

6. Strickland, "We Are Family," 64.

7. Robert J. Wicks, *The Resilient Clinician* (New York: Oxford University Press, 2008), 70.

8. Wicks, *Resilient Clinician*, 70.

9. Wicks, *Resilient Clinician*, 72.

10. Wicks, *Resilient Clinician*, 73.

11. Wicks, *Resilient Clinician*, 73.

12. Lillian Daniel, "The Rough Edges of Holy Friendship," *Faith and Leadership*, accessed April 10, 2017, https://www.faithandleadership.com/programs/spe/resources/dukediv-friendship.html.

13. Bob Wells, "It's Okay to Go There: The Place of Friendship in Ministry," *Faith and Leadership*, accessed April 11, 2017, https://www.faithandleadership.com/programs/spe/resources/dukediv-friendship.html.

14. Schwanz, *Blessed Connections,* 101–105.

15. Gary D. Kinnaman and Alfred H. Ells, *Leaders That Last: How Covenant Friendships Can Help Pastors Thrive* (Ada, MI: Baker Books, 2003), 121–123.

16. Kinnaman and Ells, *Leaders That Last*, 133.

17. Kinnaman and Ells, *Leaders That Last*, 123.

18. John Landgraf, *Singling: A New Way to Live the Single Life* (Louisville: Westminster John Knox, 1990), 117.

19. Sam Keen, *Fire in the Belly: On Being a Man* (New York: Bantam Books, 1991), 173–174.

20. Daniel Levinson et al., *The Seasons of a Man's Life* (New York: Alfred A. Knopf, 1978), 100.

21. Edward C. Sellner, *Mentoring: The Ministry of Spiritual Kinship* (Lanham, MD: Cowley Publications, 2002), 16.

22. John Donahue, *Anam Cara: A Book of Celtic Wisdom* (New York: Harper Perennial, 1997), xvii.

23. Donahue, *Anam Cara*, 13–14.

24. Sellner, *Mentoring*, 80–83.

25. Marjorie Thompson, *Soul Feast: An Invitation to the Christian Spiritual Life* (Louisville: Westminster John Knox, 1995), 114–115.

26. Spiritual Directors International, accessed December 10, 2017, http://www.sdiworld.org/.

27. Thompson, *Soul Feast*, 110–111.

28. Mark Tidsworth and Ircel Harrison, *Disciple Development Coaching: Christian Formation for the 21st Century* (Macon, GA: Nurturing Faith, 2013), 28.

29. American Association of Pastoral Counselors, accessed December 10, 2017, http://www.aapc.org/.

8. PHYSICAL SELF-CARE

1. Steve S. Ilardi, *The Depression Cure* (Cambridge, MA: Da Capo Press, 2009), viii.

2. Rae Jean Proeschold-Bell and Sara H. LeGrand, "High Rates of Obesity and Chronic Disease Among United Methodist Clergy," *Obesity* 18, no. 9 (September 2010): 1867, accessed December 17, 2017, http://onlinelibrary.wiley.com/doi/10.1038/oby.2010.102/epdf.

3. Hannah Nichols, "The Top 10 Leading Causes of Death in the United States," *Medical News Today*, February 23, 2017, accessed December 30, 2017, https://www.medicalnewstoday.com/articles/282929.php.

4. Rae Jean Proeschold-Bell, "A Holistic Approach to Wellness," *Faith and Leadership*, August 3, 2009, accessed December 1, 2017, https://www.faithandleadership.com/holistic-approach-wellness.

5. G. W. Halaas, *Ministerial Health and Wellness* (Chicago: Lutheran Church in America Division for Ministry, Board of Pensions, 2002), cited in Proeschold-Bell and LeGrand, "High Rates," 1867.

6. Duke Divinity Clergy Health Initiative, "What We're Learning: Mental Health Findings from the 2008 and 2010 Clergy Health Initiative Longitudinal Surveys," accessed December 1, 2017, http://divinity.duke.edu/sites/divinity.duke.edu/files/documents/chi/CHI%20Panel%20Survey%20Findings%20%282008%20and%202010%29.pdf.

7. Cindy Novak, "How Healthy Are Our Pastors?" *The Lutheran*, September 2002, accessed June 2, 2012, www.thelutheran.org/article/article.cfm?article_id=4464&key=19927294.

8. Sanjay R. Pate and Frank B. Hu, "Short Sleep Duration and Weight Gain: A Systematic Review," *Obesity* 16, no. 3 (March 2008): 643–653, accessed January 1, 2018, http://onlinelibrary.wiley.com/doi/10.1038/oby.2007.118/full.

9. Teresa of Avila, Goodreads Quotes, accessed December 8, 2017, https://www.goodreads.com/author/quotes/74226.Teresa_of_vila.

10. Paul Jewett, "Body," *Dictionary of Pastoral Care and Counseling*, expanded edition (Nashville: Abingdon Press, 2005), 101.

11. Jewett, "Body," *Dictionary*, 102.

12. Barbara Brown Taylor, *An Altar in the World: A Geography of Faith* (New York: HarperOne, 2009), 35–51.

13. Taylor, *An Altar in the World*, 38.

14. Taylor, *An Altar in the World*, 38.

15. Stephanie Paulsell, *Honoring the Body* (San Francisco, CA: Jossey-Bass, 2002), 18.

16. Paulsell, *Honoring*, 34.

17. Harvard T. H. Chan School of Public Health, "Staying Active," *The Nutrition Source*, accessed December 8, 2017, https://www.hsph.harvard.edu/nutritionsource/staying-active/.

18. Harvard T. H. Chan School of Public Health, "Physical Activity Guidelines: How Much Exercise Do You Need?" *The Nutrition Source*, accessed December 8, 2017, https://www.hsph. harvard.edu/nutritionsource/2013/11/20/physical-activity-guidelines-how-much-exercise-do-you-need/.

19. Herbert Benson and Eileen Stuart, *The Wellness Book: The Comprehensive Guide to Maintaining Health and Treating Stress-Related Illness* (New York: Birch Lane Press, 1992), 106.

20. Ilardi, *Depression Cure*, 116–117.

21. I. M. Lee, H. D. Sesso, Y. Oguma, and R. S. Paffenbarger Jr., "Relative Intensity of Physical Activity and Risk of Coronary Heart Disease," *Circulation* 107 (2007): 1110–1116, cited by Harvard School of Public Health, "The Benefits of Physical Activity," *The Nutrition Source*, accessed June 3, 2012, https://www.hsph.harvard.edu/nutritionsource/staying-active-full-story/index.html.

22. Marc T. Hamilton, Genevieve N. Healy, David W. Dunstan, Theodore W. Zderic, and Neville Owen, "Too Little Exercise and Too Much Sitting," *Current Cardiovascular Risk Reports* 2 (July 2008): 292, accessed December 8, 2017, https://link.springer.com/article/10. 1007%2Fs12170-008-0054-8?LI=true.

23. Ilardi, *Depression Cure*, 127.

24. Paulsell, *Honoring*, 127.

25. Harvard T. H. Chan School of Public Health, "Healthy Eating Plate and Healthy Eating Pyramid," *The Nutrition Source*, accessed December 19, 2017, https://www.hsph.harvard.edu/nutritionsource/healthy-eating-plate/.

26. Ilardi, *Depression Cure*, 70–72.

27. Taylor, *An Altar in the World*, 79–80.

28. Ilardi, *Depression Cure*, 21.

29. Thomas Dekker, *The Gull's Hornbook* (1609), accessed January 1, 2018, http://www. bartleby.com/library/prose/1607.html.

30. Division of Sleep Medicine at Harvard Medical School, "Sleep and Disease Risk," accessed January 1, 2018, http://healthysleep.med.harvard.edu/healthy/matters/ consequences/ sleep-and-disease-risk.

31. Russell Foster, interview, University of Oxford website, accessed December 9, 2017, http://www.ox.ac.uk/research/research-in-conversation/healthy-body-healthy-mind/russell-foster.

9. SELF-CARE THROUGH INNER WISDOM

1. Edwin H. Friedman, *Generation to Generation: Family Process in Church and Synagogue* (New York: The Guilford Press, 1985), 1.

2. As told by Margaret Marcuson, *Leaders Who Last: Sustaining Yourself and Your Ministry* (New York: Seabury Books, 2009), 36.

3. GenoPro. https://www.genopro.com.

4. Lisa Brookes, "What Is Family of Origin Work?" Love and Life Toolbox, December 17, 2016, accessed January 8, 2018, http://loveandlifetoolbox.com/what-is-family-of-origin-work/.

5. Margaret Marcuson, *Leaders*, 36–46.

6. Peter Scazzero, *Emotionally Healthy Spirituality* (Grand Rapids, MI: Zondervan, 2006), 106–108.

7. Scazzero, *Emotionally Healthy Spirituality*, 109.

8. Peter L. Steinke, *How Your Church Family Works: Understanding Congregations as Emotional Systems* (Bethesda, MD: Alban, 1993), 3–4.

9. Steinke, *How Your Church Family Works*, 4.

10. Friedman, *Generation*, 35.

11. As told in Arthur Paul Boers, *Never Call Them Jerks: Healthy Responses to Difficult Behavior* (Bethesda, MD: Alban, 1999), 86.

12. Boers, *Never Call Them Jerks,* 51.

13. Kathleen S. Smith, *Stilling the Storm: Worship and Congregational Leadership in Difficult Times* (Bethesda, MD: Alban, 2006), 139.

14. http://www.script-o-rama.com/movie_scripts/w/war-and-peace-script-transcript.html.

15. Friedman, *Generation*, 2–3.

16. Steinke, *How Your Church Family Works*, 12.

17. Steinke, *How Your Church Family Works*, 12.

18. As mentioned in Judith Beck, *Cognitive Therapy: Basics and Beyond* (New York: Guilford Press, 1995), 1, 14–15.

19. Beck, *Cognitive Therapy*, 166–169.

20. David Burns, *Feeling Good* (New York: Avon Books, 1980), 42–43.

21. As described in Ann Webster, Eileen M. Stuart, and Carol L. Wells-Federman, "How Thoughts Affect Health," in *The Wellness Book*, ed. Herbert Benson and Eileen Stuart (New York: Birch Lane Press, 1992), 194–195.

22. Webster, Stuart, and Wells-Federman, "How Thoughts Affect Health," 190.

23. Benson and Stuart, *Wellness Book*, 200.

24. Jon Kabat-Zinn, *Wherever You Go There You Are* (New York: Hyperion, 1994), 4.

25. Jon Kabat-Zinn, *Full Catastrophe Living: Using the Wisdom of Your Body and Mind to Face Stress, Pain and Illness* (New York: Delacourt Press, 2005), 2.

26. *Psychology Today*, "Mindfulness," accessed December 19, 2017, https://www.psychologytoday.com/basics/mindfulness.

27. Benson and Stuart, *Wellness Book*, 45–52; Elana Rosenbaum, *MSBR: Mindfulness Based Stress Reduction: Intensive 2-Day Workshop* (Eau Claire, WI: PESI: 2016), 70–71.

28. http://www.contemplativeoutreach.org/.

29. Rosenbaum, *MSBR*, 69–74.

30. Jay Dixit, "Back to the Present: How to Live in the Moment," *Psychology Today* (blog), December 17, 2008, accessed December 29, 2017, https://www.psychologytoday.com/blog/brainstorm/200812/back-the-present-how-live-in-the-moment.

31. Daphne M. Davis and Jeffrey A. Hayes, "What Are the Benefits of Mindfulness? A Practice Review of Psychotherapy-Related Research," *Psychotherapy* 48, no. 2 (2011): 198–208; Kirk A. Bingaman, "The Art of Contemplative and Mindfulness Practice: Incorporating the Findings of Neuroscience into Pastoral Care and Counseling," *Pastoral Psychology* 60 (2011): 477–489.

32. *Greater Good Magazine*, "Mindfulness: Why Practice It?" accessed December 19, 2017, https://greatergood.berkeley.edu/mindfulness/definition#why-practice.

33. S. Praissman, "Mindfulness-Based Stress Reduction: A Literature Review and Clinician's Guide," *Journal of the American Academy of Nurse Practitioners* 20, no. 4 (April 2008): 215; J. Cohen-Katz, S. D. Wiley, T. Capuano, D. M. Baker, S. Kimmel, and S. Shapiro, "The Effects of Mindfulness-Based Stress Reduction on Nurse Stress And Burnout," *Holistic Nursing Practice* 19 (2005): 26–35.

34. A. Newberg and M. R. Waldman, *How God Changes Your Brain: Breakthrough Findings from a Leading Neuroscientist* (New York: Ballantine Books, 2009), cited in Kirk A. Bingaman, "The Promise of Neuroplasticity for Pastoral Care and Counseling," *Pastoral Psychology* 62 (2013): 550–551.

35. Bingaman, "The Art of Contemplative and Mindfulness Practice," 483.

36. Bingaman, "The Art of Contemplative and Mindfulness Practice," 483.

37. Kristin Neff, "Definition of Self Compassion," *Self-Compassion*, accessed December 29, 2017, http://self-compassion.org/the-three-elements-of-self-compassion-2/#definition.

38. Kristin Neff and Oliver Davidson, "Self-Compassion: Embracing Suffering with Kindness," in *Mindfulness in Positive Psychology*, ed. I. Ivtzan and T. Lomas (New York: Routledge, 2016), 37–50. Accessible at http://self-compassion.org/wp-content/uploads/2016/07/Neff-and-Davidson.2016.pdf.

39. Kristin Neff, *Self-Compassion and Emotional Resilience* (Eau Claire, WI: PESI, 2015), 5.

40. Neff, *Self-Compassion*, 6.

41. http://self-compassion.org/category/exercises/#guided-meditations.

42. Sonja Lyubomirsky, *The How of Happiness* (New York: Penguin Books, 2007), 32.

43. Lyubomirsky, *How of Happiness*, 20–22.

44. Lyubomirsky, *How of Happiness*, 89.

45. Robert A. Emmons, *Thanks: How the New Science of Gratitude Can Make You Happier* (New York: Houghton Mifflin, 2007), 35.

46. Emmons, *Thanks*, 30–55.

47. Emmons, *Thanks*, 186.

48. Emmons, *Thanks*, 183–209; Robert A. Emmons, *Gratitude Works! A 21-Day Program for Creating Emotional Prosperity* (San Francisco, CA: Jossey-Bass, 2013).

10. SELF-CARE THROUGH LAUGHTER AND PLAY

1. Susan Sparks, *Laugh Your Way to Grace: Reclaiming the Spiritual Power of Humor* (Woodstock, VT: Skylight Paths, 2010), 6–7.

2. Sparks, *Laugh Your Way*, 6–7.

3. Richard P. Olson, *Laughter in a Time of Turmoil: Humor as Spiritual Practice* (Eugene, OR: Wipf and Stock, 2012).

4. Reported in Amy Frykholm, "The Pastors Are All Right," *Christian Century* 135, no. 10 (May 9, 2018): 23.

5. The Flourishing in Ministry Project, *Flourishing in Ministry: Emerging Research Insights on the Well-Being of Pastors* (Notre Dame, IN: University of Notre Dame, 2013), 20.

6. Flourishing in Ministry Project, *Flourishing in Ministry*, 50.

7. Wikipedia, "Flow (psychology)" accessed October 25, 2017, https://en.wikipedia.org/wiki/Flow_(psychology).

8. Martin E. P. Seligman, *Authentic Happiness: Using the New Positive Psychology to Realize Your Potential for Lasting Fulfillment* (New York: Free Press, 2002), 114.

9. Seligman, *Authentic Happiness*, 116.

10. Cynthia Lindner, "Multiple Mindedness and Ministerial Resilience," *Faith and Leadership*, November 19, 2012, accessed December 28, 2017, https://www.faithandleadership.com/content/cynthia-lindner-multiple-mindedness-and-ministerial-resilience.

11. As quoted in Daniel Amen, *Making a Good Brain Great* (New York: Harmony, 2005), 175.

12. As quoted in Leonard Sweet, *The Jesus Prescription for a Healthy Life* (Nashville: Abingdon, 1996), 28.

13. Dr. Madan Kataria, TED Talk, accessed October 26, 2017, https://www.youtube.com/watch?v=5hf2umYCKr8.

14. Evan Esar, *The Humor of Humor* (New York: Horizon, 1952).

15. Peter L. Berger, *Redeeming Laughter: The Comic Dimension of Human Experience* (New York: Walter De Gruyter, 1997).

16. Berger, *Redeeming Laughter*, 99.

17. Berger, *Redeeming Laughter*, 107.

18. Berger, *Redeeming Laughter*, 117.

19. As quoted in Tom Mullen, *Laughing Out Loud and Other Religious Experiences* (Richmond, IN: Friends United Press, 1989), 113.

20. Victor Frankl, *Man's Search for Meaning* (New York: Washington Square, 1959), 63–64.

21. Berger, *Redeeming Laughter*, 136.

22. As quoted in Berger, *Redeeming Laughter*, 129.

23. Berger, *Redeeming Laughter*, 157.

24. Berger, *Redeeming Laughter*, 157.

25. Sparks, *Laugh Your Way*, 124.

26. Sparks, *Laugh Your Way*, 124.

27. Robert McAfee Brown, *Creative Dislocation—The Movement of Grace* (Nashville: Abingdon, 1980), 134.

28. Berger, *Redeeming Laughter*, 205.

29. Annette Goodheart, *Laughter Therapy: How to Laugh About Everything in Your Life That Isn't Really Funny* (Santa Barbara, CA: Less Stress Press, 1994), 125–129.

30. John Louis Anderson, *Scandinavian Humor and Other Myths* (Minneapolis: Nordbook, 1986).

31. William Barclay, *The Gospel of Luke*, cited on Goodreads, accessed January 22, 2018, https://www.goodreads.com/quotes/227447-jesus-promised-his-disciples-three-things-that-they-would-be-completely.

11. FINANCIAL SELF-CARE

1. Lynne Twist, *The Soul of Money* (New York: W.W. Norton, 2003), 17.

2. Walter Brueggemann, *Money and Possessions, Interpretation Series* (Louisville: Westminster John Knox, 2016), 11.

3. David Gortner, *Clergy Leadership for the 21st Century*, White Paper, Virginia Theological Seminary, 2014, accessed April 27, 2017, http://into-action.net/wp-content/uploads/2014/06/Report-4-Clergy-Leadership-for-the-21st-Century-Are-We-Up-to-the-Task.pdf.

4. Lifeway Research, *Pastor Protection Research Study*, accessed April 27, 2017, http://lifewayresearch.com/wp-content/uploads/2016/01/Pastor-Protection-Former-Pastor-Survey-Report.pdf.

5. Kay Warren, "Who Pastors the Pastor? Even Ministers Suffer from Suicidal Thoughts," *Washington Post*, April 21, 2017, accessed April 27, 2017, https://www.washingtonpost.com/news/acts-of-faith/wp/2017/04/21/who-pastors-the-pastor-even-ministers-suffer-from-suicidal-thoughts/?utm_term=.37e351edb0c0.

6. Mary Pilon, "Student-Loan Debt Surpasses Credit Cards," *Wall Street Journal*, August 9, 2010, accessed October 21, 2017, https://blogs.wsj.com/economics/2010/08/09/student-loan-debt-surpasses-credit-cards/.

7. David R. Wheeler, "Higher Calling, Lower Wages: The Collapse of the Middle Class Clergy," *The Atlantic*, July 22, 2014, accessed October 21, 2017, https://www.theatlantic.com/business/archive/2014/07/higher-calling-lower-wages-the-collapse-of-the-middle-class-clergy/374786/.

8. PayScale: Human Capital, accessed October 17, 2017, https://www.payscale.com/data-packages/most-and-least-meaningful-jobs/full-list.

9. Twist, *Soul*, 17.

10. Jo Ann Deasy, Preconference Workshop at the ATS "Economic Challenges Facing Future Ministers" Gathering, Pittsburgh, October 2017.

11. Margaret Marcuson, *Money and Your Ministry* (Portland: Marcuson Leadership Circle, 2014), 79.

12. Twist, *Soul*, 120.

13. Twist, *Soul*, 121.

14. The Rev. Peter Marshall, United States Congressional Serial Set, Prayers Offered by the Chaplain at the Opening of Daily Sessions of Senate During 80th Congress 1947–1948, Senate Document 170, 80th Congress, Second Session (prayer dated Friday, April 18, 1947), (Washington, DC: Government Printing Office), 20, accessed January 25, 2018, https://quoteinvestigator.com/2014/02/18/stand-fall/.

15. Luke Timothy Johnson, *Sharing Possessions: What Faith Demands* (Grand Rapids, MI: Wm. B. Eerdmans, 2011).

16. Henri Nouwen, *The Spirituality of Fundraising* (Nashville: Upper Room, 2011).

17. Kerry Alys Robinson, *Imagining Abundance* (Collegeville, MN: Order of Saint Benedict, 2014).

18. Twist, *Soul*, 111.

19. John Wesley, "The Use of Money (Sermon 50)," accessed October 21, 2017, http://www.umcmission.org/Find-Resources/John-Wesley-Sermons/Sermon-50-The-Use-of-Money.

20. Christian Smith and Hilary Davidson, *The Paradox of Generosity: Giving We Receive, Grasping We Lose* (New York: Oxford University Press, 2014), Kindle, loc. 63.

21. Smith and Davidson, *Paradox*, loc. 72.

22. Smith and Davidson, *Paradox*, loc. 212.

12. INTELLECTUAL SELF-CARE

1. Ellen M. Umansky and Dianne Ashton, eds., *Four Centuries of Jewish Women's Spirituality: A Sourcebook* (Waltham, MA: Brandeis University Press, 2009), 295.

2. Dwight L. Moody, *Pleasure and Profit in Bible Study and Anecdotes*, cited on Goodreads, accessed October 22, 2017, https://www.goodreads.com/work/quotes/26778030-pleasure-profit-in-bible-study.

3. Richard N. Bolles, *What Color Is Your Parachute?* (Berkeley: Ten Speed Press, 2003).

4. Richard N. Bolles, *The Three Boxes of Life and How to Get Out of Them* (Berkeley: Ten Speed Press, 1978).

5. Christoforos Pappas, "The Adult Learning Theory—Andragogy—of Malcolm Knowles," eLearning Industry, May 9, 2013, accessed October 17, 2017, https://elearningindustry.com/the-adult-learning-theory-andragogy-of-malcolm-knowles.

6. "Left Brain vs. Right Brain," Diffen, accessed October 1, 2017, http://www.diffen.com/difference/Left_Brain_vs_Right_Brain.

7. Virginia Fortner, correspondence with Dick Olson, May 19, 2017.

8. Lindamood-Bell Learning Processes, accessed October 22, 2017, http://lindamoodbell.com/.

9. Open Culture, accessed October 22, 2017, http://www.openculture.com/freeonline courses.

10. David May, conversation with Dick Olson, May 8, 2017.

11. The Ministry Development Council, accessed October 22, 2017, http://ministrydevelopment.org/index.html.

12. As reported in A. Richard Bullock and Richard J. Bruesehoff, *Clergy Renewal: The Alban Guide to Sabbatical Planning* (Bethesda, MD: Alban, 2000), 19.

13. Melissa Bane Sevier, *Journey Toward Renewal: A Spiritual Companion for Pastoral Sabbaticals* (Bethesda, MD: Alban, 2002), 10–11.

14. Greg Hunt, conversation with Dick Olson, May 17, 2017.

15. Center for Pastoral Excellence, "Lilly Endowment Clergy Renewal Programs," accessed October 22, 2017, http://cpx.cts.edu/renewal.

16. Louisville Institute for Pastoral Study, "Our Programs," accessed October 22, 2017, https://louisville-institute.org/programs-grants-and-fellowships/.

17. Laura Rodgers Evans, "Curiosity Doesn't Kill Cats: Passion and Pragmatism for Adventurous Life-Long Learning," *Review and Expositor* 114, no. 3 (August 2017): 336–340.

13. BASIC STEPS TO SELF-CARE

1. As quoted in Amy Frykholm, "The Pastors Are All Right," *Christian Century* 135, no. 10 (May 9, 2018): 23.

2. Robert E. Alberti and Michael L. Emmons, *Your Perfect Right: A Guide to Assertive Living* (San Luis Obispo, CA: Impact Publishers, 1990), 7.

3. Alberti and Emmons, *Your Perfect Right*, 6.

4. Ruth N. Koch and Kenneth C. Haugk, *Speaking the Truth in Love: How to Be an Assertive Christian* (St. Louis: Stephen Ministries, 1992), 16–23.

5. As reported in Koch and Haugk, *Speaking the Truth in Love*, 116–118.

6. Robert L. Randall, *The Time of Your Life: Self/Time Management for Pastors* (Nashville: Abingdon Press, 1994), 11.

7. Randall, *Time of Your Life*, 11–12.

8. Randall, *Time of Your Life*, 24–27.

9. Heather Bradley and Miriam Bamberger Grogan, *Switch Off: The Clergy Guide to Preserving Energy and Passion for Ministry* (Nashville: Abingdon Press, 2016), 10.

10. Bradley and Grogan, *Switch Off*, 8–9.

11. Bradley and Grogan, *Switch Off*, 81–88.

12. Fred B. Craddock, *Preaching* (Nashville: Abingdon, 1985), 99–124.

13. Bruce Epperly, *A Center in the Cyclone* (Lanham, MD: Rowman & Littlefield, 2014), 57.

14. Jeremy Goldman, "6 Apps to Stop Your Smartphone Addiction," *Inc.*, October 21, 2015, accessed December 28, 2017, https://www.inc.com/jeremy-goldman/6-.apps-to-stop-your-smartphone-addiction.html.

15. Epperly, *Center in the Cyclone*, 58.

14. A THEOLOGY OF SELF-CARE

1. Charles R. Pinches, "How to Live in Hope," *The Christian Century* 134, no. 15 (July 29, 2017): 22–25, 24.

2. Gabriel Marcel, quoted in Andrew Lester, *Hope in Pastoral Care and Counseling* (Louisville: Westminster John Knox, 1995), 59.

3. Dee Dee Turlington and Michael Harvey, eds., *Learning Guide on the Covenant and Code of Ethics for Ministerial Leaders of American Baptist Churches*, November 2006, accessed January 8, 2018, http://ministerscouncil.com/wp-content/uploads/2013/03/Learning Guideontheethics06edited.pdf.

4. National Association of Evangelicals, "Code of Ethics for Pastors," June 2012, accessed January 8, 2018, http://www.nae.net/code-of-ethics-for-pastors/.

5. National Council of the Churches of Christ in the U.S.A., "A 21st-Century Social Creed," accessed January 8, 2018, http://nationalcouncilofchurches.us/christian-unity/a-21st-century-social-creed/.

6. American Association of Pastoral Counselors, "Looking Forward: AAPC Ethical Guidelines," accessed January 8, 2018, http://www.aapc.org/page/Ethics.

7. Edwin H. Friedman, *Generation to Generation: Family Process in Church and Synagogue* (New York: The Guilford Press, 1985).

8. Roy Oswald, *Clergy Self-Care: Finding a Balance for Effective Ministry* (Herndon, VA: Alban, 1991), 191.

9. Oswald, *Clergy Self-Care*, 3.

10. Julie Steenhuysen, "Pastor Who Banned Fried Chicken Leads Mississippi Obamacare Push," *Reuters*, October 27, 2013, accessed July 27, 2017, http://www.reuters.com/article/us-usa-healthcare-navigators-idUSBRE99Q03E20131027.

Bibliography

Alberti, Robert E., and Michael L. Emmons. *Your Perfect Right: A Guide to Assertive Living.* San Luis Obispo, CA: Impact Publishers, 1990.

Amen, Daniel. *Making a Good Brain Great.* New York: Harmony, 2005.

American Association of Pastoral Counselors. "Looking Forward: AAPC Ethical Guidelines." Accessed January 8, 2018. http://www.aapc.org/page/Ethics.

American Psychological Association. "Stress Weakens the Immune System." February 23, 2006. Accessed December 31, 2017. http://www.apa.org/ research/action/immune.aspx.

Anderson, John Louis. *Scandinavian Humor and Other Myths.* Minneapolis: Nordbook, 1986.

Association of Welcoming and Affirming Baptists. http://www.awab.org.

Banks, Adelle M. "Pastor-Mothers Balance Pulpit and Parenting." *Christian Century*, May 31, 2011, 15.

Bass, Dorothy C., ed. *Practicing Our Faith*, 2nd ed. San Francisco: Jossey-Bass, 1997, 2010.

Bass, Dorothy C., and Susan R. Briel, eds. *On Our Way: Christian Practices for Living a Whole Life.* Nashville: Upper Room Books, 2010.

Bass, Dorothy C., and Don C. Richter, eds. *Way to Live: Christian Practices for Teens.* Nashville: Upper Room Books, 2002.

Beck, Judith. *Cognitive Therapy: Basics and Beyond.* New York: Guilford Press, 1995.

Benson, Herbert, and Marg Stark. *Timeless Healing: The Power and Biology of Belief.* New York: Scribner, 1996.

Benson, Herbert, and Eileen Stuart. *The Wellness Book: The Comprehensive Guide to Maintaining Health and Treating Stress-Related Illness.* New York: Birch Lane Press, 1992.

Berger, Peter L. *Redeeming Laughter: The Comic Dimension of Human Experience.* New York: Walter De Gruyter, 1997.

Berkowitz, Gale. "2002 UCLA Study on Friendship Among Women." Accessed July 28, 2017. http://www.anapsid.org/cnd/gender/tendfend.html.

Bingaman, Kirk A. "The Art of Contemplative and Mindfulness Practice: Incorporating the Findings of Neuroscience into Pastoral Care and Counseling." *Pastoral Psychology* 60 (2011).

———. "The Promise of Neuroplasticity for Pastoral Care and Counseling." *Pastoral Psychology* 62 (2013).

Boers, Arthur Paul. *Never Call Them Jerks: Healthy Responses to Difficult Behavior.* Bethesda, MD: Alban, 1999.

Bolles, Richard N. *The Three Boxes of Life and How to Get Out of Them.* Berkeley: Ten Speed Press, 1978.

———. *What Color Is Your Parachute?* Berkeley: Ten Speed Press, 2003.

Borysenko, Joan. *It's Not the End of the World: Developing Resilience in Times of Change.* Carlsbad, CA: Hay House, 2009.

Boss, Pauline. *Loss, Trauma, and Resilience: Therapeutic Work with Ambiguous Loss.* New York: W.W. Norton Company, 2006.

Bowden, Paul, ed. *Telling It Like It is: A Book of Quotations.* Seattle: CreateSpace, 2011.

Boyice, Dionne. Interview with Angela Jackson. November 9, 2017.

Bradley, Heather, and Miriam Bamberger Grogan. *Switch Off: The Clergy Guide to Preserving Energy and Passion for Ministry.* Nashville: Abingdon Press, 2016.

Brookes, Lisa. "What Is Family of Origin Work?" Love and Life Toolbox. December 17, 2016. Accessed January 8, 2018. http://loveandlifetoolbox.com/what-is-family-of-origin-work/.

Brown, Robert McAfee. *Creative Dislocation—The Movement of Grace.* Nashville: Abingdon, 1980.

Brueggemann, Walter. *Money and Possessions, Interpretation Series.* Louisville: Westminster John Knox, 2016.

Buechner, Frederick. *Wishful Thinking: A Theological ABC.* New York: HarperOne, 1973.

Bullock, A. Richard, and Richard J. Bruesehoff, *Clergy Renewal: The Alban Guide to Sabbatical Planning.* Bethesda, MD: Alban, 2000.

Burns, David. *Feeling Good.* New York: Avon Books, 1980.

Carey, Peter. *Santos Woodcarving Popsicles* (blog). March 15, 2009. Accessed December 27, 2017. http://santospopsicles.blogspot.com/2009/03/every-500-years-church-has-rummage-sale.html.

Carter, Terrell. Personal conversation with Dick Olson. April 19, 2017.

Center for Lesbian and Gay Studies. https://clgs.org/about-clgs/.

Center for Pastoral Excellence. "Lilly Endowment Clergy Renewal Programs." Accessed October 22, 2017. http://cpx.cts.edu/renewal.

Center for Spirituality and Healing, University of Minnesota. "How Does Nature Impact Our Wellbeing?" Accessed June 17, 2016. https://www.takingcharge.csh.umn.edu/enhance-your-wellbeing/environment/nature-and-us/how-does-nature-impact-our-wellbeing.

Chang, Patricia M. Y. "Factors Shaping Clergy Careers: A Wakeup Call for Protestant Denominations and Pastors." *Pulpit and Pew*, Duke Divinity School, 2005.

Chapman, Gary. *The 5 Love Languages: The Secret to Love That Lasts.* Chicago: Northfield Publishing, 2015.

Cohen, Sheldon, Denise Janick-Deverts, and Gregory E. Miller. "Psychological Stress and Disease." *JAMA (Journal of the American Medical Association)* 298, no. 14 (October 10, 2007). Accessed December 31, 2017. http://sites.northwestern.edu/foundationsofhealth/files/ 2013/03/07-JAMA-Psychological-stress-disease.pdf.

Cohen-Katz, J., S. D. Wiley, T. Capuano, D. M. Baker, S. Kimmel, and S. Shapiro. "The Effects of Mindfulness-Based Stress Reduction on Nurse Stress and Burnout." *Holistic Nursing Practice* 19 (2005).

Compassion Fatigue Awareness Project. Accessed November 10, 2017. http://www.compassionfatigue.org/pages/selftest.html.

Connelly, Marc. *The Green Pastures.* Music by Hal Johnson. Produced by Laurence Rivers, Inc. Mansfield Theater, New York, February 26, 1930–August 29, 1931.

Consulting Psychologists Press. Accessed November 10, 2017. https://www.cpp.com.

Contemplative Outreach. http://www.contemplativeoutreach.org/.

Coutu, Diane. "How Resilience Works." *Harvard Business Review*, May 2002.

Craddock, Fred B. *Preaching.* Nashville: Abingdon, 1985.

Crow, Greg. "Region, Role, and Size as Risk Factors in Clergy Attrition." Association of Nazarene Sociologists and Researchers conference. March 26, 2010. Crowne Plaza Hotel, Lenexa, KS.

Daniel, Lillian. "The Rough Edges of Holy Friendship." *Faith and Leadership.* Accessed April 10, 2017. https://www.faithandleadership.com/programs/spe/resources/dukediv-friendship.html.

"Daughters Provide as Much Elderly Parent Care as They Can, Sons Do as Little as Possible." *American Sociological Association News.* Accessed on July 28, 2017. http://www.

newswise.com/articles/daughters-provide-as-much-elderly-parent-care-as-they-can-sons-do-as-little-as-possible.

Davis, Daphne M., and Jeffrey A. Hayes. "What Are the Benefits of Mindfulness? A Practice Review of Psychotherapy-Related Research." *Psychotherapy* 48, no. 2 (2011).

Deasy, Jo Ann. "How 2016 Graduates Are Faring," Association of Theological Schools, Commission on Accrediting. November 2016.

———. Preconference Workshop at the ATS "Economic Challenges Facing Future Ministers" Gathering. Pittsburgh, October 2017.

Dekker, Thomas. *The Gull's Hornbook* (1609). Accessed January 1, 2018. http://www.bartleby.com/library/prose/1607.html.

Division of Sleep Medicine at Harvard Medical School. "Sleep and Disease Risk." Accessed January 1, 2018. http://healthysleep.med.harvard.edu/healthy/matters/consequences/sleep-and-disease-risk.

Dixit, Jay. "Back to the Present: How to Live in the Moment." *Psychology Today* (blog). December 17, 2008. Accessed December 29, 2017. https://www.psychologytoday.com/blog/brainstorm/200812/back-the-present-how-live-in-the-moment.

Donahue, John. *Anam Cara: A Book of Celtic Wisdom*. New York: Harper Perennial, 1997.

Duke Divinity Clergy Health Initiative. "What We're Learning: Mental Health Findings from the 2008 and 2010 Clergy Health Initiative Longitudinal Surveys." Accessed December 1, 2017. http://divinity.duke.edu/sites/divinity.duke.edu/files/documents/chi/CHI%20Panel%20Survey%20Findings%20%282008%20and%202010%29.pdf.

Ebner, Gwen. *WHOLEness for Spiritual Leaders*. Seattle: CreateSpace, 2009.

Edwards, Dan. "The Great Emergence by Phyllis Tickle." *Bishop Dan's Blog*. March 15, 2009. Accessed July 13, 2017. http://bishopdansblog.blogspot.com/2009/03/great-emergence-by-phyllis-tickle.html.

Emmons, Robert A. *Gratitude Works! A 21-Day Program for Creating Emotional Prosperity*. San Francisco, CA: Jossey-Bass, 2013.

———. *Thanks: How the New Science of Gratitude Can Make You Happier*. New York: Houghton Mifflin, 2007.

Epperly, Bruce. *A Center in the Cyclone*. Lanham, MD: Rowman & Littlefield, 2014.

Epperly, Bruce G., and Katherine Gould Epperly. *Four Seasons of Ministry: Gathering a Harvest of Righteousness*. Bethesda, MD: Alban, 2008.

———. *Tending to the Holy: The Practice of the Presence of God in Ministry*. Herndon, VA: Alban, 2009.

Esar, Evan. *The Humor of Humor*. New York: Horizon, 1952.

Evans, Laura Rodgers. "Curiosity Doesn't Kill Cats: Passion and Pragmatism for Adventurous Life-Long Learning." *Review and Expositor* 114, no. 3 (August 2017).

Everett, Laura. *Holy Spokes: The Search for Urban Spirituality on Two Wheels*. Grand Rapids, MI: Wm. B. Eerdmans, 2017.

Faith and Leadership. "Laura Everett: Riding My Bicycle Is a Spiritual Discipline." August 8, 2017. Accessed January 12, 2018. https://www.faithandleadership.com/laura-everett-riding-my-bicycle-spiritual-discipline.

Flourishing in Ministry Project. *Flourishing in Ministry: Emerging Research Insights on the Well-Being of Pastors*. Notre Dame, IN: University of Notre Dame, 2013.

Fogoros, Richard N. "An Overview of Atherosclerosis." *Verywell*. August 7, 2017. Accessed December 31, 2017. https://www.verywell.com/what-is-atherosclerosis-1745908.

Fortner, Virginia. Personal correspondence with Dick Olson. May 19, 2017.

Foster, Richard. *Celebration of Discipline*. New York: HarperCollins, 1978.

Foster, Russell. Interview. University of Oxford website. Accessed December 9, 2017. http://www.ox.ac.uk/research/research-in-conversation/healthy-body-healthy-mind/russell-foster.

Frame, Marsha Wiggins, and Constance L. Sheham. "Care for the Care Giver: Clues for the Pastoral Care of Clergywomen." *Pastoral Psychology* 52, no. 5 (May 2004): 369–380.

Frankl, Victor. *Man's Search for Meaning*. New York: Washington Square, 1959.

Freeman, Joy M., and Tabatha Johnson, eds. *Still a Mother: Journeys through Perinatal Bereavement*. Valley Forge, PA: Judson Press, 2016.

Friedman, Edwin H. *Generation to Generation: Family Process in Church and Synagogue*. New York: The Guilford Press, 1985.

Fryckholm, Amy. "The Pastors Are All Right." *Christian Century* 135, no. 10 (May 9, 2018): 23.

Galloway, John, Jr. *Ministry Loves Company: A Survival Guide for Pastors*. Louisville: Westminster John Knox, 2003.

GenoPro. https://www.genopro.com.

Gilbert, Paul. *Overcoming Depression*. New York: Oxford University Press, 2001.

Gill, J. "Burnout: A Growing Threat in the Ministry." *Human Development* 1, no. 2 (Summer 1980): 22.

Goldman, Jeremy. "6 Apps to Stop Your Smartphone Addiction." *Inc.* (website), October 21, 2015. Accessed December 28, 2017. https://www.inc.com/jeremy-goldman/6-apps-to-stop-your-smartphone-addiction.html.

Goodheart, Annette. *Laughter Therapy: How to Laugh About Everything in Your Life That Isn't Really Funny*. Santa Barbara, CA: Less Stress Press, 1994.

Gortner, David. *Clergy Leadership for the 21st Century*. White Paper, Virginia Theological Seminary. 2014. Accessed April 27, 2017. http://into-action.net/wp-content/uploads/2014/06/Report-4-Clergy-Leadership-for-the-21st-Century-Are-We-Up-to-the-Task.pdf.

Granberg-Michaelson, Wesley. "An Anchor in the Storm." *Sojourners* 46, no. 4 (April 2017): 15–17.

Greater Good Magazine. "Mindfulness: Why Practice It?" Accessed December 19, 2017. https://greatergood.berkeley.edu/mindfulness/definition#why-practice.

Halaas, G. W. *Ministerial Health and Wellness*. Chicago: Lutheran Church in America Division for Ministry, Board of Pensions, 2002.

Hamel, Gregory. "Problems That Past Lottery Winners Have Faced," *Pocket Sense*. Accessed December 26, 2017. https://pocketsense.com/problems-past-lottery-winners-faced-8708.html.

Hamilton, Marc T., Genevieve N. Healy, David W. Dunstan, Theodore W. Zderic, and Neville Owen. "Too Little Exercise and Too Much Sitting." *Current Cardiovascular Risk Reports* 2 (July 2008): 292. Accessed December 8, 2017. https://link.springer.com/article/10.1007%2Fs12170-008-0054-8?LI=true.

Harvard T. H. Chan School of Public Health. "Healthy Eating Plate and Healthy Eating Pyramid." *The Nutrition Source*. Accessed December 19, 2017. https://www.hsph.harvard.edu/nutritionsource/healthy-eating-plate/.

———. "Physical Activity Guidelines: How Much Exercise Do You Need?" *The Nutrition Source*. Accessed December 8, 2017. https://www.hsph.harvard.edu/nutritionsource/2013/11/20/physical-activity-guidelines-how-much-exercise-do-you-need/.

———. "Staying Active." *The Nutrition Source*. Accessed December 8, 2017. https://www.hsph.harvard.edu/nutritionsource/staying-active/.

Hays, Edward. *Pray All Ways*. Leavenworth, KS: Forest of Peace, 1981.

Heifetz, Ronald A., and Marty Linsky. *Leadership on the Line*. Boston: Harvard Business Review Press, 2002.

Henderson, Nan. "What Is Resiliency, and Why Is It So Important?" *Resiliency in Action* (blog). November 2, 2012. Accessed December 26, 2017. https://www.resiliency.com/blog/.

Herbert, Tracy B., and Sheldon Cohen. "Stress and Illness." *Encyclopedia of Human Behavior*, volume 4. Cambridge, MA: Academic Press, 1994. Accessed August 12, 2017. http://kungfu.psy.cmu.edu/~scohen/encyclo94.pdf.

———. "Understanding the Stress Response." Harvard Health Publishing. 1994. Accessed December 31, 2017. https://www.health.harvard.edu/staying-healthy/understanding-the-stress-response.

Hill, Denise, Mark Jeske, and Maureen Kelly. "Compassion Fatigue." PowerPoint provided to the authors. October 6, 2017.

Hunt, Greg. Personal conversation with Dick Olson. May 17, 2017.

Ilardi, Stephen S. *The Depression Cure*. Cambridge, MA: Da Capo Press, 2009.

———. "The Diagnosis and Treatment of Depression: A Lifestyle-Based Approach." Continuing education workshop sponsored by Saint Luke's Health System. March 11, 2015.

Institute for Welcoming Resources. http://www.welcomingresources.org.

Jewett, Paul. "Body." *Dictionary of Pastoral Care and Counseling*, expanded ed. Nashville: Abingdon Press, 2005.

Jin, Young Sun. "A Study of Pastoral Burnout Among Korean-American Pastors" DMin Thesis, Liberty Theological Seminary, 26–53. http://digitalcommons.liberty.edu/doctoral/146/.

Johnson, Ben Campbell. *Hearing God's Call: Ways of Discernment for Laity and Clergy.* Grand Rapids, MI: Wm. B. Eerdmans, 2002.

Johnson, Luke Timothy. *Sharing Possessions: What Faith Demands.* Grand Rapids, MI: Wm. B. Eerdmans, 2011.

Jones, Jeffrey D. *Facing Decline, Finding Hope: New Possibilities for Faithful Churches.* Lanham, MD: Rowman & Littlefield, 2015.

Jones, Kirk Byron. *Rest in the Storm: Self-Care Strategies for Clergy and Other Caregivers.* Valley Forge, PA: Judson, 2001.

Jordan, L. G., A. M. Townsend, and E. W. D. Issac. *The Baptist Standard Church Directory and Busy Pastor's Guide.* Nashville: Sunday School Publishing Board, 1993.

Kabat-Zinn, Jon. *Full Catastrophe Living: Using the Wisdom of Your Body and Mind to Face Stress, Pain and Illness.* New York: Delacourt Press, 2005.

———. *Wherever You Go There You Are.* New York: Hyperion, 1994.

Kataria, Madan. "TED Talk." https://www.youtube.com/watch?v=5hf2umYCKr8.

Keen, Sam. *Fire in the Belly: On Being a Man.* New York: Bantam Books, 1991.

Kelly, Scott. Interview with Rachel Martin. NPR's Morning Edition, October 17, 2017. Accessed May 31, 2018. https://www.npr.org/2017/10/17/558055466/astronaut-scott-kellys-latest-mission-a-book.

Kelly, Scott, and Margaret Lazarus Dean. *Endurance: A Year in Space, A Lifetime of Discovery.* New York: Alfred A. Knopf, 2017.

Kinnaman, Gary D., and Alfred H. Ells. *Leaders That Last: How Covenant Friendships Can Help Pastors Thrive.* Ada, MI: Baker Books, 2003.

Koch, Ruth N., and Kenneth C. Haugk. *Speaking the Truth in Love: How to Be an Assertive Christian.* St. Louis: Stephen Ministries, 1992.

Krejcir, Richard. "Statistics on Pastors: 2016 Update." Francis A. Schaeffer Institute of Church Leadership Development. Accessed February 15, 2017. http://files.stablerack.com/webfiles/71795/pastorsstatWP2016.pdf.

Kruger, Tyler Lee. *Keys to Resilient Practice in Contemporary Chaplaincy.* DMin Dissertation, Lancaster Theological Seminary, 2010.

Kundtz, David J., and Bernard S. Schlager. *Ministry Among God's Queer Folk.* Cleveland: The Pilgrim Press, 2007.

Kurtz, Ernest, and Katherine Ketcham. *The Spirituality of Imperfection: Storytelling and the Search for Meaning.* New York: Bantam Books, 1992.

Lakein, Alan. *How to Get Control of Your Time and Your Life.* New York: New American Library, 1973.

Landgraf, John. *Singling: A New Way to Live the Single Life.* Louisville: Westminster John Knox, 1990.

Leas, Speed B. *Time Management: A Working Guide for Church Leaders.* Nashville: Abingdon Press, 1978.

Lee, I. M., H. D. Sesso, Y. Oguma, and R. S. Paffenbarger Jr. "Relative Intensity of Physical Activity and Risk of Coronary Heart Disease." *Circulation* 107 (2007): 1110–6. Cited by Harvard School of Public Health. "The Benefits of Physical Activity." *The Nutrition Source.* Accessed June 3, 2012. https://www.hsph.harvard.edu/nutritionsource/staying-active/staying-active-full-story/index.html.

"Left Brain vs. Right Brain." Diffen. Accessed October 1, 2017. http://www.diffen.com/difference/Left_Brain_vs_Right_Brain.

Lehman, Edward C. 2002. "Women's Path into Ministry: Six Major Studies." *Pulpit and Pew: Research on Pastoral Leadership* 1: 1–48.

Lehr, Fred. *Clergy Burnout: Recovering from the 70-Hour Work Week and Other Self-Defeating Practices.* Minneapolis: Fortress, 2006.

Lester, Andrew. *Hope in Pastoral Care and Counseling*. Louisville: Westminster John Knox, 1995.

Levinson, Daniel J., with Charlotte N. Darrow, Edward B. Klein, Maria H. Levinson, and Braxton McKee. *The Seasons of a Man's Life*. New York: Alfred A. Knopf, 1978.

Lifeway Research. *Pastor Protection Research Study*. Accessed April 27, 2017. http://lifewayresearch.com/wp-content/uploads/2016/01/Pastor-Protection-Former-Pastor-Survey-Report.pdf.

Lindamood-Bell Learning Processes. http://lindamoodbell.com/.

Lindner, Cynthia. "Multiple Mindedness and Ministerial Resilience." *Faith and Leadership*. November 19, 2012. Accessed December 28, 2017. https://www.faithandleadership.com/content/cynthia-lindner-multiple-mindedness-and-ministerial-resilience.

London, H. B., Jr., and Neil B. Wiseman. *Pastors at Greater Risk*. Ventura, CA: Gospel Light, 2003.

Louisville Institute for Pastoral Study. "Our Programs." Accessed October 22, 2017. https://louisville-institute.org/programs-grants-and-fellowships.

Louv, Richard. *The Nature Principle*. Cited by Lecia Bushak, "Benefits of Ecotherapy: Being in Nature Fights Depression, Improves Mental Health and Well-Being." *Medical Daily*, October 26, 2013. Accessed June 2, 2016. http://www.medicaldaily.com/benefits-ecotherapy-being-nature-fights-depression-improves-mental-health-and-well-being-261075.

Lyubomirsky, Sonja. *The How of Happiness*. New York: Penguin Books, 2007.

MacDonald, G. Jeffrey. "Move to Part-Time Clergy Sparks Innovation in Congregations." *Faith and Leadership*. March 21, 2017. Accessed December 26, 2017. https://www.faithandleadership.com/move-part-time-clergy-sparks-innovation-congregations?utm_source=albanweekly&utm_medium=content&utm_campaign=faithleadership.

Mahlberg, Arden. "Getting Our Bearings: Sabbath Reorients Clergy to God and to the World." *Sustaining Pastoral Excellence*. Accessed March 15, 2017. https://www.faithandleadership.com/programs/spe/articles/200707/bearings.html.

Malakh Pines, Ayala, Elliot Aronson, and Ditsa Kafry. *Burnout: From Tedium to Personal Growth*. New York: Free Press, 1981.

Marchand, Chris. *An Investigation of the Influence of Compassion Fatigue due to Secondary Traumatic Stress on the Canadian Youth Worker*. DMin Dissertation, Providence Seminary, 2007.

Marcuson, Margaret. *Leaders Who Last: Sustaining Yourself and Your Ministry*. New York: Seabury Books, 2009.

———. *Money and Your Ministry*. Portland: Marcuson Leadership Circle, 2014.

Marshall, The Rev. Peter. U.S. Congressional Serial Set. Prayers Offered by the Chaplain at the Opening of Daily Sessions of Senate During 80th Congress 1947-1948. Senate Document 170, page 20. 80th Congress, Second Session. Friday, April 18, 1947. Washington, DC: Government Printing Office. Accessed January 25, 2018. https://quoteinvestigator.com/2014/02/18/stand-fall/.

Martinez, Jose R. Chaplain 139th Airlift Wing, Air National Guard. Personal correspondence with Dick Olson. December 23, 2017.

Masci, David. "The Divide Over Ordaining Women." The Pew Research Center. September 9, 2014. Accessed July 28, 2017. http://www.pewresearch.org/fact-tank/2014/09/09/the-divide-over-ordaining-women/#comments.

Maslach, Christina, and Michael P. Leiter. *The Truth About Burnout: How Organizations Cause Personal Stress and What to Do About It*. San Francisco: Jossey-Bass, 1997.

May, David. Personal conversation with Dick Olson. May 8, 2017.

McGonigal, Kelly. *The Upside of Stress*. New York: Avery, 2016.

Meek, K., M. McMinn, C. Brower et al. "Maintaining Personal Resilience: Lessons Learned from Evangelical Protestant Clergy." *Journal of Theology and Psychology* 313, no. 4 (2009): 339–347.

Meier, Bethany. Interview with Angela Jackson. November 8, 2017.

Melander, Rochelle, and Harold Eppley. *The Spiritual Leader's Guide to Self-Care*. Bethesda, MD: Alban, 2001.

Mercadante, Linda A. *Belief without Borders: Inside the Minds of the Spiritual but Not Religious*. New York: Oxford University Press, 2014.

Michael, Cheer P., and Marice C. Norrisey. *Prayer and Temperament: Different Prayer Forms for Different Personality Types*. Charlottesville, VA: The Open Door, 1991.

Micheli, Jason. *Cancer Is Funny: Keeping Faith in Stage-Serious Chemo*. Minneapolis: Fortress Press, 2016.

Miller, Emily McFarlan. "Survey Reveals Public's Skepticism about Pastors." *Christian Century* 14, no. 5 (March 1, 2017): 13.

Miller-McLemore, Bonnie J. "Two Views of Mothering: Birthing and Mothering as Powerful Rites of Passage." In *In Her Own Time*, ed. Jeanne Stevenson-Moessner, 175–189. Minneapolis: Fortress Press, 2000.

Ministers Council. "The Covenant and Code of Ethics with Learning Guide for Ministerial Leaders of American Baptist Churches." http://ministerscouncil.com/wp-content/uploads/2013/03/LearningGuideontheethics06edited.pdf.

Ministry Development Council. Accessed October 22, 2017. http://www.ministrydevelopment.org/index.html.

Moody, Dwight L. *Pleasure and Profit in Bible Study*. Cited on Goodreads. Accessed October 22, 2017. https://www.goodreads.com/work/quotes/26778030-pleasure-profit-in-bible-study.

Mullen, Tom. *Laughing Out Loud and Other Religious Experiences*. Richmond, IN: Friends United Press, 1989.

Muller, Wayne. *Sabbath: Finding Rest, Renewal and Delight in Our Busy Lives*. New York: Bantam Books, 1999.

National Association of Evangelicals. "Code of Ethics for Pastors." June 2012. Accessed January 8, 2018. http://www.nae.net/code-of-ethics-for-pastors/.

National Council of the Churches of Christ in the U.S.A. "A 21st-Century Social Creed." Accessed January 8, 2018. http://nationalcouncilofchurches.us/christian-unity/a-21st-century-social-creed/.

Neff, Kristin. "Definition of Self Compassion." *Self-Compassion*. Accessed December 29, 2017. http://self-compassion.org/the-three-elements-of-self-compassion-2/#definition.

———. *Self-Compassion and Emotional Resilience* (Eau Claire, WI: PESI, 2015).

Neff, Kristin, and Oliver Davidson. "Self-Compassion: Embracing Suffering with Kindness." In *Mindfulness in Positive Psychology*, ed. I. Ivtzan and T. Lomas. New York: Routledge, 2016. Accessible at http://self-compassion.org/wp-content/uploads/2016/07/Neff-and-Davidson.2016.pdf.

Newberg, A., and M. R. Waldman. *How God Changes Your Brain: Breakthrough Findings from a Leading Neuroscientist*. New York: Ballantine Books, 2009.

Nichols, Hannah. "The Top 10 Leading Causes of Death in the United States." *Medical News Today*, February 23, 2017. Accessed December 30, 2017. https://www.medicalnewstoday.com/articles/282929.php.

Nouwen, Henri. *Sabbatical Journey*. New York: Crossroad Publishing Company, 1998.

———. *The Spirituality of Fundraising*. Nashville: Upper Room, 2011.

Novak, Cindy. "How Healthy Are Our Pastors?" *The Lutheran*, September 2002. Accessed June 2, 2012. www.thelutheran.org/article/article.cfm?article_id=4464&key=19927294.

Olson, Richard P. *Laughter in a Time of Turmoil: Humor as Spiritual Practice*. Eugene, OR: Wipf and Stock, 2012.

Open Culture. http://www.openculture.com/freeonlinecourses.

Oswald, Roy. *Clergy Self-Care: Finding a Balance for Effective Ministry*. Herndon, VA: Alban, 1991.

Pappas, Christoforos. "The Adult Learning Theory—Andragogy—of Malcolm Knowles." eLearning Industry. May 9, 2013. Accessed October 17, 2017. https://elearningindustry.com/the-adult-learning-theory-andragogy-of-malcolm-knowles.

Park, Samuel. Personal conversation with Dick Olson. May 11, 2017.

Pastoral Attrition Action Learning Team (PAALT). *Report on Our Survey*, 5th ed. Valley Forge, PA: American Baptist Minsters Council, June 9, 2015.

Pate, Sanjay R., and Frank B. Hu. "Short Sleep Duration and Weight Gain: A Systematic Review." *Obesity* 16, no. 3 (March 2008): 643–653. Accessed January 1, 2018. http://onlinelibrary.wiley.com/doi/10.1038/oby.2007.118/full.

Paulsell, Stephanie. *Honoring the Body*. San Francisco, CA: Jossey-Bass, 2002.

PayScale: Human Capital. Accessed October 17, 2017. https://www.payscale.com/data-packages/most-and-least-meaningful-jobs/full-list.

Petrow, Steven. "Resilience Isn't Just Being Tough. It's a Skill You Can Develop. Here's How I Did It." *Washington Post*, August 30, 2017. Accessed December 28, 2017. https://www.washingtonpost.com/lifestyle/wellness/resilience-isnt-just-being-tough-its-a-skill-you-can-develop-heres-how-i-did-it/2017/08/29/9d077a1e-881f-11e7-a50f-e0d4e6ec070a_story.html?utm_term=.748f54225475.

Pilon, Mary. "Student-Loan Debt Surpasses Credit Cards." *Wall Street Journal*, August 9, 2010. Accessed October 21, 2017. https://blogs.wsj.com/economics/2010/08/09/student-loan-debt-surpasses-credit-cards/.

Pinches, Charles R. "How to Live in Hope." *The Christian Century* 134, no. 15 (July 29, 2017): 22–25.

Pleiss-Sippola, Marggi. *The Call to Motherhood Informing the Call to Ordained Ministry*. DMin Thesis, University of Dubuque Theological Seminary, 2008.

Portnoy, Dennis. "Burnout and Compassion Fatigue: Watch for the Signs." *Health Progress*, July–August 2011.

Praissman, S. "Mindfulness-Based Stress Reduction: A Literature Review and Clinician's Guide." *Journal of the American Academy of Nurse Practitioners* 20, no. 4 (April 2008).

Proeschold-Bell, Rae Jean. "A Holistic Approach to Wellness." *Faith and Leadership*, August 3, 2009. Accessed December 1, 2017. https://www.faithandleadership.com/holistic-approach-wellness.

Proeschold-Bell, Rae Jean, and Sara H. LeGrand. "High Rates of Obesity and Chronic Disease Among United Methodist Clergy." *Obesity* 18, no. 9 (September 2010): 1867. Accessed December 17, 2017. http://onlinelibrary.wiley.com/doi/10.1038/oby.2010.102/epdf.

Psychology Today. "Mindfulness." Accessed December 19, 2017. https://www.psychologytoday.com/basics/mindfulness.

Putnam, Robert, and David Campbell. *American Grace: How Religion Divides and Unites Us*. New York: Simon and Schuster, 2010.

Randall, Robert L. *The Time of Your Life: Self/Time Management for Pastors*. Nashville: Abingdon Press, 1994.

Rassieur, Charles L. *Stress Management for Ministers*. Louisville: The Westminster Press, 1982.

Rediger, G. Lloyd. *Coping with Clergy Burnout*. Valley Forge, PA: Judson, 1982.

———. *Fit to Be a Pastor: A Call to Physical, Mental, and Spiritual Fitness*. Louisville: Westminster John Knox, 2000.

Richardson, Ronald W. *Creating a Healthier Church: Family Systems Theory, Leadership, and Congregational Life*. Minneapolis: Fortress, 1996.

Robinson, Kerry Alys. *Imagining Abundance*. Collegeville, MN: Order of Saint Benedict, 2014.

Roos, Joe, and Cheri Herrboldt. "Forced Termination: A Guide to Healing for Pastors and Congregations." *The Mennonite*, November 2017, 14–17.

Rosell, Terry. "Why People Don't Trust Preachers and What to Do About It." Class lecture and PowerPoint provided to the authors. July 3, 2017.

Rosenbaum, Elana. *MSBR: Mindfulness Based Stress Reduction: Intensive 2-Day Workshop*. Eau Claire, WI: PESI: 2016.

Roth, Nancy. *Spiritual Exercises: Joining Body and Spirit in Prayer*. New York: Seabury, 2005.

Ruger, Anthony, Sharon Miller, and Kim Early. "Taming the Tempest: A Team Approach to Reducing and Managing Student Debt." *Auburn Studies*. New York: Auburn Theological Seminary, October 2014.

Sandberg, Sheryl, and Adam Grant. *Option B: Facing Adversity, Building Resilience, and Finding Joy*. New York: Alfred A. Knopf, 2017.

Scazzero, Peter. *Emotionally Healthy Spirituality*. Grand Rapids, MI: Zondervan, 2006.

Schafer, Walt. *Stress Management for Wellness*, 4th ed. Fort Worth: Harcourt College Publishers, 1998.

Schwanz, Judith A. *Blessed Connections: Relationships That Sustain Vital Ministry*. Herndon, VA: Alban, 2008.

Script-O-Rama. http://www.script-o-rama.com/movie_scripts/w/war-and-peace-script-transcript.html.

Self-Compassion. http://self-compassion.org/category/exercises/#guided-meditations.

Seligman, Martin E. P. *Authentic Happiness: Using the New Positive Psychology to Realize Your Potential for Lasting Fulfillment*. New York: Free Press, 2002.

———. "Building Resilience." *Jay Dixit* (blog and website). Accessed August 3, 2017. http://jaydixit.com/psychology/failure-and-resilience/martin-seligman-on-building-resilience/.

———. *Flourish: A Visionary New Understanding of Happiness and Well-Being*. New York: Free Press, 2011.

Sellner, Edward C. *Mentoring: The Ministry of Spiritual Kinship*. Lanham, MD: Cowley Publications, 2002.

Selye, Hans. *The Stress of Life*, revised ed. New York: McGraw-Hill, 1978.

Sevier, Melissa Bane. *Journey Toward Renewal: A Spiritual Companion for Pastoral Sabbaticals*. Bethesda, MD: Alban, 2002.

Siebert, Al. *The Resiliency Advantage*. Oakland, CA: Berrett-Koehler Publishers, 2005.

———. "The Resiliency Quiz." The Al Siebert Resiliency Center. Accessed January 11, 2018. http://resiliencyquiz.com/index.shtml.

Skovholt, Thomas M., and Michelle Trotter-Mathison. *The Resilient Practitioner: Burnout and Compassion Fatigue Prevention and Self-Care Strategies for the Helping Professional*, 3rd ed. London: Routledge, 2016.

Smith, Christian, and Hilary Davidson. *The Paradox of Generosity: Giving We Receive, Grasping We Lose*. New York: Oxford University Press, 2014. Kindle edition.

Smith, Kathleen S. *Stilling the Storm: Worship and Congregational Leadership in Difficult Times*. Bethesda, MD: Alban, 2006.

Sparks, Susan. *Laugh Your Way to Grace: Reclaiming the Spiritual Power of Humor*. Woodstock, VT: Skylight Paths, 2010.

Steenhuysen, Julie. "Pastor Who Banned Fried Chicken Leads Mississippi Obamacare Push." *Reuters*, October 27, 2013. Accessed July 27, 2017. http://www.reuters.com/article/us-usa-healthcare-navigators-idUSBRE99Q03E20131027.

Steinke, Peter L. *Healthy Congregations*. Bethesda, MD: Alban, 1996.

———. *How Your Church Family Works: Understanding Congregations as Emotional Systems*. Bethesda, MD: Alban, 1993.

Stewart, Kristin. "Keeping Your Pastor: An Emerging Challenge." *Journal for the Liberal Arts and Sciences* (Summer 2009).

Strengthscope U.S. http://strengthscopeus.com/.

Strickland, Helyn. *We Are Family: The Significance of Fictive Kinship on Longevity Among Twenty Year Invested Employees in a Minimum Security Psychiatric Hospital*. DMin Dissertation, Central Baptist Theological Seminary, 2016.

"Study Finds Clergy Sexual Misconduct Widespread." *Christian Century* 126, no. 21 (October 20, 2009): 14.

Sweet, Leonard. *The Jesus Prescription for a Healthy Life*. Nashville: Abingdon, 1996.

Taylor, Barbara Brown. *An Altar in the World: A Geography of Faith*. New York: HarperOne, 2009.

———. *Leaving Church: A Memoir of Faith*. New York: HarperOne, 2012.

Teresa of Avila. Cited on Goodreads. Accessed December 8, 2017. https://www.goodreads.com/author/quotes/74226.Teresa_of_vila.

Thompson, Marjorie. *Soul Feast: An Invitation to the Christian Spiritual Life*. Louisville: Westminster John Knox, 1995.

Tickle, Phyllis. *Emergence Christianity: What It Is, Where It's Going, and Why It Matters*. Ada, MI: Baker Books, 2012.

Tidsworth, Mark, and Ircel Harrison. *Disciple Development Coaching: Christian Formation for the 21st Century*. Macon, GA: Nurturing Faith, 2013.

"Top 2 Causes for Pastors Leaving Ministry and More Statistics." Standing Stone: Strengthening Shepherds. Accessed February 28, 2017. https://www.standingstoneministry.org/top-2-causes-for-pastors-leaving-ministry-and-more-statistics/.

Turlington, Dee Dee, and Michael Harvey, eds. *Learning Guide on the Covenant and Code of Ethics for Ministerial Leaders of American Baptist Churches*. November 2006. Accessed January 8, 2018. http://ministerscouncil.com/wp-content/uploads/2013/03/LearningGuide ontheethics06edited.pdf.

Twist, Lynne. *The Soul of Money*. New York: W.W. Norton, 2003.

Umansky, Ellen M., and Dianne Ashton, eds. *Four Centuries of Jewish Women's Spirituality: A Sourcebook*. Waltham, MA: Brandeis University Press, 2009.

Ungersma, Aaron. *The Search for Meaning: A New Approach in Psychotherapy and Practical Psychology*. Sydney: Allen and Unwin, 1961.

Veterans Administration. https://www.ptsd.va.gov/professional/co-occurring/moral_injury_at_war.asp.

Warren, Kay. "Who Pastors the Pastor? Even Ministers Suffer from Suicidal Thoughts." *Washington Post*, April 21, 2017. Accessed April 27, 2017. https://www.washingtonpost.com/news/acts-of-faith/wp/2017/04/21/who-pastors-the-pastor-even-ministers-suffer-from-suicidal-thoughts/?utm_term=.37e351edb0c0.

Webster, Ann, Eileen M. Stuart, and Carol L. Wells-Federman. "How Thoughts Affect Health." In *The Wellness Book*, ed. Herbert Benson and Eileen Stuart. New York: Birch Lane Press, 1992.

Weems, Lovett H., Jr., and Ann A. Michel. *The Crisis of Younger Clergy*. Nashville: Abingdon, 2008.

Weise, Michael. "Murmurs from the Outside: What Former Pastors are Saying to the Church." *Comparative Report of Six Studies on Pastoral Attrition*. 2004. Submitted to the Pastors Institute and symposium participants in response to the October 4 and 5 symposium, Lousville Institute for Pastoral Study.

Wellman, Jack. "Average Pastor Salaries in United States Churches." *Christian Crier* (blog). December 15, 2013. Accessed January 5, 2017. http://www.patheos.com/blogs/christian crier/2013/12/15/average-pastor-salaries-in-united-states-churches/.

————. "Why We Are Losing so Many Churches in the United States?" *Christian Crier* (blog). October 26, 2013. Accessed January 5, 2017. http://www.patheos.com/blogs/christiancrier/2013/10/26/why-we-are-losing-so-many-churches-in-the-united-states/.

Wells, Bob. "It's Okay to Go There: The Place of Friendship in Ministry." *Faith and Leadership*. Accessed April 11, 2017. https://www.faithandleadership.com/programs/spe/resources/dukediv-friendship.html.

Werner, Emmy. "Resilience and Recovery: Findings from the Kauai Longitudinal Study." *Focal Point: Research, Policy, and Practice in Children's Mental Health* 19, no. 1 (Summer 2005): 11–14.

Wesley, John. "The Use of Money (Sermon 50)." Accessed October 21, 2017. http://www.umcmission.org/Find-Resources/John-Wesley-Sermons/Sermon-50-The-Use-of-Money.

Weston, Sean. Interview with Angela Jackson. November 9, 2017.

Wheeler, Barbara G., Sharon L. Miller, and Daniel O. Aleshire. "How Are We Doing? The Effectiveness of Theological Schools as Measured by the Vocations and Views of Graduates." *Auburn Studies*. New York: Auburn Theological Seminary, December 2007.

Wheeler, David R. "Higher Calling, Lower Wages: The Collapse of the Middle Class Clergy." *The Atlantic*, July 22, 2014. Accessed October 21, 2017. https://www.theatlantic.com/business/archive/2014/07/higher-calling-lower-wages-the-collapse-of-the-middle-class-clergy/374786/.

Wicks, Robert J. *The Resilient Clinician*. New York: Oxford University Press, 2008.

Wikipedia. "Herbert Freudenberger." Accessed November 3, 2017. https://en.wikipedia.org/wiki/Herbert_Freudenberger.

Wilson, Michael Todd, and Brad Hoffmann. *Preventing Ministry Failure: A ShepherdCare Guide for Pastors, Ministers, and Other Caregivers*. Westmont, IL: Intervarsity, 2007.

Wright, Wendy. *The Rising: Living the Mysteries of Lent, Easter, and Pentecost.* Nashville: Upper Room Books, 1994.

————. *The Time Between: Cycles and Rhythms in Ordinary Times.* Nashville: Upper Room Books, 1998.

————. *The Vigil: Keeping Watch in the Seasons of Christ's Coming.* Nashville: Upper Room Books, 1998.

Yu X., Fumoto M., Nakatani Y., Sekiyama T., Kikuchi H., Seki Y., Sato-Suzuki I., and Arita H. "Activation of the Anterior Prefrontal Cortex and Serotonergic System Is Associated with Improvements in Mood and EEG Changes Induced by Zen Meditation Practice in Novices." *International Journal of Psychophysiology* 80, no. 2 (May 2011). Abstract accessed December 31, 2017. https://www.ncbi.nlm.nih.gov/pubmed/21333699.

Index

Index of Bible Passages

About the Authors

Richard P. Olson has served as pastor or staff member in churches in Massachusetts, South Dakota, Wisconsin, Colorado, and Kansas. He has also been a pastoral counselor, a teacher in college, and most recently the distinguished professor of pastoral theology at Central Baptist Theological Seminary. He received his bachelor's degree from Sioux Falls College, MDiv and STM from Andover Newton Theological School, and his PhD (social ethics) from Boston University. He and Mary Ann, his wife of sixty years, have three daughters and six grandchildren. He is the author or coauthor of eighteen previous books, the most recent being *Laughter in a Time of Turmoil* and *Side by Side: Being Christian in a Multifaith World*.

Ruth Lofgren Rosell is associate professor of pastoral theology at Central Baptist Theological Seminary, Shawnee, Kansas, and teaches in the area of pastoral care and counseling. She also serves as an associate pastor at Prairie Baptist Church in Prairie Village, Kansas. She received her BA in nursing from Gustavus Adolphus College in St. Peter, Minnesota; her master of divinity degree from Gordon-Conwell Theological Seminary in Massachusetts; and her PhD in religion and personality from Vanderbilt University. She is a certified pastoral counselor and fellow with the American Association of Pastoral Counselors. She also has many years of experience as a psychiatric nurse. Ruth was ordained in 1983 by the American Baptist Churches, USA. In shared ministry with her husband, Tarris, she has served churches in upstate New York and Kansas. Previous pastoral experience has included small church ministry, refugee resettlement, new church development, and small group ministry. Ruth and Tarris have four adult children.

Nathan S. Marsh serves as the associate executive minister for the American Baptist Churches of the Central Region. Nathan has served three pastorates but five churches in various ministry contexts. He holds a bachelor's degree in psychology and biblical studies, a master's degree of Christian leadership studies, a master's degree of religious education, a master's degree of divinity, and a doctorate of ministry. In his doctoral research, Nathan worked with the question, "What can be done to support pastoral retention within the first five years of ministry?" Nathan has been married to his wife, Cosette, for six years. Together they have two children, elementary age and younger.

Angela Barker Jackson is a graduate of Indiana University (BS Ed 1993) and Central Seminary (MDiv 2014, DMin 2018). She is an ordained minister in the American Baptist tradition with experience in the areas of youth, poverty, and pastoral ministries, as well as theological education. For the last several years, she has served Gage Park Baptist Church (Topeka, Kansas) as copastor and Central Baptist Theological Seminary (Shawnee, Kansas) as project director for a program aimed at addressing the economic challenges facing future ministers. Angie has been married for twenty-three years, and she is the proud mother of adult children. When she has free time, she loves to travel, cook sumptuous food, read good books, and play word games.